"In an age when well-chosen words can be misinterpreted as inauthentic, *Worship Words* makes a dramatic case for the opposite. Followers of the Word made flesh, Jesus Christ, need to be attentive to the words used in worship. Theological and practical insights work hand in hand in this volume as it shatters the myth about the powerlessness of our words. See and hear the possibilities for well-chosen worship words in a text that is itself a fine example of verbal craftsmanship."

—**Lester Ruth**, Lily May Jarvis Professor of Christian Worship,
Asbury Theological Seminary

"In *Worship Words*, the Rienstras present an elegantly written and masterful study of words that will assist the 21st century Christian worship leader. Learning how to use words meaningfully in worship is vitally important, and the Rienstras bring fresh, clarifying, practical insight to that endeavor."

—**Charles E. Fromm**, publisher, *Worship Leader Magazine*,
Song DISCovery, and *The Worshiper Magazine*

## engaging
## worship

### series editors
Clayton J. Schmit
Todd E. Johnson

Engaging Worship, a Brehm Center series, is designed to promote reflection on the practice of Christian worship by scholars, artists, and practitioners, often in conversation with each other. Each volume addresses a particular liturgical issue from one or multiple academic disciplines, while exploring ways in which worship practice and leadership can be renewed. Volumes in this series include monographs and edited collections from authors of diverse theological and ecclesial communities. The goal of this series is to bring scholars, students, artists, and church leaders into conversation around vital issues of theology and worship.

The Brehm Center for Worship, Theology, and the Arts is an innovative space for the creative integration of worship, theology, and arts in culture. It is located at Fuller Theological Seminary in Pasadena, California.

# Worship
# WORDS

## DISCIPLING LANGUAGE
## FOR FAITHFUL MINISTRY

### DEBRA RIENSTRA
### AND RON RIENSTRA

**Baker Academic**
a division of Baker Publishing Group
Grand Rapids, Michigan

Published by Baker Academic
a division of Baker Publishing Group
P.O. Box 6287, Grand Rapids, MI 49516-6287
www.bakeracademic.com

Printed in the United States of America

Library of Congress Cataloging-in-Publication Data
Rienstra, Debra.
    Worship words : discipling language for faithful ministry / Debra Rienstra and Ron Rienstra.
       p.  cm. — (Engaging worship)
    Includes bibliographical references and index.
    ISBN 978-0-8010-3616-3 (pbk.)
     1. Public worship. 2. Language and languages—Religious aspects—Christianity. I. Rienstra, Ron,
1965– II. Title.
BV15.R54 2009
264.001′4—dc22                                            2008038276

For John D. Witvliet

*Blessed are those whose strength is in you,*
*who have set their hearts on pilgrimage.*

Psalm 84:5

# Contents

# Preface

By the age of twenty-seven, I had attended my share of Christmas worship services. Every year they came around—the plump-cheeked children draped in white polyester and crowned with tinsel halos, the candlelit church decked out in pine boughs, the choir processing in robes, the familiar nativity passages read once again. So as I walked through the wintry Iowa darkness to yet another candlelight service, I was not expecting any new revelations. I had seen it all before.

Two things were different this time though. First, this was a service on a college campus, so those leading and attending worship were almost all college students and faculty. Second, I was pregnant with my first child.

The choir lifted its communal voice, the service began, and something happened to me. The harmonies of the choir and the hearty singing of the congregation filled the small chapel so full of sound, I thought the roof might fly off and our voices would burst into the sky, blending with the heavenly host and all creation. As we sang the familiar songs and my own child rolled and squirmed in my rounded belly, I heard words I had never attended to before: "infant holy, infant lowly," "newborn," "mother and child." I was astonished: Christmas was about *a baby*.

After several choral and congregational flourishes of song and spoken word, a small group of students offered a quieter song, a setting of the familiar text from Luke 1, Mary's Magnificat. A young female soloist sang the verses, and the congregation responded:

> And holy is your name
> through all generations!
> Everlasting is your mercy
> to the people you have chosen,
> and holy is your name.*

---

*David Haas, "Holy Is Your Name," based on Luke 1:45–55; text and music copyright © 1989 by GIA Publications, Inc., 7404 S. Mason Ave., Chicago, IL 60638 (www.giamusic.com; 800.442.1358). All rights reserved. Used by permission.

There among those young people, filled with my own growing child, I heard Mary's words as never before: words of a young woman with quiet and persistent faith, praising a creating and redeeming God whose tender mercy reached down the generations.

My passion for the topic of language in worship comes from deep hunger and thirst. I understand that at its heart, what I am feeling when I go to worship is spiritual longing—the hunger and thirst of my soul for the presence of God, for Jesus, the Bread of Life and the Living Water. Many times in my life, this longing has been deeply satisfied through worship words: an expressive song, Scripture read well, a thoughtful and emotionally engaging sermon, a deeply meant prayer. These things have fed me, sometimes far beyond my expectations, sometimes just enough to get by. All of us need, perhaps not a gigantic banquet feast of delectable words at worship every week, but at least a steady diet of a few wholesome morsels to sustain us.

Since you are reading this book, you probably know exactly what I mean. God has fed you through words, both satisfying you and awakening your longing for more. Perhaps you also know the mystery of words: how words combine with place, time of day, and personal mood to startle us into understanding; how tired and familiar words can suddenly spark into life again; how the untraceable histories of our lives intersect with the worship of the assembled body of Christ and reshape us, again and again.

I recognize, of course, that words are not the only things that satisfy our longing for God. We can feel our souls revived through music, in the companionship and touch of people we love, by serving others, or by entering a beautiful garden or mountain path or cathedral. I have come to understand as an adult how deeply I love the nonverbal elements in worship. I love the exuberant sound of voices joined in singing, the hushed communion of a congregation in concentrated prayer, the splashing of the water during a baptism, the blessing of a Christian brother's kind eyes meeting mine as he offers me the bread and wine.

Still, as Christians we are people of the Book, a book that testifies to Jesus Christ, the Word. There's no getting around the fact that words are a vital means through which God has chosen to reveal to us and bless us. Those of us in Protestant traditions claim in our theology the primacy of the Word. Words, naturally enough then, are the primary medium in which we carry on our spiritual practice, our worship and devotion.

Even so, trends in North American Protestant worship in the last thirty years have focused heavily on shifting musical styles and new ways to organize the time, emotional contours, and architectural spaces of worship. Some people have attended to words, too, especially in the 1980s when arguments about inclusive language were flourishing. However, it's my impression that attention to words has tended to lag behind attention to other things. This book, then, is a call to renewed appreciation of words in worship: how they bless us and how we can use them well, to the glory of God and for the building up of God's people.

This book was written in response to an invitation from John Witvliet, director of the Calvin Institute of Christian Worship. John and his staff have been concerned about words, too, and have been busy developing varied and creative resources for helping congregations do words better. In addition to the many resources available through the institute and elsewhere, John felt that pastors and worship leaders would appreciate a single text summarizing the issues and offering examples and exercises to help people apply good ideas about worship words to particular worship contexts.

I accepted the task of creating such a book as a way to make use of an odd combination of expertise, background, opportunity, and experience. As a writer and literary scholar, I have a particular sensitivity to words as well as professional training in language theory and literature. I also have the blessing of being married to Rev. Ron Rienstra, a pastor and educator whose specialties are preaching and worship. This marriage partnership has transformed my love for worship, developed in childhood, into a more mature love that has become both personal and professional.

Though the main text of this book is in my voice—primarily because this is most comfortable and personable for the reader—in every way the book represents a collaborative effort. Every paragraph has benefited from Ron's editing and expertise, from our conversations over the years, from his library, and from many direct suggestions and examples. Early in the process we decided that Ron would write sidebars and appendixes 2 and 3 in his own voice, though these also were collaboratively finished. All of this is meant to create a richer resource for the reader. We have tried to provide a fresh approach based on my literary training and experience as a writer while also bringing to bear Ron's study and experience as a pastor, worship educator, and homiletician.

In addition, we wanted to model appropriately the kind of conversational format in which all good ideas develop. No expert writes in a vacuum, nor does any worship leader or planner work in a vacuum. Worship arises out of the community, and thus our reflection about worship should as well. So the primary conversation in the book between my voice and Ron's helps model that principle.

This book has also grown out of many wider conversations. Ron and I share roots in the Reformed enclaves of West Michigan, which gave us a strong theological background even before our professional training. We like to think we have inherited the best of the Reformed tradition: intellectual rigor, love for the Bible, and faithfulness in the practices of the faith. Our Reformed background, then, is the source of sturdy tools and abiding passions. These tools and passions are in turn responsible for sparking a desire to explore the theology and practices of many Christian traditions.

During the years of our marriage, we have lived in New Jersey, Iowa, and Michigan, experiencing many kinds of churches and worship styles. For four years, from 2003 to 2007, our family embarked on a series of adventures: Ron and I taught a short travel course in the UK on worship reform; I directed Calvin College's Semester in Britain program, so that we returned to the UK with our three children for a five-month period; and we lived in Los Angeles for two years while I was on sabbatical and Ron began his PhD work at Fuller Theological Seminary. These travels have afforded us an even more concentrated opportunity to experience different kinds of worship.

By now we have attended, as a family, too many different churches to count. We have experienced a soul-boggling range of worship styles: Anglo-Catholic cathedral worship, bilingual charismatic worship, chill-track-enhanced alternative worship, expertly creative praise-band style worship, jazz-inflected folk-liturgical worship, Texan Episcopal worship, and many more. Not all of it has been great, of course. We have been bored or exasperated as often as we have been deeply moved and inspired. It's a wry species of mercy that the Spirit enables us all to worship through what could be called bad worship as well as through what we might consider good worship—and we can learn from all kinds of worship too.

During our travels, our three children (now ages fifteen, thirteen, and nine) came to appreciate our home church in Grand Rapids, Michigan, and missed the groundedness of returning to the same place and people every week. On the other hand, they have received an invaluable glimpse of the breathtaking variety in Christian worship. They have some sense of how big and complicated the church is, and a keen realization that although we have worshiped in many ways among many people, we have still only experienced a tiny fraction of our country's Christian assemblies, not to mention the world's. Limited as our experience is on that global scale, we are glad to put to use our adventures in worship over the years as well as our reading and research into the subject.

In addition to our own experiences and study, an enormous body of research, wisdom, and energy stands behind this book in the form of the Calvin Institute of Christian Worship. We are grateful for the practical support and warm encouragement of John Witvliet and the institute staff. Special thanks are also due to the small but lively group of Los Angeles–area pastors I convened in the early stages of writing. Our discussions helped clarify the issues and test ways of discussing them, and their suggestions and examples have greatly enriched this book. Meanwhile, Ron and I together also had the privilege of teaching a class on worship words at Fuller Theological Seminary in Pasadena in the spring of 2006. Our students in that class were true inspirations; their wisdom and commitment would give anyone hope for the future leadership of the church. Their ideas and insights will also be apparent throughout.

Whatever knowledge and expertise Ron and I have gathered along the way from pastors, scholars, and experts of all sorts, we still try to represent here the perspective of the pew (or folding chair, or padded seat), as two of a large body of people who go to worship always hopeful, expectant, longing. We hope that you will find this perspective valuable and that the ideas and examples offered here will provide challenge, encouragement, and inspiration to you.

When Jesus instructed Peter to "feed my lambs," he was pointing, ultimately, to our hunger and thirst for the person of Jesus himself. When we preach, pray, sing, and speak in worship, we are using words to receive that Bread of Life, that Living Water, that Word. May we all do it well.

# Acknowledgments

This book is only the latest installment in a growing library of resources available today that would not exist except for the vision, inspiration, and leadership of Dr. John Witvliet. John's unique gift for turning trouble into blessing has benefited us personally many times over the years. We are grateful both to the Lilly Foundation for its support of the Calvin Institute of Christian Worship and to John as director of the Institute for suggesting this project and for shepherding it along with funding, vision, ideas, and all manner of practical help.

In the early stages of the writing, we enjoyed much inspiration from our class at Fuller Theological Seminary in the spring of 2006: Ryan Bailey, Drew Bannon, John Dudich, Mark Finney, Luke Hyder, Marla Hyder, Lauren Mayfield, Brenda McGee, and Rebecca Russo. We are also grateful to the pastors who, in exchange for a few humble catered lunches, generously gave of their time and wisdom to review early manuscripts and offer sage advice: Moses Chung, David Lemley, Rebecca VerStraten-McSparran, and Norberto Wolf. The good people of the Brehm Center at Fuller, especially Fred Davison and Clay Schmit, also supported the early stages of research. All these amazing and gracious people added light and color to this book but even more so to our lives.

At the Calvin Institute of Christian Worship, the intrepid Emily Cooper labored · through a terrible thicket of citations and permissions, rescuing us from certain madness. Nathan Bierma offered important early scouting for the bibliography.

At Baker Academic, many thanks to Bob Hosack and Jeremy Cunningham for their professionalism and personal grace. Because of this book's deep California connections, we are delighted that it appears in Baker Academic's Engaging Worship series. Many thanks to Clay Schmit for enthusiastically gathering this project into the inaugural installations of the series.

We would also like to express our appreciation to the many people at Church of the Servant CRC who have contributed insight, study, and creativity over the years to the congregation's worship practice. We are especially grateful to Jack Roeda and, in recent years, Greg Scheer. Thanks to your faithful service, every week we come to the banquet.

This book is dedicated, with great affection and gratitude, to John Witvliet. Our prayer is that God will use it in some small way for the building up of the church and the glory of Christ.

# How to Use This Book

We worked through an early version of this material with a class of seminary students in ten weeks in the spring of 2006. By about week five, we all felt overwhelmed, as though we were drinking from a fire hose. There was *so much* to think about. Those of our students who were leading worship at churches every week that semester felt helpless to put into practice what they were learning: they hardly knew where to begin!

So our primary advice is to work through this book with others—and do so very slowly and patiently, perhaps over the course of an entire year.

1. Work through the book with a group, such as the church staff, the worship leadership group, or—ideally—a group representing staff and congregants.
2. Read one chapter at a time, discuss it, and then take a few weeks to do the exercises and let the ideas sink in.
3. Plan as a group how you will implement any changes. You may wish to read through the entire book before making any changes. Or you may wish to try a few things as you go along, and then, once you have finished the book, hold an additional planning session to discuss longer-term change. Be sensitive to your context and your own role in the congregation. Even with larger changes, work on one thing at a time. Better to make three genuine improvements that "stick" than to try thirty things that are forgotten in a year.
4. Find ways to communicate to the congregation what your group is doing and to explain with enthusiasm and sensitivity any changes you might make. Seek ways to invite everyone into ownership.

# Introduction

The purpose of this book is to help pastors and worship leaders attend carefully to the words used in prayers, songs, sermons, and other spoken elements in worship—and to use words more intentionally. The many people who helped develop the material in this book share a sincere desire to help leaders across a broad range of worship styles: traditional, contemporary, charismatic, liturgical, alternative, emerging, and so on. Our goal is to help all of us remain true to the best of our own traditions while also gathering wisdom from other Christians.

Our conviction is that the basic principles governing good worship language remain about the same no matter what the style or tradition in question, and that they can be adapted to the different emphases of many theological commitments. Whether words are scripted or extemporaneous, old or new, formal or colloquial, taken from a service book or composed for the occasion, they can be done well or done badly. They can serve to heal, feed, and challenge the people of God, or they can bore, confuse, or mislead them. What is good or bad does depend partly on context, but no particular style or tradition has a monopoly on the best worship words.

Theological differences among traditions do have a bearing on worship words, and if anything, this book will highlight the importance of worship words in teaching theological conviction. But it is possible to discuss worship language with reference to many basic Christian convictions that we largely agree on (though we may not all practice what we say in some cases). You and I might disagree, for

"The cheaper our language the less it will accomplish. God is purposeful with words. We should be, too. Good worship language is not cheap, but costly: it costs our time and care."

—Mark Finney, seminary student

### Speaking of Speaking in Tongues

In this book, we will explicitly steer clear of one important aspect of language in worship: the charismatic gift of speaking in tongues, also known as *glossolalia*. This is the practice, attested in the New Testament (Acts 2:1–11; 1 Cor. 12; 14), in which a believer, in the power of the Holy Spirit, speaks fluidly in an unknown language.

*Glossolalia* is a key part of the worshiping experience for vast swaths of the Christian world. As a liturgical phenomenon, the practice of speaking in tongues raises fascinating theological questions about the use of language in worship and its ability to both glorify God and build up the church. Though some reject the practice outright and others demand it as a sign of the Spirit's presence and power in worship, we do not wish in this text to make judgments about its validity or significance.

*Glossolalia* is best understood and considered by those for whom it is a living experience. Deb and I may witness it, read books about it, and be in conversation with those who know and cherish it, but this practice is not part of our personal lived tradition. Therefore, we would not be able to speak of it with any legitimate authority. So even at points where it might seem natural to do so, we will refrain from addressing the practice, not out of disregard, but out of profound respect.

example, on whether a song should ask God to "Let us find that second rest" as a reflection of Wesleyan sanctification theology. But in this book we are more interested that our worship words faithfully convey, for example, the humanity and divinity of Christ. At any rate, if certain ideas or examples don't make sense to you because of your particular theological convictions, I hope you will still find helpful ideas or examples elsewhere in that chapter or the book.

One of the great challenges of the broader Protestant tradition is our freedom to shape the way we worship. Many of us strive earnestly to be biblical in our worship, but the results of those strivings look very different. Weekly Eucharist, a cappella singing, and speaking in tongues are all considered deeply biblical and necessary practices by one or more branches of Protestantism, while other branches regard the same practices as optional or even suspect. While respecting these differences, Ron and I will be seeking to promote here worship that is biblical insofar as it is

- guided by Scripture's themes, principles, and stories as well as its specific instructions concerning worship;
- informed by the rich and varied history of Christian worship, since that history reflects previous generations' wisdom on how Scripture guides us to worship;
- drenched in the words of Scripture, inspired by the words, images, and literary modes of this book we love;
- responsive to Scripture's directive to "sing a new song."

We trust that this approach will allow readers to gain from the general principles explored here and then apply them in a way that respects their own contexts.

## Analysis and the Spirit

Some of us resist the idea of analyzing what is "good" or "bad" in worship words. The point, after all, is whether the Spirit is present and whether we follow the Spirit's leading in worship. Perhaps all of us believe at least some of the time that too much analysis and planning can cause paralysis: "a read prayer is a dead prayer." If we take this concern to its logical conclusion, then, a book like this one is based on a mistaken premise and not worth anyone's time.

However, we would like to invite a very wide and joyful view of the Spirit's many means of being present in worship. The Spirit works through spontaneity and improvisation but also through planning and careful preparation. We know from our own experience and the testimony of many others that the Spirit comes to the preacher as he prepares his sermon on the days before Sunday; comes to the songwriter as she works out a lyric at the piano in her living room; comes to the elder as he reads Scripture and writes down thoughts in preparation for leading a congregation's prayers; comes to the musicians as they rehearse together and practice on their own.

In short, when we seek to make our worship Spirit-filled, our seeking must not begin at ten on Sunday morning, but must drive all we do, all week long. Any musician who is expert at improvisation will tell you that true freedom, true spontaneity in performance only comes through years of constant practice in the "woodshed." The same is true of worship. Whether we favor planned worship or spontaneous worship, either way we must seek the Spirit both outside and within the worship assembly.

Part of that seeking involves deliberate effort. For worship leaders across traditions, putting together a worship service involves drawing on resources—songbooks,

"The Bible is the source of our knowledge of God and of the world's redemption in Christ. Worship should include prominent readings of Scripture. It should present and depict God's being, character, and actions in ways that are consistent with scriptural teaching. It should obey explicit biblical commands about worship practices, and it should heed scriptural warnings about false and improper worship. Worship should focus its primary attention where the Bible does: on the person and work of Jesus Christ as the Redeemer of all creation and the founder and harbinger of the kingdom of God through the work of the Holy Spirit."[1]

—The Worship Sourcebook

> "The purpose of worship is to bring healing and change to people. Language either aids or detracts from that. I don't want to be petty, but to prepare for revival."
>
> —*John Dudich, seminary student*

prayer books, sermon commentaries, worship music CDs, oral tradition, and of course the Bible—as well as composing original words for the occasion, either written down or improvised. Thus, the chapters, examples, and exercises that follow will emphasize careful evaluation, selection, and adaptation of word resources as well as the development of original resources, including ways to become a more skilled improviser of worship words. We will also consider the ways in which words are contextualized in worship: who is speaking or singing them, at what point in the service they are spoken or sung, and what other sensory elements support (or compete with) them. If we wish our words to mean something, we have to attend not only to the words themselves but also to the way that all language is embedded in meaning-making contexts.

### Organization of the Book

The book is organized into twelve main chapters. The chapters move roughly from general principles such as repetition and authenticity to more specific categories of practice such as global awareness and lament. Chapters 1–7 are lengthier because they cover more theoretical ground, a foundation on which later chapters build. Chapters 6 and 7 in particular, on figurative language and naming God, discuss heavily theoretical and even controversial material, but we hope the challenging nature of the material will be matched by the useful insights resulting from studying it. Every chapter is designed to combine larger issues and principles with more practical ideas about selecting and creating worship words. Each chapter concludes with exercises tested on students and participants in various workshops Ron or I or others have led. These exercises include

- discussion questions for personal or group reflection;
- exercises that invite observation and reflection on particular worship services;
- exercises for creating and adapting worship resources, including songs, prayers, and in-between words;
- exercises designed specifically for preachers.

Icons identifying each type of exercise appear in the margin. The key is as follows:

- 𝄂 an exercise for group discussion
- 👁 a participant-observer exercise to be done at a worship service
- 📖 an exercise for developing resources to be used in worship
- ⛪ an exercise especially designed for preachers

## On Being a Participant-Observer

A word about doing exercises: Many of the exercises in this book require you to become a participant-observer at worship services. Students often lament that when they do these exercises they are in "analysis" mode and can't actually worship. Yes, this is true. It is very difficult to observe worship and participate in it at the same time. The best strategy is to recognize this from the outset and make peace with the problem. The analysis mode is not always comfortable, but it is necessary if we want to lead worship that is rich, meaningful, healing, and challenging. Ron and I have witnessed over and over again those wonderful "aha!" moments when people notice for the first time what they have formerly taken for granted. We are both strong advocates of the participant-observer process because we know that people learn from it in life-changing ways.

You might think of going to services in analysis mode as a kind of sacrifice you make as a leader for the sake of others. Still, please do it only for a season or only occasionally. Worship leaders have a hard enough time simply worshiping. They are always worried about sound balance or whether the Scripture reader showed up or whether the grape juice got to the table or any of a million other things. It's important for worship leaders to have some Sundays or Wednesdays or Saturday nights when their only task is to worship. We hope the exercises in this book are helpful and eye-opening and inspiring. But we also hope that you will make an effort as you go through the book and do the exercises to care for yourself spiritually and make sure you do not get analysis paralysis.

## What Is Good?

As we seek to make our worship *better*, it's important to consider exactly what *better* might mean. What are we after, really, as we plan and lead worship? In one sense or another, we are after some kind of *best*. We want worship to be biblical, meaningful, comforting, challenging, inspiring, instructive, memorable—all kinds of worthy things. These goals require our best efforts. At the same time, we don't want worship to be fake or to be a show or a series of merely correct rituals.

### "New York Quality"

Years ago, I interviewed for a position at a large church in New York City. They boasted to me after a stunning choral piece was performed in worship that all their music had to be excellent—"New York quality." I felt squeamish about this, but didn't know why in the moment. Later, upon reflection, I realized that this church's practice associates *excellence* with what some cultural observers call "high art," and then appears to value that art for its own sake. This approach rightly puts people off or leaves them in despair if they don't have the kind of resources necessary to meet such standards. "We just don't have anyone who can play the piano that well!" a worship leader might lament. But no church needs to live by some other church's definition of excellence. Furthermore, we should be careful about borrowing any definition of excellence unquestioned from some nonchurch sphere—such as the classical music world, the recorded pop music world, or the network television production world. Our goals in worship are not always the same as the goals of those other spheres. Our task as worship leaders is not to impress or entertain our congregations, but to enable and encourage them to worship fully. All the excellences we pursue strive toward that end.[2]

Some worship leaders use the word *presentational* to describe worship that serves as a wonderful performance on the part of the pastor or choir or worship band, but fails to empower the people of God to participate fully and authentically. The opposite of presentational might be *authentic* in a broad sense. Authentic worship is fitting to its context and fully participative. Worship arises genuinely from the people. Of course, people need the guidance and assistance of informed leaders and wise traditions. So perhaps what we all strive for in worship is a healthy tension between excellence and authenticity.

Taking the terms one at a time, then, what does it mean to be excellent? Excellence depends on context. In one church, excellence might mean a wisely selected and beautifully read prayer from the Book of Common Prayer. In another context, it might mean a prayer improvised in simple language, honestly expressing the longings and troubles of that congregation. Excellence could mean an expertly performed choral anthem, or it could mean a simple, guitar-led "He's Got the Whole World in His Hands," sung joyfully at an infant baptism or dedication—and including the "little bitty babies" verse. Excellence means doing very well what is fitting to the context. It requires both intentionality and sensitivity to the congregation's comfort zones and growing edges.

What is authentic then? We often hear people, especially young people, describe good worship in terms implying that excellence and authenticity are opposed to each other. If a choir sings with precision, its members can't really mean what they are singing. If a person leading prayer stumbles and hesitates and struggles for words—well, she is obviously authentic.

It's true that excellence and authenticity are not the same thing: excellence is not necessarily authentic; authenticity is not necessarily excellent. Excellence without authenticity is merely polish; authenticity without excellence devolves into sloppiness. Either without the other is distracting and gets in the way of worship.

Perhaps we should propose, therefore, that these two notions do not represent opposite ends of the same spectrum. They can merge together, and they should. Authenticity-with-excellence (or excellence-with-authenticity) should be our goal. When we reach this goal, worship achieves the quality of transparency. This means that a particular prayer or sermon or song becomes not only a good thing in itself, but more important, it becomes transparent to God's self-disclosure. Authenticity-with-excellence, therefore, is the most effective way to help worshipers stay in full, conscious, active participation.

**authenticity + excellence = transparency → participation**

We will consider this tension again in the chapters ahead, particularly the chapter on authenticity. Meanwhile, at the outset of this book—a book advocating excellence as well as authenticity in worship words—we should remind ourselves of something else: God can work through lousy words too. We all know this from experience. After one especially tough week, our family heard a sermon that made us think, "For a bad sermon, that sure was something we needed to hear." Everything was wrong with the sermon—it was disorganized and shallow and hardly touched the Scripture text—and yet the preacher had one excellent insight that God used to speak to and reassure our whole family that day.

Though we rightly desire to give God our best, God's favor toward us does not depend on our reaching some threshold of excellence. On the contrary, God's attitude toward our worship exemplifies grace and acceptance.[3] As theologian James B. Torrance explains, our worship does not have to be perfect because it is perfected through Christ.[4]

One more thing: when the text or sidebars here set forth an example of a "bad" worship song, for instance, we might be naming one of your favorites, a song that moves you to tears whenever you sing it. If you find yourself disagreeing with the examples, please forgive. We may disagree on what is bad or good, but we hope we can agree that we depend on the Spirit to work through our efforts, however

"I feel as if we've opened Pandora's box, but in a good way. I can see now how much we're missing out when we settle for thoughtless clichés."

—Drew Bannon, seminary student, on the final day of our class fine or clumsy, to awaken worshipers' hearts. Some songs and prayers and sermons present the Spirit with challengingly meager raw material—but we have to admit that anything is possible.

Nevertheless, so much is lost when we don't care. When we don't care, people grow up in the faith with a truncated view of God as the bearded man in the sky. When we don't care, young people turn away because constant talk of blood and sacrifice seems far distant from their everyday longings and hopes. When we don't care, older people limp along spiritually, barely challenged and rarely reawakened to the wonders of God. When we don't care, people wonder why they should bother with church at all.

When we do care, however, we are given a humbling and thrilling privilege: the Spirit will work through our words to bless and transform the sons and daughters of God. We have to care, as Clay Schmit writes, "for the sake of the people who have gathered and for the sake of their faith."[5]

The example of Scripture itself, with its inexhaustible treasury of image, story, and compelling voices, tells us that God chooses to work through powerful words, and so we are invited to cooperate with the Spirit as best we can, using all the God-given creativity, discernment, and wisdom we can muster.

### Exercises

1. Describe a time when you were especially blessed by the words of a worship service. How do you think the work or wisdom of the worship leaders contributed to that blessing?

2. In seeking excellence-with-authenticity, what do you think your church does well? What are some areas that need improvement?

# 1

# The Dimensions of Language in Worship

Last autumn at our home church, we began the worship service each week by singing a worship song from Zimbabwe:

| | |
|---|---|
| Uyai mose, tinamate Mwari; | Come, all you people, come and praise your Maker; |
| Uyai mose, tinamate Mwari; | Come, all you people, come and praise your Maker; |
| Uyai mose, tinamate Mwari; | Come, all you people, come and praise your Maker; |
| Uyai mose Zvino. | Come now and worship the Lord.[1] |

As we sang this joyful yet solemn processional song, first in the original language and then in English, musicians played African drums and dancers arrayed in colorful sashes made their way from the back of the congregation to the front, swaying and stepping and spinning in time with the music. Their movements drew on traditional African dance, representing how we come together from all directions and meet in God's presence for worship. Each week, once we had cycled through the song (substituting *the Savior* and *the Spirit* for *your Maker* on subsequent verses), the drums died out, and a worship leader spoke words of Scripture as God's invitation to worship. Then we sang a hymn, usually a familiar one from our denominational hymnal.

In the rest of the service, we sometimes used practiced words, and at other times more informal, extemporaneous language. Our pastor preached from memory, improvising based on that week's study and preparation. A member of the congregation offered a congregational prayer, usually improvising from notes and incorporating that week's requests. During communion (which our church celebrates each week), we sang a variety of songs, including contemporary praise-and-worship songs.

Our church's worship style is rather unusual; it could be called "eclectic folk-liturgical." But in just about any church, worshiping in any style, we can observe language performing a variety of functions. The words of the sermon serve to teach and explain. The words of an opening hymn might express praise in a poetic way, but also remind us of generations past who worshiped the same God with that same hymn. The words of an improvised intercessory prayer express the holy longings of the leader on behalf of the congregation, and the words of our praise-and-worship songs express our individual dedication, love, and thankfulness. Many words that help us act as worshipers might also delight us because of their vividness or beauty—and that sensory engagement is a valid part of worship.

It's fascinating to observe how all these dimensions of language can come together, even in a single moment. For me, the most moving part of our autumn worship services was often that opening song. Though the words were not my native language, I soon came to adopt them as my own. Those words, along with the drums and dancing, the voice of the congregation, the dignified spirit of praise—all of it together awakened in me a vision of the whole body of Christ gathered, with a sense of deep gratitude and joy, around the throne of God (Rev. 7:9). The song prepared me for worship, but also lingered with me throughout the week.

The challenge of working toward good worship words, in essence, is that language in worship operates on many levels at once. Language helps us perform certain actions in worship, actions that include praising, interceding, confessing, listening, celebrating, and thanking. But as we experience those actions, the language with which we experience them simultaneously works on us to form our spiritual and devotional life, our patterns of thought and feeling. In a fundamental sense, worship language, like all of worship, is *formative*.

The words we hear, sing, and speak in worship help form

- our images of God;
- our understanding of what the church is and does;
- our understanding of human brokenness and healing;
- our sense of purpose as individuals and as a church;
- our religious affections: awe, humility, delight, contrition, hope;
- our vision of wholeness for ourselves and all creation;
- our practices of engaging with God, with each other, and with the world.

**Schooled in Worship**

"Worship both forms and expresses the faith-experience of the community. Worshipping God involves telling stories, singing praise and trust and hope, sorrow and joy, delight and wonder. It trains us in lamenting, confessing, adoring, and lifting our cries for the whole world. At its best, Christian worship presents a vision of life created, sustained and redeemed and held in the mystery of grace. What we do together in acknowledging God 'schools' us in ways of seeing the world and of being in it."[2]

*—Don E. Saliers*

Our words form us whether or not we pay attention to how they are doing so. Just as children quickly learn to speak with the vocabulary, tones, and inflections of their parents, so we learn to "speak" our spiritual lives with the words and tones, with the emotional and theological range of what we experience at worship. It's true that worship is not the only part of our church experience that forms us in the faith—Bible studies and shared meals and casual conversations after services also shape our spirits. Nevertheless, worship is the central shared act in a congregation's life. What we do there matters because we do it together, and we do it repeatedly. The formative nature of worship and of worship words in particular is a compelling reason to pay careful attention to our weekly practice.

Under that main heading of language as formative, we can consider several more specific ways in which language works in worship. This chapter highlights four dimensions of language: the *expressive, aesthetic, instructive*, and *memorial*.

It is rather difficult to distinguish among these; the nature of language is such that its various qualities operate simultaneously. However, some styles of worship emphasize some dimensions of language and dismiss others, and other styles of worship do quite the opposite. Yet *all* these dimensions are important. Once we are aware of the various dimensions and how each is formative, we have one good framework for evaluating worship language broadly, as well as some guidelines for choosing language that supports worship actions faithfully and well.

## Language Has an *Expressive* Dimension

Those who argue against the use of formal language and older songs and prayers in worship point out that we can't genuinely express ourselves through language that feels too foreign from our everyday speech. Instead, we want the language we use in worship to reflect who and where and when we are. We want our language to be alive, to speak authentically—in our own voices—of our joys, griefs, worries, and hopes. God invites us to come as we are to worship and delights in our particularity. After all, the gospel is for us, here and now, and our words should reflect that immediate relevance. Thus, some worshipers would reject a prayer of confession from a service book because of its formal language ("wash me thoroughly from mine iniquity"), and prefer the more straightforward expression of a contemporary song:

> Change my heart, O God;
> make it ever true.
> Change my heart, O God;
> may I be like you.*

The arguments for expressive language in worship are strong ones. If we believe that worship is *primarily* expressive, however, we run into some immediate difficulties. For worship language to be purely expressive, all words for every worship service would best be improvised on the spot. *That* would be as immediate and relevant and particular as we could get. In practice, of course, this would be impossible. It would be very difficult to sing together, for one thing. Could we even speak together? In any congregation, we bring a variety of expressive language patterns with us—idiolects, as the linguists call them. Teenagers speak differently from seniors, history professors from electricians, immigrants from long-established locals, extraverts from introverts—and sometimes, pastors from laypeople. Finding words that are expressive for all of us is quite a challenge.

This underlying desire and expectation—that worship be expressive—is at the heart of many conflicts over worship. It is one crucial reason churches are splintering along generational lines: believing that worship language must be primarily expressive, each generation insists that worship be expressive *for them*, and no one wishes to make the effort to speak in someone else's language. In order to understand and perhaps even heal these conflicts, we have to recognize that, indeed, worship language should be expressive, but that is not its only important quality. Moreover, worship language ought to be expressive for the whole local body and not only some small demographic segment of it.

This means that we all face the challenging task of adapting our natural idiolects when we go to worship. We arrive in church carrying language patterns from outside, for better or worse. The language we find expressive is formed to some extent by the music we listen to, by the things we read, by our schooling, by our families and neighborhoods, and by the media. Meanwhile, we all learn patterns of language particular to the worship style and tradition we are used to. Some of

---

*Eddie Espinosa, "Change My Heart, O God," © 1982 Mercy/Vineyard Publishing (ASCAP), admin. in North America by Music Services o/b/o Vineyard Music USA. All rights reserved. Used by permission.

us have learned a prayer-book-and-hymnal language that becomes, over the years, expressive for us. Other worshipers, such as those in charismatic, free-church, or African American traditions, even without the use of written prayer books or preachers' manuscripts, still have a shared worship language: a storehouse of words and patterns, metaphors and images, an oral tradition stored in ears and hearts. All of us are constantly adapting in worship, learning to express our own devotion through someone else's song lyrics, someone else's prayer—even if that person's idiolect is much like our own. Every congregation has crisscrossing patterns of many inherited expressive dialects—and language itself is amazingly diverse and dynamic. So is every worshiping community.

Thus, worship leaders have to recognize that we cannot simply take "every-day" language and assume it will be expressive in worship for everyone. There is no single or constant everyday language. Instead, a better goal is to remember that together we are always in the process of forming a communal expressive language. No matter what our predominant worship style, all of us, in going to worship, are doing much more than merely expressing what we personally feel or think. We are also having our expressive ability expanded by learning patterns of language, old and new, healthy and unhealthy too, that eventually begin to feel natural.

This is actually a marvelous opportunity, not only for preachers, but for pray-ers and songwriters and all sorts of worship leaders. We have the chance to help people learn forms of expression that will deepen their knowledge and love of God. We can place the words of Scripture on people's lips so that these ancient words over time become expressive for them. We can form a community of believers precisely through this effort to find a shared communal language, drawing on many sources. Finally, we can use expressive language to form our devotion. We have all had the experience of responding to something we have read by exclaiming, "That's exactly what I feel, except I didn't know how to say it!" Our worship language can give

### Language Creates Gospel Meaning

"We are not simply beings who use language. We are beings whose capacity to see the world in certain ways depends upon having that world first 'named' for us linguistically by others. We cannot think what we cannot say. . . . This understanding of language profoundly affects our understanding of worship. It means that the language of worship generates a world of meaning grounded in the revelation of the gospel and draws us into this new world where our religious affections are trained properly, thereby moving us from the fragmentation of humanity's fall to the new wholeness and integrity made available through the incarnation."[3]

—*Kendra G. Hotz and Matthew T. Mathews*

people that same gift, helping us all find the words we cannot find on our own. Together we can learn how to express ourselves to God and to one another.

## Language Has an *Aesthetic* Dimension

Words are not merely little suitcases that "carry" meanings for instructive purposes. They have aesthetic qualities: sounds, rhythms, and networks of meaning. Some words are smooth and noble, some are rough and vulgar, some are rich in meaning, others are worn out from overuse, and still others, entirely technical. All these qualities affect how we respond to words. It is useful therefore to pay attention to the way words create an aesthetic effect—the way they play on our senses, emotions, and subconscious associations.

For instance, all of us desire to experience some beauty in worship. This is appropriate because, after all, beauty helps point us to the grandeur of God. So beautiful words certainly have a place in worship. This is one important argument used by those who favor formal language in worship; they seek words that have been composed by poets and polished through centuries of use and refinement. This prayer of confession, for instance, was composed in its original form by Thomas Cranmer for the English Book of Common Prayer in 1559:

> Almighty and most merciful Father,
> we have wandered and strayed from your ways like lost sheep.
> We have followed too much the devices and desires of our own hearts.
> We have offended against your holy laws.
> We have left undone those things that we ought to have done;
> and we have done those things that we ought not to have done;
> and there is no health in us.
> But you, O Lord, have mercy upon us sinners.
> Spare those who confess their faults.
> Restore those who are penitent,
> according to your promises declared to mankind
> in Christ Jesus our Lord.
> And grant, O most merciful Father, for his sake,
> that we may live a disciplined, righteous and godly life,
> to the glory of your holy name. Amen.[4]

Many congregations appreciate the elegance of formal words like these. They are smooth, decorous, rhythmically pleasing, and cover a lot of ground in a few words.

On the other hand, rough and common words also have a place in worship. The Bible is full of rough-edged language, used to convey God's judgment on sin or the realities of a fallen world or that which is merely humble. "My strength is dried up like a potsherd," writes the psalmist, "and my tongue sticks to the roof of my mouth" (Ps. 22:15).

So rather than claiming that all worship words must be beautiful, perhaps we could say instead that the aesthetic qualities of worship words must be fitting to the purpose. We cannot rightly speak of God's majesty in silly, sloppy, or stupid words. This is why some[5] cringe at these lines in the popular song "Awesome God":

> When He rolls up His sleeves
> He ain't just puttin' on the Ritz.[6]

That cute, idiomatic phrase (which has prior associations with a movie, of all things) detracts from the song's effort to declare God's majesty. There is a place for humor and playfulness in worship songs, especially those meant for children, but not in a song about majesty, please. In cases such as this, the aesthetic qualities of the words undercut the truth we wish to declare through them.

Similarly, we can sometimes hide the blunt truths of suffering in flowery euphemisms. Imagine this prayer offered on behalf of an older woman who has recently been admitted to hospice care:

> O most magnificent and holy God, we beseech thee to pour out thy divine balm upon Mrs. Williams, for she languishes in the wastelands of life's afflictions, awaiting that day when she shall crest the hill of the Promised Land. By your mighty Providence raise her up to climb that steep mountain path to glory.

Among congregations accustomed to densely metaphorical language, this could be a powerful and appropriate prayer, particularly if everyone already knows exactly what Mrs. Williams is going through. The metaphors might serve to draw her particular suffering into a story of redemption larger than her own life. Yet the bald truth about Mrs. Williams's condition is important too: we should not neglect to say at some point that Mrs. Williams is suffering constant pain from her bone cancer, pain so severe she can barely speak or think. In other words, it is possible to use formal language to turn away from pain, and in so doing we hide the important truth that the Christian life includes, embraces, and finally redeems experiences that are anything but pleasant, beautiful, or elegant. To pray and worship genuinely, we need to get some grit between our teeth, as it were.

Kathleen Norris likes to say that language in worship ought to be "incarnational."[7] This means not only that it ought to reflect our condition as unique created beings, but that our language ought to awaken our senses to the presence of God in the *matter* of this world. When we use incarnational language in worship, we attend to the sounds of the words as well as to the images and other perceptions they create

> ### Crying Our Lament
>
> The Brazilian lament "Um pouco além do presente"[8] is a wonderful example of a song whose language precisely fits its function in worship. In a minor key, the verses speak of our hope in Jesus Christ, and the time when there will be "no war, no disaster, no crime, no more desolation, no sadness." But here and now, before that time, the chorus cries out in a phrase that rises to the song's musical high point: "Venha teu Reino Senhor" (your kingdom come, Lord). The lament concludes in an extended cry of sorrow and longing—a longing that is too deep for words, and so no words are used, but sobbing syllables: Ai-eh, ei-ah, ai-eh, a-eh, a-eh.

in our minds. What do these words make us see, taste, hear, smell, and feel—in the sense of touch and in an emotional sense? Are the words' sounds and sensory qualities fitting to the act of worship in question?

Attending to the aesthetic dimension of language helps form in us an attentiveness to the world and an honesty about our own spiritual lives. Using language fitting to the purpose helps us know that we can be *real* in worship, that different tones and emotional ranges are fully appropriate for a worshiping body. If worship is always entirely exuberant or always entirely solemn, we send the message to God's people that only certain emotions are religiously acceptable. But God invites us to bring our whole selves to worship—surely the chaotic emotions expressed in the book of Psalms amply demonstrate this. In the presence of God, as God's people, we can feel sadness, joy, contrition, thankfulness, peace, grief, agitation, anger, reverence, assurance, determination, and every nuance of human experience. Using vivid language avoids a kind of bland sameness that associates being in worship only with a detached pose of religiosity.

### Language Has an *Instructive* Dimension

Perhaps all Christian traditions would agree that one important function of language in worship, particularly in the homily or sermon, is to instruct. We need to understand a whole range of facts and ideas in order to believe and practice our faith well: salvation by grace, the Trinity, the historical background of the book of Jeremiah, first-century Jewish customs, and so on. We also need instruction to apply biblical knowledge to our daily lives. When Jesus warns his listeners not to give money or pray or fast in public like the Pharisees, for example, what does that mean for me? We need instructive words to be formed into better disciples.

Some congregations seem almost exclusively focused on instruction—instruction in biblical knowledge, doctrine, and ethics. Singing makes up the "worship" part of the service, and then comes the "teaching," which, by measure of dramatic centrality and time investment, is clearly the central purpose of the gathering. However, since *everything* spoken or sung in worship has an inherently formative dimension, not just the obviously instructive words, to call only one part of the service "the teaching" is a little misleading.

We ought to ask about *all* our worship words: How do these words, over time, instruct worshipers? "Rejoice, the Lord Is King," for instance—a beautiful hymn written by Charles Wesley in the eighteenth century—is sung often in some churches. But if our songs and prayers over time only picture God as king, and never, for example, as servant, we are instructing the congregation in an unbalanced,

---

### "Open Your Books, 'Cause Now It's Time to Sing": Directive Words

One subset of instructive words is what we might call *directive* words. These are the incidental words that worship leaders use to give people directions during worship. They're the words sometimes squeezed between songs or other acts of worship:

- "You can sit down now."
- "Turn in your hymnbooks to number 368."
- "Why don't you turn to your neighbor, shake his hand, and say to him 'God loves you'?"
- "Those wishing individual prayer from our prayer leaders may proceed during communion to the prayer chapel."

These words may be necessary to help congregants worship, but they can often be a distraction from the more important business of actually worshiping. One way to ease this discomfort is to consider how to make the directive words instructional not just about physical actions, but about the *worship action* about to be performed.

For example, instead of saying,

> "Now let's sing 'Open My Eyes, Lord,'"

the worship leader might say,

> "In order to prepare our hearts to receive God's Word, let us pray together, singing 'Open My Eyes, Lord.'"

The key is to identify the worship action—praise, confession, dedication, adoration—that a particular physical action is serving. Ask yourself, "Why are we doing this?" (If you can't think of a good answer, perhaps you might consider doing something else instead.) If you can keep instructional words to a minimum without leaving the congregation feeling uncomfortably unguided, you can help people focus on worshiping and not on "what are we doing now?"

Finally, when using in-between words, even when instructing, it is most hospitable to do so not by pleading ("Would you please sit down?") or coercing ("I'll bet you can sing louder than that!"), but by *inviting* the congregation into the next act of worship ("Will you join together in prayer?").

and in the end insufficiently biblical, view of God. Or, to give a positive example, if every week we speak words of repentance and confession, and hear in response God's words of grace, then over time we are forming people who know how to say "I'm sorry," seek forgiveness, and try to start over. We are teaching a fundamental dynamic of Christian faith.

Sometimes our words do not reflect what we actually believe about God, ourselves, the church, and the world. For example, if we believe that God calls us not only as individuals but as a *community* of Christians, then we ought to sing and pray with the pronoun *we* sometimes and not only with *I*. If we believe that God is three-in-one, then we should focus our worship on the Spirit as attentively as on the Father and the Son. If we believe that we are a small group of Christians among millions throughout the world, then we should rejoice and suffer with our brothers and sisters on the other side of the planet regularly through prayer and other means.

So as we choose and create worship words, we have to understand that our words *all* have an instructive dimension. They teach our children and newcomers, and they continually shape all of us in the faith. Therefore, we must aim not only our

### "Go in Peace and Be Sure to Buy Raffle Tickets": Dealing with Announcements

Nearly every worship leader has struggled with the vexing problem of announcements—those bits of information about a church's programs and the life of the congregation. "Announcement time" can often be boring, as information overload interrupts a congregation immersed in worship. It can also be awkward, as when someone gives the hard news of a church member's recent hospitalization followed by the comparatively trivial detail of a Sunday school classroom change, or when the congregational charge at the end of the service to live in the power of the Holy Spirit is appended with a request to remember the youth fund-raising event being held right after the service concludes.

Unfortunately, there is no easy solution to the announcement problem. Almost anywhere they are offered they are likely to kill the dramatic momentum of a service, no matter how enthusiastic or upbeat the person who delivers them. Some churches solve the problem by printing important congregational information in the bulletin or projecting it onto a screen before the service and avoiding any spoken announcements in worship at all. Others confine spoken announcements to a window of time directly before or after the worship service itself. These are fine solutions.

Another solution, which recognizes the importance of connecting the weekly worship hour to our daily lives of worshipful service, is to restrict announcements to only those intended for the whole congregation, and then to speak them in the context of the church's intercessory prayer. Information about the fund-raiser can be spoken as a way of guiding the church's prayers for its youth program. If an announcement seems jarring as a platform for prayer, it probably belongs outside worship.

deliberately instructive words, but *all* our words toward the kind of people God wishes us to become. We are pilgrims on the way to God's kingdom, and we must begin to speak the language of that realm while we are still on the way.

### Language Has a *Memorial* Dimension

One of the most important things we do together as Christians is remember. If we seek in worship only a "mystical . . . experience of God apart from histori-cal time," we are abandoning the pattern of Christian worship established in the Psalms and observed throughout the centuries and across traditions.[9] The Psalms, and indeed the whole Bible, celebrate a God who acts in history, and our Scriptures teach us to remember in our worship words the mighty acts of God. To understand God's nature and to prompt our fitting gratitude, in worship we remember the sweep of salvation history, we remember what God has done for us in our specific traditions, and we remember the promises of God fulfilled in our own lives. Language itself, in fact, always carries memories with it. Words and patterns accumulate meaning through a constant process of passing down former meanings as well as gaining new associations. Children and adults who are learning to write in English face this problem every day with English spell-ing. Even in their spelling, our words remember their past. The English word *knight*, for example, remembers its Anglo-Saxon heritage with that silent *k* (it used to be pronounced "k-nicht"). The name *Watergate* evokes a whole historical period, so much so that even attaching the suffix *-gate* to something can carry the meaning of scandal. So how can we skillfully wield, in worship, this power of language to remember?

We can honor the memorial function of worship language by connecting our own lives to the stories of ordinary saints who have gone before us. We can talk about them, use words they have left for us, or both. This kind of remembering is important not only for older worshipers but also for young ones. Placing our stories into the larger story of God's purposes grants us both dignity and humility. It blesses us with meaning: we are part of a story that began long before us and will continue as long after us as God wills. It reminds us that we are responsible to the past, to the present, and to the future. In worship, we must tell the story of God's redemption, both in its grand sweep and in its specifics for us, over and over again. Memorial language forms us into a people who belong to each other and to the larger story of God's grace. (For more ideas on how to remember in worship, see chapter 8, "Something Old.")

Our family has attended otherwise lively and wonderful contemporary wor-ship services that unfortunately left the impression that as Christians we have no history. We could easily have come away from these services thinking that the Bible was compiled by several New Testament apostles and then plopped directly into our midst—yesterday. It's easy to feel uncomfortably unmoored in such worship services. What happened in all those centuries between the New Testament writers and today? Tradition must not become an idol we defend for its own sake, of course; but on the other hand, we must not act as if those many generations who came before us—poor benighted souls—have nothing to teach us.[10]

Therefore, it is fitting that at least some of our language in worship should borrow from sources before our time. Yes, we must evaluate old sources; after all, the saints of the ages made mistakes too. They had their biases and blind spots (as do we). But we ought to hear what our forebears have to teach us, those from the ancient days right up to those from our parents' generation. Even churches that consider themselves traditional have to be careful not to get completely stuck in the mode of only one, usually fairly recent tradition.

Remembering in worship is a matter not merely of looking backward toward the past but of bringing the truth of the past into the present. This is what we do, for example, when we celebrate communion. As the apostle Paul writes, "For I received from the Lord what I also passed on to you . . ." (1 Cor. 11:23). In communion, we remember Jesus's death and resurrection, but we also celebrate its

### "Traditional" and "Contemporary": Term Trouble

Many churches found an uneasy truce in the last decades' "worship wars" by splitting into two subcongregations. At different hours on Sunday, each group worships in its own expressive idiom, sometimes labeled with terms like *traditional* and *contemporary*. These terms, however commonly used, may be more trouble than they are worth. They are not only imprecise, but they also have polemical overtones.

The word *contemporary* refers to anything "with the times," anything happening now. By this definition, whatever worship is being offered by God's people will be contemporary, whether it is a centuries-old liturgy of the Armenian Orthodox Church or the we-just-nailed-down-our-praise-set-five-minutes-ago worship at a community church.

Similarly, the term *traditional* is often invoked without much clarity about *whose* tradition is under consideration. If a worship service, or a song, or a prayer, or a sermon style is "traditional," what does that mean? Is it in the tradition of 1950s New England Presbyterianism? Or 1820s Baptist Revivalism? Or medieval French monasticism? The words *contemporary* and *traditional* mean very little, even when we think we know what they mean.

And worse, these terms are most often used in an unhelpful way: as code words that pit one generation over against another—"newfangled" and "old-fashioned"—in a way that divides rather than unites the body of Christ.

In this text we will try to use other, more precise terms in the hope that we can encourage others to do the same.

> **Anamnesis**
>
> "Jesus said: TOUTO POIEITE EIS TEN EMEN ANAMNESIN ['Do this in remembrance of me'] (1 Cor. 11:24ff.). This anamnesis or memorial . . . is something quite different from a mere exercise of memory. It is a restoration of the past so that it becomes present and a promise. In the world of biblical culture 'to remember' is to make present and operative. As a result of this type of 'memory,' time is not unfolded along a straight line adding irrevocably to each other the successive periods which compose it. Past and present are merged. A real actualization of the past in the present becomes possible."[11]
>
> —J.-J. von Allmen

reality in our present community as well as its promise for the future, the hope that it makes real for us. Events in the past flow forward in meaning through time. By using language of remembering, we welcome those meanings into our midst. This practice of remembering helps form us into a people who know their place in history, a people of both humility and great hope.

To sum this up, we can say that language in worship forms us with all its dimensions—aesthetic, expressive, instructive, and memorial. Sometimes these actions of language feel comfortable and sometimes they stretch us uncomfortably. The important thing is not necessarily to gain an even balance among the dimensions; this would be difficult to calculate anyway, as any given worship element operates in more than one dimension simultaneously. Instead, the important thing is not to completely neglect any one dimension at the expense of others.

The Iona Community, an ecumenical worship reform group based in Scotland, has taken as its emblem an ancient Celtic symbol for the Spirit, the wild goose. This free and beautiful creature is also unpredictable; it sometimes has a way of disturbing the peace. It reminds us that the Spirit is not under our control. Alison Adam, a founding member of the Wild Goose Worship Group connected with the Iona Community, likes to say that we can expect worship led by the Spirit to both "bless and disturb" us. Language in worship should not only please and uplift us, serving as a means of God's comforting grace, but also challenge and transform us, serving as a means through which God works out our salvation in us.

## Summary Calls to Action

> → Seek continuously to develop as a congregation a communal language that all worshipers can find expressive of their devotion.

→ Attend to the aesthetic dimension of words by using vivid language fitting to the purpose.

→ Let directive language teach the actions of worship whenever possible.

→ Use language to connect the congregation to the bigger story of God's redemption and God's saints of all generations.

### Exercises

1. Which of the four dimensions of worship language described here seems most natural to you? to your congregation? Are there any dimensions you or your congregation tend to neglect? What effect might your congregation's strengths and weaknesses have on the faith formation of your congregants?

2. During the next worship service you attend, keep tabs on the four dimensions of worship words discussed here. On a piece of paper, make four columns labeled *aesthetic, expressive, instructive, memorial*. As each element of worship is enacted, jot a few words of description under the column or columns where you think it best fits. You might judge a choir anthem, for instance, to be primarily aesthetic and memorial. The song "Here I Am to Worship" might be primarily expressive. The sermon might use language primarily for its instructive dimension.

Of course, this is somewhat artificial as words perform these functions to some degree all at once, but it can still be useful at the end of the service to consider, roughly drawn, whether each dimension was present. Did the service seem to leave some dimensions out?

3. As you do exercise 2, take special note of elements in the service where each dimension of language was honored well. What was the best instance of each dimension?

4. Which dimensions are most comfortable and uncomfortable for you? During a worship service, take notes during moments you feel uncomfortable, bored, offended, or otherwise displeased. Later, analyze possible reasons for your feelings. Is it possible that you are resistant to the language dimension this worship element appropriately performs?

For instance, perhaps you rolled your eyes through an emotional worship song because you resist the expressive function of language. Perhaps you disliked the Fanny Crosby hymn with organ because you are not much interested in the memorial dimension.

Of course, it's possible that you are responding to the *content* of the song or prayer. For instance, you appreciate the expressive dimension but you thought the sentiment expressed in the song was shallow or inappropriate. Test this by asking yourself how you might have replaced what bothered you with something else that performed the same function(s).

See if you can distinguish content from the principal dimension of language expressed in order to discern your own feelings about the various dimensions of language in worship.

5. Write a sermon in which you invite your congregation to remember the mighty acts of God. (Possible texts: Ps. 78; 136; Heb. 11.) What do we learn about God's nature when we recall how God acts in history? How might you invite your listeners to catalog, in a spirit of wonder and praise, the mighty acts of God in your own congregation's history? in their personal histories?

# 2

# Worship as Dialogic Encounter

*"Biblical faith . . . is uncompromisingly and unembarrassedly dialogic."*[1]
—Walter Brueggemann

Good thing he was only a guest pastor. Maybe no one told him how the service was supposed to conclude, or maybe he chose to try something different that week, but when this guest pastor did not end the service by raising his hands and pronouncing a blessing, my mother was not happy. Fortunately, her own pastor was seated right behind her that day, so as the postlude played, she turned around to him and demanded, "Where was my blessing? I want a blessing before I leave!" Her pastor laughed and offered to bless her himself, right then and there.

My mother was good-natured about the guest minister's lapse, but she was very serious about wanting a blessing as she prepared to leave worship. Why? What was the big deal? I think my mom recognized that the blessing is one important way God acts upon us in worship: God blesses us and promises loving faithfulness to us as we go out into the world. The words used in parting blessings are often prayers: "May the Lord bless you and keep you. May the Lord make his face to shine upon you and be gracious to you. . . ." (Num. 6:24–25). But when the pastor speaks these words, we understand them as the conduit of God's action in the moment: through these words God *is* blessing us.[2]

## Worship as Mutual Action

Worship is fundamentally a series of actions. We sing, we pray, we praise, we confess, we cry out to God. But none of our actions would mean much if God did not act as well. We worship not a dumb idol but a living God. This God acts in the world—and in worship. In fact, we could not worship at all if God did not invite us and enable us to do so. God's grace comes first; then we respond. David Peterson summarizes his careful survey of the Bible's teachings on worship with this statement: "The worship of the living and true God is essentially *an engagement with him on the terms that he proposes and in the way that he alone makes possible*."[3] God acts first, and we respond with worship. This is why some kind of call to worship and parting blessing are important elements. They frame the service with the actions of God, reminding us of the fundamental shape of the Christian life: God reaches out to us, we respond through grace, and God blesses us for service in the world. This is why the view of worship in which we are the actors, so to speak, and God is the audience—a view attributed to the Danish philosopher Søren Kierkegaard—is not quite adequate. It's a good way to counter our tendency to make leaders the actors and the congregation the audience. But maybe we need to get rid of the theater metaphor altogether. Worship is a dialogic encounter, a loving conversation between God and the people of God.[4]

In worship, much of this exchange of actions happens through words. Words are performative; as we speak them, we are doing what they say. We praise and confess and cry out in words. God speaks to us in words too—primarily in the words of Scripture and in the words of the sermon, but also in words of forgiveness, blessing, welcome, and healing. We also speak to each other, encouraging each other, confessing to each other, and sharing joys and burdens. So it's appropriate

---

### God Is Not the Object of Our Worship

"If God is the object of worship, then worship must proceed from me, the subject, to God, who is the object. God is the being out there who needs to be loved, worshiped, and adored by me. Therefore, the true worship of God is located in me, the subject. I worship God to magnify his name, to enthrone God, to exalt him in the heavens. God is then pleased with me because I have done my duty.

"If God is understood, however, as the personal God who acts as subject in the world and in worship rather than the remote God who sits in the heavens, then worship is understood not as the acts of adoration God demands of me but as the disclosure of Jesus, who has done for me what I cannot do for myself. In this way worship is the doing of God's story within me so that I live in the pattern of Jesus' death and resurrection."[5]

—*Robert E. Webber*

to think of worship as the kind of ongoing dialogue that characterizes any loving relationship. As worship scholar John Witvliet writes: "The God of the Bible is not interested simply in having us contemplate him or appease him. This God desires the give and take of faithful life together, with good communication right at the center."[6] This suggests that one fundamental consideration for our worship words is how they reflect that ongoing dialogue.

Some churches, very keen to make this dialogic aspect of worship unmistakable to everyone present, use bold, all-caps print in their bulletins. The elements of worship are grouped under huge headings, something like this:

GOD INVITES US TO WORSHIP
    call to worship
    songs of praise

WE CONFESS OUR SINS
    song of confession
    prayer of confession

GOD SPEAKS TO US
    assurance of pardon
    Scripture reading
    sermon
    reading of the law

WE RESPOND IN GRATITUDE
    song
    offering
    passing of the peace

WE REMEMBER GOD'S GRACE AT THE LORD'S SUPPER
    institution
    invitation
    communion

GOD SENDS US OUT INTO THE WORLD
    closing hymn
    blessing

Helping worshipers understand the different actions of worship is a wonderful practice, and most churches could do it better. We stay attentive and worship more fully when we are given cues and when we recognize that the service has a meaningful order. Bulletin headings are only one way to do this, of course. Leaders can guide the congregation orally with simple words such as "Let's respond to God's word with praise," for example. And there are many other ways. But before worship leaders can begin drawing attention to the loving dialogue of worship, they need to make sure it is actually there.

### But What Is *God* Saying?

Perhaps you have attended very fine worship services that were, unfortunately, not very attentive to worship as dialogue. In a typical scenario, the service begins when the music leader steps up to the microphone, people stand, the drums and guitars burst into action, and words come up on the screen:

> Come, now is the time to worship.
> Come, now is the time to give your heart . . .*

The next song continues:

> Here I am to worship
> here I am to bow down
> here I am to say that you're my God . . .†

Then the worship leader prays, asking God to be present among us and accept our praise. Then we sing:

> God of wonders beyond our galaxy,
> You are holy, holy.
> The universe declares your majesty . . .‡

So far, who has done all the talking? We have. It's true, we have been saying worthy things: We have invited each other to worship. We have told God we are here to worship. We have praised God. But what has God said to us so far? No one in the congregation and certainly not in the leadership actually believes that we come to worship out of our own strength and that we call God down to be with us from some far-off realm using rituals and incantations. And yet, doesn't this way of opening worship subtly dramatize those very notions?

---

*Brian Doerksen, "Come, Now Is the Time to Worship," © 1998 Vineyard Songs (UK/EIRE) (PRS) admin. in North America by Music Services. All rights reserved. Used by permission.

†Tim Hughes, "Here I Am to Worship," © 2001 Thankyou Music (admin. by EMI Christian Music Publishing c/o: Music Services). All rights reserved. Used by permission.

‡Marc Byrd and Steve Hindalong, "God of Wonders," © 2000 New Spring Publishing, Inc. / Never Say Never Songs (ASCAP) (admin. by Brentwood-Benson Music Publishing, Inc.) Storm Boy Music / (BMI) / Meaux Mercy (admin. by EMI Christian Music Group c/o Music Services). All rights reserved. Used by permission.

## A Prayer Is a Promise

When pastors or worship leaders pray before the sermon or message, they signal to the congregation what the church—or at least the pastor—imagines the sermon will actually do. The prayer, in other words, sets the congregation's expectations. It can claim God's promise to work through the Holy Spirit and open our hearts to hear, understand, love, and obey the Word about to be spoken, or it can do . . . something else.

One week when I was visiting a huge church that boasted a semiprofessional orchestra and thousands of worshipers each week, the pastor prayed before his sermon a prayer that was probably aiming for humility, but ended up hitting insignificance. He prayed that God would bless "this little bit of information to help us live better lives this week."

"That's what a sermon is?" I thought. "Not the living Word of God? Not the very presence of Jesus Christ? Not the power of the Holy Spirit to bless and disturb? Just 'a little bit of information'?"

Despite the low expectations the pastor telegraphed for his . . . talk, I decided to listen hard for what God wanted to say to me. But after a half hour of Scripture-neglecting, simplistic, self-help drivel—targeted to a very small demographic sliver of those assembled—what God said to me was: "You're angry. That's all right; you should be angry that my hungry people, who come here to be fed by my Word, get this instead."

As preachers, our humility is appropriate. But so is our desire to claim God's promise in the living and active Word. We must pray, in the people's hearing, that God will help us speak the Word, and then we must speak it.

Even in those parts of the service that are obviously supposed to be God talking to us—the Scripture and sermon—there can be little sense of God's action. This is not uncommon, unfortunately, across a range of worship styles. In both high-liturgical churches and charismatic free churches, I've heard terrible sermons that barely refer to the Scripture and reveal more about the speaker's "issues" than anyone needs to know. Instead of hearing God's Word to us, the congregation hears irrelevant jokes and sentimental, vaguely spiritual stories.

It's possible for a worship dialogue to be one-sided the other way, too, with the congregation doing little besides sitting, standing, listening, and occasionally mumbling through a dusty old hymn or two. This gives the picture that we come to church only to go through ancient motions, or to receive instruction—and perhaps a scolding—to which we barely have the means to respond. This is not as common anymore, thankfully; the increased levels of participation for worshipers in Christian churches across the spectrum can certainly be regarded as a healthy development. Still, we have to be careful that in our words and in all other ways, we don't make worship all about us and the wonderful stuff *we* are doing.

### The First-Words Test

The British Christian satirical Web site Ship of Fools operates a serious worship observation-and-reporting enterprise called "the Mystery Worshipper." It is composed of a group of "intrepid" volunteers who visit worship services all around the globe incognito, and then write a report on the Web site. "Mystery Worshippers" are required in their reports to answer a series of questions designed to elicit telling details about the service. The reports are funny and entertaining, but they also give a revealing, composite insight into Christian worship (in English) around the world.

One of the required questions is this: "What were the exact opening words of the service?" This question may seem trivial, but the opening words of worship reveal much about the congregation's notions of what worship is supposed to be and do. Just as the first minute can set the tone for a sports game, a business meeting, a job interview, or a musical performance, so the opening words of a worship service communicate expectations that will influence worshipers' experience of the whole service. Think about these opening words, and imagine what is being communicated in each case about what worship is:

- "Alleluia, Sing to Jesus" (lyrics to an opening song)
- Good morning, and welcome to worship!
- There's plenty of room up front!
- Blessed be God: Father, Son, and Holy Spirit.
- We're going to start now, so a bit of quiet please.
- Hey, good morning. I said *good morning*! Welcome to Vanguard Church. There seems to be a lot of energy in the room. Let's start off by standing and singing "You Are Worthy."
- Grace to you, and peace, in the name of our Lord Jesus Christ.

For the whole list of questions and to read worship reports, visit http://www.shipoffools.com/Mystery/index.html.

Perhaps the question to ask is whether we actually expect God to speak. If we wish to invite worshipers into that expectation, then the opening words of the service are especially important. A blessing and invitation from God, in the words of Scripture, set the expectation that God is already speaking in this place, today. This prepares worshipers to hear God in any element of the service, even those not specifically thought of as God's Word to us.

## What Should We Say?

Good worship words not only reflect the dialogic nature of worship, they also help us learn what to say in this loving exchange. John Witvliet, who besides being a worship scholar is also the father of four small children, draws a helpful analogy between worship words and teaching small children to speak. We teach our children to say

---

**But What Does the Song Actually *Say*?**

Congregational song can perform a wide range of actions within a service. Offering loving, intimate praise is an important one, but not the only one. Songs can also

- gather people together and focus attention;
- adore God's holiness;
- confess personal and corporate sin;
- lament brokenness;
- celebrate God's grace;
- tell stories;
- ask God for something;
- make promises;
- bless and encourage others.

It's important, then, for those planning and leading worship to know the liturgical *purpose* a song has, that is to say, its function within a service. The lyrics are key to discerning this, and perhaps most important in figuring this out is knowing *who is speaking*, and *to whom* and *for what purpose*.

For more on this, see exercise 2 at the conclusion of this chapter; "Using Repetition Well," point 5, in chapter 4; and appendix 3 at the conclusion of the book.

---

"Please," "Thank you," "I'm sorry," and the other phrases fundamental to human relationships long before our children actually mean those words when they say them. At first these words are, you might say, only rituals. Eventually, though, if we do our job well, our children say these words on their own and even mean them. The rituals become meaningful. They *grow into* the important relational values and practices that these word-rituals represent. The same is true of the basic words we speak in worship. For example, praise, confession, thanksgiving, and service can all be distilled into basic things we say to God: "I love you," "I'm sorry," "Thank you," and "How can I help?" As Witvliet observes, "Good worship services make room for these essential words. They help each of us express our particular experience, but they also help us practice forms of speech we're still growing into."[7] One important thing that worship leaders and pastors do is help congregations learn those basic words, and a broad vocabulary of them. We can teach people how to say "I love you" to God through praise, for example, but can we also teach them how to say "I'm sorry" and how to offer their dedicated service in words?

## The "I" and the "We"

I recently heard a Roman Catholic nun and worship scholar eloquently describe the profound changes brought about in Roman Catholic worship since Vatican II. She drew a distinction between what she called "liturgical prayer" and "devotional

|            | Liturgical prayer | Devotional prayer |
|------------|-------------------|-------------------|
| **Similarities** | personal | personal |
|            | essential | essential |
| **Differences** | enacts paschal (Easter) mystery by its very structure | enacts individual affectivity and relationship |
|            | is source and summit of Christian living | flows to and from liturgy |
|            | ecclesial | individual |
|            | transcultural | cultural |
|            | rhythmic | sporadic |
|            | it shapes us | we shape it |

prayer," and pointed out that Roman Catholics have recently been working to make worship a place of devotional prayer as well as liturgical prayer (see the above chart that she used to explain the distinction).

### Dialogue Puzzlers

Sometimes when the Bible is read in worship, worship planners will wisely use multiple readers to help the congregation understand that the passage involves a conversation among different persons. This is often fairly obvious, as when Jesus is talking to the woman at the well in John 4. It's less obvious in other places in Scripture. Psalm 95, for instance, like many psalms, has an internal dialogic character to it; it begins with a call to praise from one worshiper to others:

Come, let us sing for joy to the LORD

At verse 8 God's voice is heard:

Do not harden your hearts as you did at Meribah.

In the same way, some songs have a dialogic character to them. They too are led best when the congregation is helped to understand and participate in the conversation. The verses of the song "Here I Am, Lord" by Dan Schutte are in God's voice:

I, the Lord of sea and sky,
I have heard my people cry.

Each verse concludes with a question: "Whom shall I send?" The refrain, in another voice, is meant as the congregational response:

Here I am, Lord . . . I will hold your people in my heart.*

This song, then, is much better understood as a dialogue when a soloist—or perhaps a trio representing the Trinity?—sings the verses, and the congregation the refrain. Creative leaders may be able to think of other musical adaptations that allow the dialogic character of the song to come through.

---

*Daniel L. Schutte, "Here I Am, Lord," text and music © 1981, OCP Publications. Published by OCP Publications, 5536 NE Hassalo, Portland, OR 97213. All rights reserved. Used with permission.

Her distinction, based on Roman Catholic theology and experience of worship, seemed instructive and helpful to me as a Protestant.[8] It prompted me to reflect that free-church Protestants have made worship almost entirely a place of devotional prayer. In other words, we come to worship expecting a subjective, emotional, and individual experience of God's presence. We are looking for intimacy with God, and meanwhile the other people nearby—well, they're doing the same thing for themselves. We wind up having personal devotions together in the same room. Meanwhile, we have forgotten that worship is a place where God acts on us objectively—that is to say, divine action is happening whether we "feel" it or not. We shouldn't forget this, because there's something very comforting about God's objective action, particularly on those inevitable down days when worship—for whatever reason—feels blah and routine.

Early Reformers such as John Calvin, Martin Luther, Thomas Cranmer, and others demonstrated an urgent concern to combine both the liturgical *and* the devotional into Christian worship. The early sixteenth-century Reformers retained a strong Roman Catholic sense that in worship, God acts apart from any feelings or thoughts we may or may not be having as individuals. On the other hand, they also recognized that worship has a crucial educational (or, as we have been calling it, formative) function: in worship we learn how to have a personal devotional life as well. We learn *how* to pray, *how* to read Scripture, *how* to see God acting in our own lives. Moreover, the Reformers strongly emphasized that in worship, God forms us *as a people*. It's a matter not of doing personal devotions in the same room but of *becoming* the community, the body, that God desires us to be.

All of this has very practical implications for worship language. If God is forming us into a body in worship, yet we are also being strengthened and educated in our individual walks with God, do we sing and pray and speak using *we* or *I*? What is the proper personal pronoun for worship words?

In recent years, critics of popular praise-style worship music have complained that virtually all the songs are in the first person. "It's all 'me-n-Jesus,'" people complain. This is not entirely true, of course, but worship music from publishers like Maranatha, Vineyard, Integrity, and so forth has indeed tended to emphasize a personal, emotive expression of devotion (see chapter 6 for more on this). This is partly a function of how this music gets created: musicians have been using a singer-songwriter model taken from folk and pop music, which tends to produce lyrics in what is called, in fact, the lyric mode—that is, the expressions of a single voice.

So is this a problem? Well, yes and no. It is a problem if we use only *I* in our prayers and songs. This suggests, after all, that there is nothing distinctive about the body gathered for worship. It suggests that we are merely a group of individuals with

### The Psalmic "I"

Psalm 25 is not unusual as a psalm in its frequent shifting of address. The psalm begins as a personal address to God:

> To you, O LORD, I lift up my soul;
>> in you I trust, O my God.

By verse 3, the address shifts. The speaker is still speaking to God, but making a general statement of faith rather than conveying a personal circumstance:

> No one whose hope is in you
>> will ever be put to shame.

In verse 8, another form of address appears. This time, the speaker is addressing an audience of peers, offering words of wisdom:

> Good and upright is the LORD;
>> therefore he instructs sinners in his ways.

The psalm alternates among these varying forms of address throughout.

Any use of a psalm in worship—whether as a reading, the basis of a sermon, or the source of a song or litany—must take into account who is speaking to whom at each given point.

For examples of ways to adapt a psalm as a worship resource with attention to forms of address, see exercise 7 at the end of this chapter.

something in common, and we go away from worship as individuals. But this view of ourselves ignores passages like 1 Corinthians 12 from which we learn that we are Christ's presence in the world as a body of believers. We go to worship partly to be formed into that body by the Spirit. So it is appropriate that we use *we* in our prayers and songs in worship in order to remind us that God calls us as a people, together.

At the same time, the use of *I* is also appropriate in worship. After all, the tradition of using *I* in communal worship goes back to the original composition of the Psalms. However, we should note from the example of the Psalms that the lyric voice of the psalmist never stays focused on himself for long. The "I" of the Psalms always turns outward to consider the mighty deeds of God, God's faithfulness to God's people, and the way in which God's relationship with the speaker is surrounded by broader purposes for the world.

As Ruth Duck points out in her comments on the communal "I," our use of the first-person pronoun should reflect the African philosophy of *ubuntu*, summed up in the proverb "I am because we are."[9] So when we use *I* in worship, especially in song, we must let our individual "I" become a communal "I." When I sing words from Psalm 51 in worship—

> Create in me a clean heart, O God,
> and renew a right spirit within me.

—I am joining my voice not only with the others singing that day, but with thousands upon thousands of worshipers from ancient times to the present who have prayed these words. My "I" joins their "I"s and becomes a "we." The same can be true of other songs we sing, old and new, that use the first person:

| | |
|---|---|
| ¡Santo, santo, santo, | Holy, holy, holy, |
| mi corazón te adora! | my heart, my heart adores you! |
| Mi corazón te sabe decir: | My heart pours out my praise to you; |
| santo eres Señor. | you are holy, Lord.[10] |

Nothing could be more intimate than this Argentinian love song to the Lord; yet when I sing it in worship with my brothers and sisters in Christ, it becomes *our* love song to our God, together.

So there are at least two good reasons to continue using the personal pronoun in our communal worship. First, one legitimate purpose of worship is to help us gain the devotional vocabulary we need for our individual relationship with God. Second, the *I* in worship can become a communal "I" when used appropriately. However, there are also compelling reasons to use *we* deliberately in worship, the most important of which is that the use of the plural reminds us that in worship, we are being formed into Christ's body.

Perhaps *we* is the appropriate choice in songs sung near the beginning and end of the service. At the beginning of the service, we need to be reminded that we are coming together to worship. We may have thought of ourselves as individuals in the parking lot, but now we are a congregation. If not, we might as well have stayed home and prayed on our knees in our bedrooms. Also, at the end of the service, we need reminding that we go out into the world not as individuals, on our own, but as part of a dispersed body. We support one another, we belong to one another, even when we are not in a room together. Finally, *we* is the appropriate choice in prayers spoken aloud together by the congregation as well as in prayers spoken by a leader on behalf of the congregation. If the leader is praying his or her

"The African philosophy of *ubuntu* ('I am because we are' or 'A human is a human through other humans') as it finds expression in worship services is important in social capital formation, but the Biblical notion of hospitality to the stranger, remembering that we are all sojourners with God as our Host, should complement and enrich this philosophy towards an all inclusive bonding capital generation."[11]

—Cas Wepener

---

**The Baptismal Door**

Many churches embody—in their architecture and ritual as well as in their words—the conviction that we come to worship as individuals but are then made into a people. One way churches do so is to position the baptismal font at the very door of the sanctuary, saying, in effect, that each of us enters into God's presence only through the grace of Jesus Christ, and at church we become part of Christ's body.

A pastor I know served a church whose font was placed not at the entrance to the sanctuary, but at the front, near the pulpit and communion table. He would begin every service with the same words and actions. He would walk slowly to the font from his seat, and as he visibly and audibly poured a pitcher full of water into the font, he would say: "We gather today as God's forgiven people. The sign of that forgiveness (*pouring*) is the water of baptism. Come, let us worship God."

---

own prayer in front of the congregation, he or she is not leading. Leading means guiding the congregation to pray along with the leader, through the leader's words. The use of *we* is both an invitation to pray along and a reflection of the purpose of communal prayer.

One of our students, Brenda McGee, coined the helpful phrases "I-experience" and "we-experience." Brenda wrote a reflection on a Palm Sunday worship service she attended and described the early parts of the service as creating a "we-experience": the congregation sang Hosanna hymns, the children processed with palm branches, and the Scripture reading and sermon invited the congregation to imagine being in the crowd that day as Jesus rode into Jerusalem. Later elements of the service, particularly the communion, created an "I-experience" as the congregation sang first-person songs of adoration and commitment while receiving the elements. As we discussed Brenda's reflection in class, we noted that communion is not primarily an individual experience, but in this case the dimension of communion involving repentant reflection was appropriately emphasized. We also discussed how the leaders of the service might have made an even more meaningful transition between the "we" of Palm Sunday and our individual reflections on and responses to those stories.

On any Sunday, Christian worship fulfills its purposes best when it invites worshipers to interweave the "I" of their individual devotion with the "we" of the assembled people of God.

## Summary Calls to Action

→ Frame the worship service with words indicating that God is acting to gather and send us, and to set the expectation that God is speaking to us throughout the service.

### "Gather Us In" as a Gathering Song

The song "Gather Us In," by Marty Haugen, is a wonderful song that can be used well at the opening of a service to signal that we are individuals forming into a communal body. Directed to God, it prays

> Gather us in, the lost and forsaken,
>> gather us in, the blind and the lame;
>> call to us now, and we shall awaken,
>> we shall arise at the sound of our name.

Later verses identify things that separate us—both from God and from one another: our age, our health, our pride or fear or pasts. The third verse describes the sacramental activity in worship by which God helps us to fashion holy lives and true hearts. In the fourth stanza, the congregation pleads to be gathered as God's own—not into a place, but into a people, animated by God's Spirit:

> Not in the dark of buildings confining,
>> not in some heaven, light-years away—
>> here in this place the new light is shining,
>> now is the kingdom, and now is the day.
>> Gather us in and hold us forever,
>> gather us in and make us your own;
>> gather us in, all peoples together,
>> fire of love in our flesh and our bone.*

Though the song is directed to God, it never explicitly *names* or addresses God. So when used at the opening of worship, it's best to offer a fitting prayer either before or afterward to give the song proper context.

---

*Marty Haugen, "Gather Us In," text and music copyright © 1982 by GIA Publications, Inc., 7404 S. Mason Ave., Chicago, IL 60638 (www.giamusic.com; 800.442.1358). All rights reserved. Used by permission.

→ Consider the form of address in worship songs so that they fit smoothly into the overall dialogue of worship.

→ Invite the congregation to "say" a number of basic, relational words to God through worship.

→ Balance the use of *I* and *we* in worship so that worshipers see themselves as individuals and as part of the larger worshiping body.

## Exercises

1. What do you wish to say to God in worship? What do you wish God would say to you? Describe a specific time in which you heard God speaking to you in worship. What was the role of worship leadership in making that experience possible?

2. Using the chart below as a model, make a list of each worship element in a worship service you attend.[12] For each element, draw an arrow indicating which direction the dialogue of worship moves in that element. Notice that some elements may have more than one arrow. The passing of the peace and the communion, for example, are worship actions in which God speaks to us and we respond by speaking to one another. In confession, we confess to one another and to God.

| Gathering | Call to Worship ▾ |
| | Greeting ▾ |
| | Prayer of Adoration or Prayer of Invocation ▴ |
| | Call to Confession ▾ |
| | Prayer of Confession and Lament ▴ ◄► |
| | Assurance of Pardon ▾ |
| | Passing of the Peace ▾ ◄► |
| | Thanksgiving ▴ |
| | The Law ▾ |
| | Dedication ▴ ◄► |
| Proclamation | Prayer for Illumination ▴ |
| | Scripture Reading ▾ |
| | Sermon ▾ |
| Response to the Word | Profession of the Church's Faith ◄► ▴ |
| | Prayers of the People ▴ |
| | Offering ▴ |
| The Lord's Supper | Declaration of God's Promises and Invitation ▾ |
| | Prayer of Thanksgiving ▴ |
| | Breaking of the Bread ▾ |
| | Communion ▾ ◄► |
| | Response of Thanksgiving ▴ |
| Sending | Call to Service or Discipleship ▾ |
| | Blessing/Benediction ▾ |

Key:  ▴   we are speaking to God
      ▾   God is speaking to us
      ◄►  we are speaking to one another

Looking at your finished chart, do you think the worship service is creating a dialogic encounter between God and God's people?

3. Using the chart below as a model, make a list of fundamental worship words.[13] During a service you attend, write down examples from the service of elements that represent each worship word. For instance, if you sing "Let All Things Now Living," that would be an example of "thank you." The prayer of intercession would go under "Help." Notice that some of the words can be spoken by either God or us, some only by us, some only by God. After the service, consider the balance of the service. Were some basic words spoken and not others? Were there any elements that surprised you?

|   | Relational words | Worship words |
|---|---|---|
| 1 | *Love You.* | **Praise** |
| 2 | *Sorry.* | **Confession** |
| 3 | *Why?* | **Lament** |
| 4 | *I'm Listening.* | **Illumination** |
| 5 | *Help.* | **Petition** |
| 6 | *Thank You.* | **Thanksgiving** |
| 7 | *What Can I Do?* | **Service** |
| 8 | *Bless You.* | **Blessing** |

4. What would be the most appropriate, brief, and unobtrusive way in your worship context to help the congregation understand what they're doing during each element of worship?

Examples:

- *spoken transitions*

  A leader invites worshipers into the next action by bridging from the previous action. Spoken transitions can be very simple, like this sentence from a traditional liturgy:

  > As the risen Savior gives us his peace, let us share that peace with each other . . .

  Or they can be richer, using words of Scripture and the words of a song. The transition below serves the liturgical function of absolution, moving seamlessly from a spoken or sung confessional prayer to the song "Mourning into Dancing." Along the way, it makes use of Romans 6:8, 11; Psalm 30:5, 12; and the lyrics of the song:

  > Scripture tells us this great good news: we have died with Christ, and we shall also live with him. We are now dead to sin—forgiven and freed—we are alive to God in Jesus Christ. His anger lasts only a moment, but his favor lasts a lifetime. Weeping may linger for the night, but joy comes with the morning. I can't be silent, I must sing, for his joy has come![14]

- *printed indications*

  Headings in the bulletin indicate the purpose of each element. In contrast to spoken words of transition or projected words, a printed order of service has the advantage of giving worshipers a map they can see all at once. For some people, this can be especially helpful and instructive in conveying the overall shape of worship.

- *projected words*

Words appear on the screen(s) to help orient worshipers as they move into the next worship action:

> God invites us into his presence.
>
> We confess our sins.
>
> God assures us we are forgiven.
>
> God speaks to us through Scripture.
>
> We listen for the Word of God.
>
> We rededicate our lives to Jesus.
>
> God sends us out into the world.

Choose one of these methods and sketch out how you would make the method work in a particular service. Or, think of a different way to "cue" the congregation and describe your alternative.

5. Write transitional words for a service that not only cue the congregation to perform the worship action, but also fit with the liturgical season or theme for the day. For instance, in a service focused on Jesus as master, a fitting departure prayer and blessing might be:

> Good Shepherd, you have promised never to leave us or forsake us. Lead us out into the world. Protect and comfort us. Show us your paths. Amen.

Choose a theme or Scripture passage and write transitional elements appropriate to your worship context that fit the theme or passage.

6. Keep track of the number of *I*'s and *we*'s in a particular service. Were the pronouns used in appropriate places both to help form the congregation as a people and to teach a language for devotional prayer? If you think the pronouns were too heavily weighted toward either *I* or *we*, suggest some changes. Suggest different prayers or songs that would have been better, adapt what was used, or compose new prayers or lyrics.

7. Read through some psalms and observe the relationship of "I" and "we" in the psalms. Notice that even the most intimate psalms, such as Psalm 30, place the cries of the psalmist in the context of God's people (v. 4) and the history of God's faithfulness (vv. 1–3, 5, 11–12), so that the immediacy of individual expression is framed with a broader view. Choose a psalm that means something to you and adapt it into a song or prayer for use in worship, mindful of this interplay between

the individual voice and the broader context of God's action in and through God's people.

---

### Psalms for Worship Attending to the I/We Question

#### Responsive Prayer Adapted from Psalm 121

The psalm shifts from first-person singular to second-person singular. Here the psalm is adapted to shape the words of a communal prayer of trust, using first-person plural and direct address to God.

*Leader:* In the morning, we lift our eyes and see the mountains before us—work and trouble, obstacles and fear, worry and burdens—all that overwhelms us. Where will we find help?

*People:* Our help comes from El Shaddai, Maker of heaven and earth.

*Leader:* You, our God, are greater than the mountains.

*People:* Do not let our feet slip as we journey along.

*Leader:* Watch and keep us with your unsleeping eye.

*People:* We are weary, but you never tire of loving us.

*Leader:* Be our shelter and shade; grant us rest.

*People:* Guard us from all evil.

*Leader:* Our lives are hidden in your hand.

*People:* Watch over our coming and going, now and forever. Amen.

#### "Foothold" (based on Psalm 25, sung to the tune "Kingsfold")

This hymn uses *I* in the first verse, then shifts to *we* in the second and third verses, signaling the way in which our individual spiritual struggles are caught up into our shared struggles as a body. Direct address to God governs the whole.

vrs. 1  To you, O Lord, I lift my soul, let me never sink in shame.
Keep your strong hand near and my hope secure on the foothold of your name.
Remember, Lord, your mercies old for the failures of youth weigh down.
Show me truthful ways and fearless days; lead me to the higher ground.

vrs. 2  All the paths of God lead the lost along through the knotted snares of death.
As you free our song and untie our bonds, you confide a mystery yet.
O school us, Lord, in your healing word; make us humble, holy, wise
To the gentle grace of your tear-stained face in its every grim disguise.

vrs. 3  In our loneliness, in the world's distress, to you, our hope, we turn.
Let us spread the fire of the Spirit's power and a fiercer courage learn.
Redeem us soon from affliction's rule, for we trust in you alone.
May we bear your peace till we dwell at ease in you, our surest home.

*—Debra Rienstra*

# 3

# On Chatter and Patter

In prayer we come to God freely and boldly in the name of Christ. Even when we do not have the words, the Holy Spirit "intercedes for us with groans that words cannot express" (Rom. 8:26). Without this promise, we would be lost indeed.

In the worshiping assembly, however, our words of prayer, song, and proclamation—all part of the larger prayer of worship itself—help to form the devotion of the people. We attend to our words because while they address God, they also teach the people how to pray. We do not want to take the promise of Romans 8 as an excuse to be lazy or thoughtless about the words we speak in prayer.

So with respect and delicacy, I want to offer a careful evaluation of language often heard in churches, such as the language in this prayer offered for the young people of a congregation:

> Father-God, we just thank you for this time together Lord and we thank you for our young people and for all their gifts Lord and for their families and all the ways they support these young servants Lord, and we just ask that you would be with us now Lord as we talk about how we can bless our young people and help them grow Father-God and help them find the wonderful plan Lord that you have for their lives. In the name of Jesus our precious Lord and Savior we pray: Amen.[1]

It's a wonderful thing to pray for one another aloud in worship, sincerely and with feeling. Bringing our requests freely before God is a blessed part of the Christian tradition, particularly among evangelicals, and the plain language and spontaneous address of an improvised style can be perfectly fitting both for prayer and for other words in worship. However, the virtues of this mode of worship language can sometimes devolve into what might be called chatter and patter.

Without criticizing the motives or even the basic content of worship words like the example above, it will be helpful for us to consider some of the problems behind patter prayer and chatter in worship generally.

## Cultural Sources and Learned Responses

No speech style is neutral. Not only do the *words* we pray have theological force behind them, but so does the *style* in which we pray. Except in the most formal churches, chattiness has permeated Protestant worship across many traditions and styles. The worship leader might begin the service by addressing the congregation, welcoming them, greeting visitors, remarking on various matters of church life that week, then handing the service off to the music leader. The music leader then takes over, chatting or inserting a brief prayer between songs. Then back to the pastor for the sermon, whose style—casual language, conversational feel—might also verge on the chatty.

The worship chattiness prevalent today seems to have developed in reaction to the formality of some Protestant worship styles practiced commonly before the 1970s. People began to experience that formality as cold, distant, stiff, and unemotional. So congregations legitimately sought ways to make congregants feel welcome, warm, and "real" in worship services. One way to do that was to make worship language more relaxed and informal. While in some churches the pendulum is now swinging back toward planned liturgies and formality, the casual style is still common in Protestant worship.

Relaxed, informal, and casual can be an appropriate style. When that style devolves into a constant patter of language, trouble begins. The trouble with chattiness is that our feelings of comfort with it come from other cultural sources with purposes quite different from those of worship. Where else do we hear a constant patter of language? Radio talk shows, news broadcasts, advertisements, television shows of all kinds with chatty hosts, and sports commentary, among other things. There's nothing wrong with chattiness in these contexts. The problem comes in taking a style derived from these other cultural sources and transplanting it into worship.

When we hear a constant flow of language, a comfortable stream of "upbeat" words, we associate this with entertainment. And we have learned, through much

"It is not easy to alter one's speech, but keeping one's brain ahead of one's mouth is hardly the most terrifying lion that Christians have had to face."[2]

—*Gail Ramshaw*

---

### The Chatty Preacher

Chatter-patter in worship does not prepare congregations well for God's transforming power. But just as important for those of us who preach, chatter-patter does not function well as a *conduit* of God's transforming power, either. Our words, in sermons, testify to, and by God's grace carry, the divine Word. Are we diminishing that power with chatty language? Easy-breezy-style sermons may be carrying so much other baggage that they have less capacity to bear the word of grace, and doubly so if that word is an unsettling one—as it often is.

---

practice with the media, to respond to chattiness either by expecting entertainment—our attention constantly stimulated—or, if that fails, by tuning it out. Obviously, neither of these attitudes is among those we wish to cultivate in worship.

True, we can say to ourselves, "Well, I'm in church now. This is different." But learned responses are not entirely conscious. Anthropologists who study ritual tell us that we learn how to respond to stimuli *in our bodies*. This includes our ears and eyes and other sense organs and the kinds of attention they allow us to pay consciously to what is around us. So if we usually respond to chatter by turning the radio dial or sitting on the couch and expecting amusement, we will respond to chatter in church unconsciously and physically in similar ways, even when our conscious minds tell us: This is worship! Pay attention![3]

Chatty worship may make newcomers feel comfortable. Of course. They've heard this style of language before. It's the same patter and noise they hear everywhere, and they know it is harmless. It is easily digested or ignored and therefore completely safe. Maybe the words are churchier in a worship service, and that's nice. But there's no need to expect anything uncomfortable to happen in one's soul.

So the most serious problem with chattiness is this: we do not expect chatty language, ultimately, to transform us. Pique our curiosity and interest briefly, perhaps, or offer tidbits of information, but not transform. Both the words and the emotional blandness of chatter trigger expectations of ease, maybe temporary excitement, but not deep, divinely designed change.

Do chatty worship words make use of the crucial dimensions of language outlined in chapter 1? Not very well. Such a style might seem wonderfully expressive, but in fact it is expressive mostly for the individual speaking. It is actually more difficult for a congregation to enter this kind of idiosyncratic expressiveness, especially when it flows so easily and familiarly that it hardly holds attention. Chatty language might be instructive, but the kinds of instruction we are accustomed to receiving through chatter have to do with products, local events, diet plans, light relationship advice, business objectives, and so on—hardly things of deep mystery and import. In the end, chatter-patter, as a style, simply does not prepare us well for God's transforming power.

## Chatter and Sloppiness

Besides evoking learned responses not conducive to worship, chatter-patter often devolves into sloppy use of language and clichés. This is not necessarily true, but because people improvise chatty language based on what they have heard over and over, careless word usages tend to get perpetuated.

The use of the word *just* as an intensifier is a commonly criticized case in point. "We just want to praise you, Lord" is meant to express greater earnestness than "We want to praise you, Lord" or the more direct "We praise you, Lord." The Christian satire Web site Holy Observer posted a stinging send-up of this habit, critiquing the way this use of the word *just* creates grammatical nonsense.

### Just What Do You Mean?

#### God to Intercessors: Just Stop Saying "Just"

> For decades, God has lavished his followers with linguistic grace regarding what could be considered an epidemic in the prayer world—the use of the word "just." Usually found in a pattern similar to "God, please just [insert petition] and just [insert another petition]," the word "just" has made answering prayers a confusing and tedious process for the Almighty. In response, God declared earlier this month that Christians everywhere may no longer use the word "just" during intercessory prayer, effective immediately.[4]

The article from which the above quote is excerpted goes on to have great fun with this "pronouncement" from heaven. The joke is based on the multiple ways the word *just* is used in prayer. The common confusion is between *just* as an intensifier and as a restrictive word. When we say, "I'm just going to brush my teeth," we use the word as a restrictive, to signal that toothbrushing is the *only* thing we are about to do. When we say, "Lord, we just want to thank you for your grace today," that doesn't mean that we want to thank God only and do nothing else, or that we want to thank only for grace. Here the word is an intensifier. The word is also used as an *ironic* intensifier, meant as a mark of alleged humility: "Lord, we know you're awfully busy today, but we just have this one thing we'd like to ask." Finally, of course, the word *just* can also be used as an adjective, describing either the world for which or the God to whom we pray.

If you're wondering whether it's possible to use all of the above forms of *just* in one sentence, the answer is yes: "God, we'd just like to just thank you for giving us knowledge of the just war tradition."

Of course, words do come to be used in new ways, and probably most of us use *just* as an intensifier at least sometimes in informal speech or writing. Besides, in some churches, phrases including the word *just* have become part of a cultural heritage dear to worshipers. However, like anything, it can be overdone. The use of the word *just* in church—almost always to express earnestness in prayer—makes many people grit their teeth because it is dropped in so constantly that it has ceased to mean much. If used very sparingly, particularly for memorial reasons having to do with cultural heritage, it may be possible to rescue some of its effect as an intensifier.

Actually, the constant use of the names *Lord* and *Father-God* is more troublesome. These are, after all, names for God. When they are used not as an address but as a comma, semicolon, and period, then it's legitimate to wonder whether this might not be a mild instance of using God's name in vain. Are we addressing the majesty of heaven, the Triune Godhead, and our merciful Master? Or are we simply using these names carelessly as fillers? Apart from any issues related to gender inclusiveness (which will be addressed in chapter 7), constant use of the names *Lord* and *Father-God* serves, in a way, to infantilize us as pray-ers. Imagine a child who says "Mommy Mommy Mommy Mommy Mommy" between every phrase. Wouldn't that be annoying? Fortunately, God is not easily annoyed. But we do not want to pray like whiny toddlers, either.[5]

Careless use of *just* and *Lord* and *Father-God* is worth avoiding, even in contexts where some use of this style is part of a cultural connection to the past. However, these are not the only phrases that can become troublesome bad habits. Another example is the phrase *be with* ("Dear God, please be with Michelle as she awaits the birth of her baby . . ."). I use this one too frequently myself and have managed to teach it to my children unintentionally.

The desire behind the phrase is a good one, of course. We want those we love and care for to receive God's presence and blessing. Unfortunately, by asking God to *be with* these people, we give the subtle impression that God is always wandering off and we have to keep calling God back to attention. This makes God out to be a little like the mom trying to play Candy Land with her three-year-old for the hundredth time and repeatedly getting distracted by laundry folding or dishwasher loading. Don't we believe that God is always present with us, whether we perceive that presence or not? Maybe it would be better to bypass formulaic phrases as much as possible and instead say more exactly what we mean, giving our prayers more vivid verbs:

- Dear God, work in Paul so that he is more aware of your presence . . .
- Dear Lord, please free Shawnda and James from obstacles as they serve on the mission field . . .

---

**What about "The Lord Be with You"?**

Having said that *be with* is a rather weak prayer phrase, what are we to make of those traditions that make frequent use of the liturgical exchange: "The Lord be with you/And also with you"?

The phrase "The Lord be with you" is found in many places in Scripture (Ruth 2:4; 1 Sam. 17:37 [Saul blesses David before he fights Goliath]; 2 Thess. 3:16; and, in some translations, Luke 1:28, the Annunciation). Other variations are "peace be with you" (John 20:19, 21) or "grace and peace to you," as Paul opens and closes many of his epistles.

The phrase itself does two things. It is a prayerful petition in the subjunctive mood: *may* the Lord be with you. It is also a statement of faith in the indicative mood: as you assemble for worship, the Lord *is* with you (where two or three are gathered . . .). In both senses, it is a form of blessing.

The response ("and also with you" or "and with your spirit") is also a blessing. It is not scriptural, but we find it used already in third-century liturgical documents, and it has been in constant use ever since. For this reason, the phrase operates well in the memorial dimension of worship language. It is a mutual acknowledgment that the worship we offer as both congregation and as clergy is activated by the living Spirit of God.

---

- Holy Spirit, open Esteban's heart to the grace we know you are eager to give . . .
- Savior, bless Dawn and Andrew with patience as they wait for their baby . . .

While there are occasions in a worship setting in which we might pray that God "be with" or "come" among us (see sidebars on this page and the next), for ordinary prayers we do better to strive for more vivid and specific language.

Those of us who value extemporaneous prayers and transitional words in worship for their immediacy and authenticity must recognize that our words are sometimes not particularly original, genuine, or thoughtful. We learn habits of speech from others and then we adopt those into our own worship words. Chatter and patter happen when we stop thinking about exactly what we are saying and instead remain content merely to create an effect: a style and "feel" valued for its own sake and for reasons we have not carefully considered.

## The Virtues of "Flow"

Recently I was duly chastised in my prejudices against chatter-patter by a friend who teaches at an evangelical college. She was describing her preparations for a study-abroad trip involving a large number of students, and she mentioned in particular her efforts to find students who could serve as chaplains for the trip, leading others in prayer and Bible study. As she asked who among the group might be suitable, several people suggested certain students who were known as "good pray-ers." It turned out that the students had earned their reputation as good pray-ers because they had mastered an emotionally intense style of patter prayer. My friend explained to me that the students in her group, who came largely from charismatic and Pentecostal church traditions, considered this good prayer because, for them, an emotionally charged flow of words resembles speaking in tongues and is therefore more "in the Spirit" than other forms of prayer.

This raises an important issue: the sheer music of language. Words have an aesthetic quality. In some worship contexts, the aesthetic quality of word flow is particularly valued. Words in sermons and prayers rise and fall, spin and settle, ascend on thunderous crescendos and then ease down diminuendos into whispers. All this creates dramatic emotional effects. African American preaching has long been studied for its music; in fact, one researcher went so far as to analyze African American sermons using the tools of musical analysis such as tone, cadence, tempo, even key.[6]

The virtue of this style of preaching is that while the words, as units of meaning, are engaging the intellect, the music of the voice speaking the sounds of the words is engaging the emotions as well. Mastery of this dual effect characterizes the best orators in every field and certainly the best preachers. In the African American tradition generally, preachers learn not only to create music with their voices but also to value rich words: they learn through listening and studying a variety of rhetorical schemes and tropes—like extended metaphor and parallel repetition—and steeping themselves in the words of Scripture. They also learn standard sermon

### Come, Holy Spirit?

Having said that God is always present at our worship services and does not need to be summoned, what are we to make of congregations that use prayers invoking the presence of the Holy Spirit at different points in their worship services?

This sort of prayer is called an *epiclesis*, from the Greek word for "to call upon." We call upon the Holy Spirit's special work at many points in our worship: at the very beginning of the service, just before the reading and proclamation of Scripture, before we participate in the Lord's Supper, and more. During Pentecost season, congregations may pray general prayers that the Holy Spirit come upon the congregation as it worships.

Such prayers can suffer from the same vagueness that the "be with" prayers do. The most fitting invocations of the Holy Spirit say more than "come and be here"; they say "come, and inflame our waiting hearts" or "come, and sharpen our minds to understand what you would say to us today" or "come, and bless this bread and wine so that those who share in them may also be sharers in Christ."

shapes. As Cleo LaRue describes it: "Start slow, rise high, strike fire. Sit down in a storm."[7] Of course, African American preaching does have its own tired clichés, but the tradition is still well known for its many excellent preachers who learn to improvise effective word music through listening and practice.

The potential problem with any style that emphasizes word music, however, is that when the words are not particularly meaningful, you are left with only sound effects. When a preacher or pray-er abuses the music of speech by saying *nothing* in dramatic fashion, then this devolves into emotional manipulation. Preaching and prayer can disintegrate into mere schmaltz just as much as music can, as the schmaltzy preaching of some religious broadcasters on cable television unfortunately demonstrates.

It's worth asking which is more difficult: to speak worthy words or to whump up emotional fervor? I think we too often attribute emotional highs to the Spirit's

---

### Tips for Better Improvisation in Prayer

A friend of mine who teaches worship tells of an exercise he gave one of his students who came from a "read prayer is a dead prayer" tradition. The student taped his extemporized prayers in worship four weeks in a row. When he listened to them, he realized that he was praying almost exactly the same prayer—spontaneously—every week. *Good* improvisation is more difficult than you might think. Here are a few tips:

- Do what my friend's student did: listen to a tape of yourself praying a few weeks in a row. You might be surprised by what you discover.
- When you're asked to improvise a prayer, spend time beforehand thinking about that prayer and its context in worship. Does the prayer have a particular *purpose* within the service? What might be its emotional tone?
- Spend some time before worship remembering (or even composing) memorable and meaningful phrases that you can use in your prayer. Avoid clichés, but there is nothing wrong with the purloined phrase (e.g., "O God, our help in ages past") that connects congregations to larger webs of meaning.
- Some people benefit from using an outline to guide the flow of the prayer into particular channels so it doesn't become a puddle of words. The outline could be written out, or a simple structure that one can easily keep in mind. So, for example, some will follow the familiar ACTS (Adoration, Confession, Thanksgiving, Supplication) structure during the congregational prayer, or visualize a widening series of circles, representing congregational concerns that spread from the most immediate (Mrs. Johnson's upcoming surgery); to local, national, and international concerns; and concluding, perhaps, in prayers for the church that extends beyond bounds of time and space.
- Another structure one can use to improvise a prayer is the *Collect* form, which grounds our petitions in the nature of God and in God's past actions. See "The Collect Form: Names to Verbs" on p. 159.

work and neglect to honor the miracles of the Spirit that occur in worthy words. Those who practice musical rhetorical styles with skill and integrity are aware of the dangers of empty fervor and strive to avoid it. Less-scrupulous people (and no style or tradition is free from this danger) are happy to imitate legitimate rhetorical power for the purposes of manipulation and self-glory.

So in discussing the effect of word flow, we have to distinguish dramatic, musical preaching and prayer from chatter-patter. Chatter-patter has questionable cultural origins whether it is practiced by sincere people or not. Musical preaching and prayer have their dangers; however, they do derive legitimately from traditions of the church and can certainly represent an effective rhetorical style in the right context and for a receptive congregation.

## Some Ways to Limit Chatter in Worship

Well-known Presbyterian preacher Tom Long preached a sermon at Princeton Seminary in 1991 called "Words, Words, Words." In his sermon, which was addressed to an audience of seminary students, Long warned that in our culture, we "use words by the bushel." The members of our congregations swim in words all day, he observed, and so many of those words are false, shallow, and careless. As a result, people enter the church not entirely trusting words. After many rather depressing paragraphs about the debasement of words in our culture, Long turned the corner toward hope: "That is why it is important to hear this day the claim of the gospel that, in Jesus Christ, we get our words back, that the words we speak can become filled with grace and truth, instruments of redemption."[8]

It's true; people are quite accustomed to slovenly words, yet they are dying for good language used well. Nowhere is this more true, perhaps, than in church. Newcomers and old-timers alike come to church with their thirsts, their longings, and their discontents near the surface. If they find there the same old patter and noise, except with churchy words rather than advertising slogans and talk show banalities, then what happens? They give shallow attention or stop listening altogether, just as they would at home in front of a TV infomercial.

How thrilling it would be if in church, language itself was charged and alive again. What if newcomers and old-timers could find that in church, at last, words have substance and meaning? How can we make this happen? How can we make language vital and arresting?

1. Slow down. We are afraid of the power of words spoken slowly and attentively. We might have to listen. Yet words offered this way can capture our attention better than upbeat patter, partly because this style is so different from the common noise of popular culture.

We once attended a bilingual service in which the pastor preached in English and an interpreter translated, sentence by sentence, into Spanish. It was wonderful! The pastor, knowing that his sermon would be dispensed in small morsels like this, took special care over his words that week. And while the interpreter was speaking, we English-speakers had a chance to think over each sentence. The Spanish-speakers had the same opportunity while the preacher was speaking his English words. As a result, we were all obliged to listen and absorb, and we were given the time to do so.

2. Use silence to frame words. Long ago I played in an orchestra with a wonderful conductor who had many wise sayings. One of his favorites was: "Music is a picture painted on the background of silence." This was his elegant way of reminding one hundred high-energy high schoolers to resist our impulse to crash through our music without giving full value to the rests. But what he said applies to words as well. Words are more dramatic when they are given room to breathe on a background of silence. Silence is part of the meaning, just as rests are part of the music.

Try placing a few moments of silence before a prayer, and perhaps between the sentences of a prayer. Leave a few moments of silence after the sermon for reflection. Give people a way of using the silence so it feels more comfortable: "Let us listen now in silence for how God is speaking to us today in this word."

A common feature of some worship styles is the use of soft music behind prayers, which can also be an effective background to silent reflection. The point is that we are squandering the power of words when we stir them together in a thick soup of chatter and patter. They become mush, and we can't chew on them at all.

3. Frame words with other elements. Just as an appropriate frame can bring out a painting's beauty, so also other elements of worship can frame words. Music and visual arts are especially helpful for this. For instance, I have come to appreciate sung responses in worship. In my home church, each season of the church year we follow a different liturgical pattern, each of which comes with short sung prayers and other sung responses. Because they are short and we sing them repeatedly for several weeks, they enter my memory and I find myself humming them all week, therefore meditating on the words as well.

Another way to frame words in worship is to ask visual artists to incorporate key words or phrases into their art. We heard a powerful sermon once on Isaiah 41; it was part of a service whose theme was "I am with you always." The preacher reminded us that "our stories do not end in suffering," and she showed us how God gave the Israelites hope in exile by reminding them of the story of Ruth. Then she connected that story with the stories of many faithful servants of God before us, and with our own stories. It was an encouraging, moving, deeply comforting

## Sung Responses

Some congregations sing a particular song every week—a particular setting of the Doxology, for example ("Praise God, from whom all blessings flow"), or an "Alleluia" after the reading of the gospel. Roman Catholic liturgies have sung responses at many key points: an Agnus Dei as a frame for prayer ("Lamb of God who takes away the sin of the world, have mercy on us"), or a Sanctus ("Holy, holy, holy is the Lord God of Hosts!") as a response to the story of God's saving work in history.

Many moments in worship can benefit from a musical frame. One verse from the hymn "Take My Life and Let It Be" works well as an accompaniment to the congregation's offering of their gifts. Or the African processional "Uyai mose" ("Come, all you people, come and praise your Maker!") as an opening call to worship, or this riff on Psalm 51 as a frame for the congregation's confession of sin:

### People sing (silent confession between verses):

Coni Huisman, "Create in Us," text and music © 1974. Used by permission.

sermon. After the sermon, we listened to quiet music while a series of slides appeared on the screens. They were drawings and photographs of great figures of the Bible and saints from all periods of history—from Moses to Mother Teresa to ordinary faces we might see in the pew beside us. Each slide carried just a few words: I am with you. I am with you, Martin. I am with you, Teresa. I am with you, John. By framing those few words with the images of the saints, the key words of the sermon sunk into our hearts powerfully and unforgettably.

Good teachers know that in order to learn something well, students need to receive the knowledge a little bit at a time and repeat it until they know it well. Framing helps us notice words again, receive them, meditate on them, and get them permanently in our memories.

4. Limit the number of words in a service. When the words in a service are mostly chatter, the sheer number of them transforms into mere noise, indistinguishable background static. This can create the "glazed-eyes" effect in the congregation.

However, even when the words are carefully chosen and beautiful, there can be too many of them. This may depend largely on congregational capacity, but there are times I have come away from worship feeling as if I have been to a fabulous buffet, about half of which I missed because I was too full to eat more.

5. Balance slow, careful words with relaxed, more extemporaneous speech. Some traditions favor set prayers and words for the whole service; other traditions favor extemporaneous words for the whole service. In each case, some moves toward the other end of the spectrum would combine the benefits of both while eliminating many of the pitfalls.

Our family often attended an evangelical Anglican church in the Los Angeles area that followed the traditional patterns of Anglican liturgy but also found times for more relaxed, conversational words. Before the service began, the pastor would stand below the altar and greet the congregation briefly and personally; then he would use words from Scripture as a more formal signal that God was calling us to worship. Then we would sing two contemporary praise songs and transition to a hymn. As we sang the hymn, a small processional of clergy and choir brought the Bible and cross to the altar in traditional fashion, and the service proceeded with words for various prayers and responses, most of them from Scripture or the Book of Common Prayer, projected onto screens. The sermon was, once again, in a more informal style. The pastor had notes for what he planned to say, but he improvised the precise words while speaking. At the end of the service, after communion, the pastor would once again stand below the altar and offer announcements. People celebrating birthdays or anniversaries that week would be invited forward and the pastor would improvise a short prayer for them. Then we concluded the service with an organ-led recessional hymn.

This is an illustration of how a congregation with a tradition of formal words can make the best of that tradition while still enjoying the advantages of spontaneous words. Churches with a tradition of extemporaneous words can certainly find good occasion in a service to slow down the flow and use planned words. Reading Scripture well, writing out and perhaps projecting on a screen memorable phrases or sentences in the sermon, reading a poem that fits the service's theme, or teaching the congregation a repeated prayer response are some examples. Offering carefully chosen words slowly, framing them, and repeating them are excellent ways to send people away with the sense that they have heard something valuable and memorable—that in worship, words can mean something again.

### Summary Calls to Action

- → Eliminate careless use of common filler words, particularly God's name, in prayers and other worship words.
- → Use the aesthetic effects of word flow to support, not replace, good words.
- → Slow down.
- → Frame words with silence.
- → Frame words with music, art, and other elements.
- → Limit the number of words overall.
- → Balance slow, careful words with relaxed, extemporaneous speech.

### Exercises

1. Describe some times when words seemed particularly substantive and real for you, either in worship or in some other context. What was it about the words and the situation that gave the words power and meaning?

2. Chatter often happens at the opening of a service or between songs. In the next service you attend, observe these transitional words. Do they serve a purpose? Do they point the congregation's attention to the next element of the service as an act of worship? Do they help the congregation understand what it is doing and why?

Example: Which is better?

"OK, now we're going to sing 'Lord, I Lift Your Name on High.'"

or

"Let's respond to God's forgiving grace with praise."

3. Write down an order of service for a service you attend (or bring home the printed one) and color-code it to show degrees of "tension" in the language. Does the service on the whole tend toward the careful and formal or toward the chatty and loose? Were there variations along the spectrum? Were they appropriate? What do you think could change to improve the balance so that the congregation gains a sense of warmth and spontaneity and also gets to hear, meditate on, and remember important words?

4. Take a written prayer that you are going to offer in a service and enlarge it on the page with your computer program or a copy machine. Make the words very large with much space between the lines. Now read it aloud. Do you say the words differently when there is more space on the page? Do some words seem especially extraneous now? Revise until you can speak each word with attention and confidence.

5. If you are a "Father-God/just/Lord" pray-er, see whether you can improvise a prayer without using the words Lord or just at all. You will have to think of other ways to address God. Try to use at least three different names for God in your prayer besides Lord, Father, or Father-God. (See chapter 7 for ideas.) You will also find yourself looking for new verbs to express God's action. See if you can do all this while also retaining the emotional intensity that is important to you. Don't be afraid of a little silence as you think of the next thing to say.

6. Most public speakers dislike listening to recordings of themselves; but there is no better way for a minister to become aware of how his or her preaching actually sounds. So (especially if you are someone who preaches extemporaneously), get a tape of one of your sermons and, as you listen to it, identify the places where you fall into patterns of chatter or patter, where the language seems bloated with extraneous material, even verbal tics (e.g., "um" or "you know"). Likely these are speech patterns you import from your everyday life. Work on being aware of them and excising them. For example, ask your children to repeat the word "um" after you every time you say it. Soon, it will be gone from your everyday speech, and it will begin to fall away when you step into the pulpit as well.

# 4

## On Repetition

When Ron was in seminary, he served as an intern at a small Reformed church in New Jersey, working with a wonderful pastor named Paul Walther. One Sunday a particularly difficult middle schooler approached Paul after the service and demanded, "After you read the Bible in church, why do you always say, 'The grass withers and the flower fades but the word of our God will stand forever'?" Paul looked the young person right in the eye and replied, "*That's* why."

This young fellow was complaining about what appeared to him to be a meaningless ritual, a thoughtless repetition. But it wasn't thoughtless or meaningless at all, not from Paul's point of view. Paul repeated these words every week because he felt it was a fitting way to conclude the reading of Scripture. When his young parishioner questioned this practice, Paul realized that by his repetition, he was also making sure that even a kid not particularly open to learning about Scripture wound up carrying in his mind a profound truth.

Repetition is a powerful teacher. What is constantly repeated will stick with us, whether we like it or not. If we took an inventory of the words lodged in our minds, probably all of us would be embarrassed. For instance, I have no problem singing along with advertising jingles from decades ago. Ron can sing all the lyrics perfectly to dozens of top 40 songs from the 1970s, even after not hearing them for years. My children can recite whole scenes from *Star Wars* movies, and they know the theme song to *Gilligan's Island* better than any praise song—although it must be said that they can sing the first verse of "Amazing Grace" to the same catchy tune. (Please don't do this in worship.)

In a media-saturated culture, spiritual words—words of Scripture, hymns and worship songs, creeds, liturgical words, and prayers—compete for space in our heads with a random heap of other stuff—most of it related to entertainment and advertising. Savvy corporations know the power of repetition, study it, and deploy it strategically. Author Malcolm Gladwell, in the chapter called "The Stickiness Factor" in his book *The Tipping Point*, describes the development of the wildly successful children's show *Blue's Clues*. The makers of the show discovered that if they aired the same episode every day for a week, their little viewers' "attention and comprehension [of the show] actually increased over the course of the week."[1] It seemed counterintuitive at first to the show's producers, but they came to understand that preschoolers *like* repetition. It helps them feel that the world is predictable and that they can interact successfully with it.

Repetition is valuable not only for small children, of course. Any foreign language teacher can attest to the importance of repetition in helping students learn to speak and understand a new language. Any athlete or musician can verify that repetition is the only way to build muscle memory, and muscle memory in turn creates the instinct and ease required to perform complex skills at a consistently high level. Our son, who is now thirteen years old, has been studying violin in a Suzuki program since he was five. The Suzuki philosophy is based on the idea that every child is talented, every child can learn. All it takes is patience, love, breaking down every skill into very small parts, and a great deal of repetition. The founder of the Suzuki method, Dr. Sinichi Suzuki, believed that a correct violin-bow hold, for example, does not become natural and secure until a student has repeated it a thousand times. Although I knew this from my own experience as a violist, watching my son gain skill and confidence over the years has caused me to marvel again over the magic of repetition.

Repetition is a powerful teacher. Surely it is appropriate and wise, then, to use repetition in worship in order to sink worthy words into our souls. We should be eager to replace the advertising jingles and pop songs rattling around in our brains with something more spiritually edifying.

So there is a powerful pedagogical argument for wise use of repetition in worship. But even more important, there is a theological argument. Repetition is a way of remembering and carrying on our Christian story. We remember in order to be a countercultural witness. This is why God was always calling the ancient Israelites to remember: remember that you were slaves, remember that I rescued you, remember the law that protects you and sets you apart. The Israelites did much of their remembering through worship rituals—as do we.

In worship, we need to repeat the words of Scripture, the story of the gospel, the promises of the Bible, the comfort and inspiration of our songs, the wise peti-

---

***"Hey nony nony," or "Oo ee oo-ah-ah, ting tang walla-walla bing bang"***

Nonsense lyrics that stick in one's head through repetition are not a unique feature of silly music from the 1960s. Miles Coverdale, the English Reformer, composed a volume of metrical psalms and songs in about 1535. In the introduction to the volume, Coverdale explains that one of his goals is to give people something to sing other than tawdry love songs. His commentary on what proceeded from the popular mouth turned out to be the opening salvo in a long rivalry in the sixteenth century between pious and secular lyrics. It was a rivalry over what stuck in people's minds through much repetition:

> Yea, would God that our minstrels had none other thing to play upon, neither our carters and plowmen other thing to whistle upon, save psalms, hymns, and such godly songs as David is occupied withall! And if women, sitting at their rocks, or spinning at the wheels, had none other songs to pass their time withall, than such as Moses's sister, Elkanah's wife, Debora, and Mary the mother of Christ, have sung before them, they should be better occupied than with *hey nony nony, hey troly loly*, and such like fantasies. [spelling modernized]

—Goostly Psalms and Spirituall Songes, *1535*

---

tions of our prayers. We, too, are a forgetful and distracted people, and we need to remember.

However, if repetition is such a useful and necessary part of the Christian life, why do worship leaders often hear complaints about repetition in worship? "Why do we always sing the same songs?" people ask. Or "Why do we always have to say the Lord's Prayer?" "Why does the service always follow the same order?"

Of course, the problem is that we also love novelty. A consumer culture puts a high premium on novelty, so we have learned to demand a constant flow of new movies, books, TV shows, music, restaurants, cars, fashion, electronics, razors, and toothpaste dispenser technology. Our thirst for novelty in consumer goods tends to leak into areas of life where the virtues of stability used to be taken for granted: homes, jobs, relationships—even church. We have learned to be easily bored, and this puts worship leaders in a quandary. Worship leaders know very well that many people have a low tolerance for repetition in worship, and if they get too much of it, they will complain—or worse, they will leave, looking for something fresh elsewhere.

## Everybody's Doing It

The topic of repetition in worship is particularly amusing because everyone is "guilty," but everyone blames others for being worse offenders. In the 1980s, young

### "The Cows in the Corn"

An old farmer went to the city one weekend and attended the big city church. He came home and his wife asked him how it was.

"Well," said the farmer, "it was good. They did something different, however. They sang praise choruses instead of hymns."

"Praise choruses?" said his wife. "What are those?"

"Oh, they're OK. They are sort of like hymns, only different," said the farmer.

"Well, what's the difference?" asked his wife.

The farmer said, "Well, it's like this—If I were to say to you 'Martha, the cows are in the corn'—well, that would be a hymn. If on the other hand, I were to say to you:

'Martha, Martha, Martha,
Oh Martha, MARTHA, MARTHA,
the cows, the big cows, the brown cows, the black cows,
the white cows, the black and white cows,
the COWS, COWS, COWS
are in the corn,
are in the corn, are in the corn, are in the corn,
the CORN, CORN, CORN.'

Then, if I were to repeat the whole thing two or three times, well, that would be a praise chorus."

The next weekend, his nephew, a young, new Christian from the city, came to visit and attended the local church of the small town. He went home and his wife asked him how it was. "Well," said the young man, "it was good. They did something different however. They sang hymns instead of regular songs."

"Hymns?" asked his wife. "What are those?"

*(continued on next page)*

adults complained that they were sick and tired of singing the same old hymns over and over, so they left the hymnals in the pew racks and started composing brand-new praise-and-worship songs. As praise-and-worship songs made their way into worship services, the old-timers started complaining about having to sing the same words over and over again instead of having four or five distinct verses. There were many factors in this major shift in musical styles, but repetition troubles were surely part of it. My mother, who is now eighty-two years old, cheerfully accepts the need for younger people to pray and offer praise in a musical language they find meaningful. "But please," she says, "three times through one of those songs is enough!"

Despite sometimes scornful finger-pointing from all corners, we must admit that everybody uses repetition in worship. Prayer-book-style worshipers use the same prayers, hymns, and forms for baptism and communion that have been used for generations. They repeat words across the weeks and the decades. Praise-band-style

"Oh, they're OK. They are sort of like regular songs, only different," said the young man.

"Well, what's the difference?"

The young man said, "Well, it's like this—If I were to say to you 'Martha, the cows are in the corn'—well, that would be a regular song. If on the other hand, I were to say to you:

'Oh Martha, dear Martha, hear thou my cry
Inclinest thine ear to the words of my mouth
Turn thou thy whole wondrous ear by and by
To the righteous, inimitable, glorious truth.

'For the way of the animals who can explain
There in their heads is no shadow of sense
Hearkenest they in God's sun or His rain
Unless from the mild, tempting corn they are fenced.

'Yea those cows in glad bovine, rebellious delight
Have broke free their shackles, their warm pens eschewed
Then goaded by minions of darkness and night
They all my mild Chilliwack sweet corn have chewed.

'So look to the bright shining day by and by
Where all foul corruptions of earth are reborn
Where no vicious animals make my soul cry
And I no longer see those foul cows in the corn.'

"Then if I were to do only verses one, three and four and do a key change on the last verse, well that would be a hymn."[2]

worshipers also use the same songs repeatedly, though a particular song's shelf life may be shorter. The songs themselves, however, tend to involve more repetition of lines and phrases than strophic hymn forms. Even worshipers who enjoy extemporaneous prayers and sermons every week will notice that particular phrases and patterns of speech get repeated frequently: *Almighty God and Father, we ask your blessing upon . . . Grant healing to . . . Let your Spirit fall upon . . .* and so on.

So there's no point in criticizing repetition of words per se. Everyone does it, and there are excellent reasons to embrace the practice.

Even the most innovative churches these days have similarly discovered that some kind of patterning and repeated elements are necessary. Repeated elements serve several useful and important functions: they give worshipers a sense of comfort and security; they serve to settle important words in people's minds and hearts; they provide a structure within which it is possible to innovate; and they help relieve leaders of the need for constant innovation in every part of a service. In fact, it is much easier and more meaningful to introduce innovative elements

### Cyclical versus Strophic Music

Many of us who grew up with a strong heritage of European hymnody expect that any rich worship song will include a number of verses, each of which will successively build on the last as it develops a theological theme. Hymns of this sort are known as *strophic*.

Folk music, on the other hand, is often *cyclical* and works in a fundamentally different way. What appears to be mere repetition is actually a complicated theme-and-variation structure that allows worshipers to focus not on singing the song, but on engaging God. When well led, each cycle through the song adds or subtracts an element: a rhythmic complexity, a harmonic improvisation, a small lyrical substitution (Father/Jesus/Spirit, for example), hand-clapping or swaying, and so on. This variety allows the song to "heat up" as the congregation enters more deeply into it.[3]

in worship when they fit into an already familiar pattern. A new song expressing lament, for example, may introduce an unfamiliar mode in worship, but singing the song before the familiar time of intercessory prayer helps the congregation, simply through the song's placement in the overall pattern of worship, understand that the song is helpful and appropriate in preparing them to pray for those who suffer.

An "emerging church" group in Los Angeles called Tribe has found that following a similar pattern of worship three weeks per month helps ground them and create a context for innovation. On the third Sunday of each month, they often plan something different—a foot-washing ritual, a guest pastor, the creation of a group artwork, for example. Even on those Sundays, worship usually still

### Creative Burnout

In the 1970s my parents were part of an organ-and-hymn church whose young people were leaving in droves because church no longer felt "relevant" to them. In the anti-institutional spirit of the times, a small group of adults and young people decided to start a new service based on egalitarian leadership and layperson-led worship. (The group eventually became its own daughter congregation.)

These enthusiastic and energetic folks divided up the worship-planning duties among the members so that each week someone else was in charge. At first it was creative and innovative, eclectic and exciting. It wasn't long, though, before everyone was pretty much exhausted. The constant surprises in worship became tiresome and disorienting for worshipers, and the constant pressure to come up with something new left the planners frustrated and upset. Everyone realized that trying to reinvent the wheel every week quickly resulted in both worship-leader and congregational burnout.

Many churches committed to liturgical experimentation are discovering these same realities and find that they have energy "emerging" to do something entirely innovative only about once a month.

---

**The Virtues of Repetition**

Repeated elements in worship

- give worshipers a sense of comfort and security;
- serve to settle important words in people's minds and hearts;
- provide a structure within which it is possible to innovate;
- help relieve leaders of the need for constant innovation in every part of a service.

---

begins with a shared meal, which serves as the setting for communion. A prayer of blessing over the meal and the familiar words of institution repeated from 1 Corinthians 11 frame the meal. "The Lord Jesus, on the night he was betrayed, took bread . . ." signals the beginning of the meal and leads into prayer and the silent sharing of a large loaf. After the meal, the pastor stands and speaks these words: "In the same way, after supper he took the cup. . ." and the wine is shared to close the meal.

Repetition has great value in worship, but it also has potential vices, some of which we'll explore in a moment. So we face the challenge of how to do it well. What words are we repeating? Are we thoughtful about it? Are the words that worshipers carry home with them worthy of remembering? Are they helping people remember the larger Christian story? If repetition is a powerful teacher, what are we teaching? What is sinking into the souls of our people? What will they know by heart?

## Vain Repetition

One of the main objections to repeated words in worship, particularly prayers, is the possibility of "vain repetition." We have all experienced the validity of this objection: if you repeat the same thing often enough, it is certainly tempting to stop paying attention. Free-church traditions especially put a premium on improvised prayers, partly in order to avoid meaningless repetition of familiar words. An improvised prayer must by definition be truly felt—the assumption goes—since the pray-er is making up the words on the spot.[4]

Unfortunately, of course, this isn't always true. My two older children say that in their Christian-school classrooms, when students are asked to lead in prayer they often begin by rattling off the words, "Dear-God-thank-you-for-this-day . . ." "They're not even thinking about what they say!" complain my children. "They're on autopilot!" These are young kids, of course, in what is for them an uncomfortable situation; they are not practiced and called worship leaders. Good worship leaders do indeed think about what they are saying when they improvise a prayer, even if they are using familiar phrases. They recognize that whether or not the leader is concentrating on the words is critical both to that leader's devotion and to the devotion of those he or she is leading. But of course even the best, most earnest worship leader cannot control the attention of all congregants. Those praying *through* the leader's prayer are responsible for their own attention level. Do improvised prayers, in fact, help them pay attention better?

"Vain and meaningless repetition" is a well-worn concern in the Christian church. When Thomas Cranmer set out to write a prayer book for the newly independent English church in the 1530s and 1540s, he complained about the "vain repetitions" of the Roman Catholic rite.[5] Yet he never dreamed of solving the problem by allowing leaders to improvise prayers. To the early Reformers, the solution to "vain repetition" was a new kind of "common prayer": prayers and forms for worship that were in English (rather than Latin), reflected right doctrine, were thoroughly biblical, and could be shared across all the regions of England. To leave worship words up to individual priests, the Reformers thought (with good reason), would surely invite a frenzy of heretical teachings. Common prayer instead was meant to create a new church unified at least in part by its shared worship words. The common prayer of the church would keep it pure in the wake of enormous upheaval as well as teach right devotion to all the people.

Common prayer has some appealing advantages, especially in the hands of someone like Cranmer, who had a brilliant gift for elegant, concise, yet accessible language (more accessible in the sixteenth century than today, admittedly). I have myself experienced the joy of speaking the same prayers and liturgical words from the Book of Common Prayer with fellow Christians in greatly different assemblies in the United States and Britain, knowing all the while that we were praying the same words that many had prayed before us. However, despite the excellence of the first English Book of Common Prayer in 1549 and its enduring revision of 1559,

### Growing into the Lord's Prayer

Annie Dillard speaks about set pieces of liturgy as "certain words which people have successfully addressed to God without their getting killed."[6] How might our souls be shaped within us if the only words we dared speak to God in prayer were the words Jesus gave us—the Lord's Prayer? How would we be formed differently if we spent a lifetime growing every day into the depths of meaning to be found there? I am glad that I can express myself to God, both privately and publicly, in a broader range of words and phrases. But I would bet that my prayer life as a whole would be a good deal richer if I spent some years with the Lord's Prayer every day, meaning it more and more each time I said it.

some leaders immediately resisted it, seeking the freedom to improvise prayers. Despite the efforts of Queen Elizabeth I to unify the English church, various groups of nonconformists arose in England who resisted the English Book of Common Prayer and emphasized the importance of improvising prayers. They wished to avoid the terrible danger, in their minds, of speaking words when one's heart was not in them. And they wanted to make their prayers specific to the needs of their congregations on each particular day.

### It's Only Meaningless If You Don't Mean It

The words of Jesus from Matthew 6 are often cited to support criticism of prayer-book or written prayers: "And when you pray, do not keep on babbling like pagans, for they think they will be heard because of their many words" (Matt. 6:7). Of course, one can "babble" a long, extemporaneous prayer as easily as a written prayer. But just as the first assumption against composed prayers—that an improvised prayer must be truly felt since the pray-er is making up the words on the spot—is not necessarily true, neither is the second assumption: that anything inherited cannot be truly meant when it is spoken in the service. Repetition is only mean-ingless *when we don't mean it*.

When we use words commonly repeated in services, such as the Apostles' Creed, the Lord's Prayer, the familiar words of an ancient communion rite, or the reading of familiar Scripture passages, the challenge is to *grow into* these words, to *learn* to mean them more and more every time we say them. This has always been the genius of liturgical traditions. Not only do the standard liturgies of the Orthodox, Roman Catholic, Lutheran, Episcopal, and some parts of the Presbyterian traditions assure that worship words are assessed for their doctrinal soundness, these liturgies also teach by repetition.

Of course there are potential drawbacks to standard liturgies, including the temptation to jog-trot through them without really thinking about the words. This is why we must be careful not only to repeat worthy words but to help people understand what they are saying. For instance, however sincerely spoken by the leader, the invocation of the Trinity—Father, Son, and Holy Spirit—can feel like vain repetition to the worshiper unless she has been taught to understand *how* God is three persons and yet one, how the three persons interrelate, and what it all means for her personal devotion and for the church's. When leaders and con-gregants perform the words attentively and well, and when they make an effort to explore and explain what we repeat, then we not only remember the words, but we give them a chance to sink in, to shape and change us, to fund our spiritual vocabulary.

---

### An Advocate for the Same Old Thing

"I think our business as laymen is simply to endure and make the best of it. Any tendency to a passionate preference for one type of service must be regarded simply as a temptation.

"A good shoe is a shoe you don't notice. . . . The perfect church service would be one we were almost unaware of; our attention would have been on God. But every novelty prevents this. It fixes our attention on the service itself; and thinking about worship is a different thing from worshipping. . . . I can make do with almost any kind of service whatever, if only it will stay put. But if each form is snatched away just when I am beginning to feel at home in it, then I can never make any progress in the art of worship."[7]

—*C. S. Lewis*

---

In her spiritual memoir *Girl Meets God*, author Lauren Winner recalls an occasion on which she came to understand the importance of repeated worship words:

One day, when I was full in the flush of agony about what I should do with my life, whether I would always be alone, whether I should become a nun, whether I should drop out of graduate school, and other high-pitch anxieties, I heard, reverberating around my brain, "Go out to do the work I have given you to do." *The work I have given you to do. The work I have given you to do.*

*What an ingenious sentiment,* I thought. *I can't believe I dreamed that up. Maybe I should drop out of grad school and enter a poetry-writing Master's of Fine Arts program.* All day, all week I heard those words, *the work I have given you to do,* heard them, and was deeply consoled by them. . . . Not only had God given me work to do, He had given me little poetic snatches of reassurance, too.

That Sunday, Winner showed up at her Episcopal church. After the communion, she spoke with the rest of the congregation the same prayer of thanksgiving she had spoken many times before: "Father, send us out to do the work you have given us to do." So much for her own poetic genius. Winner comments: "It was the liturgy that had lodged in my brain, words of the liturgy I barely noticed Sunday to Sunday when we said them, but here I was, noticing them raptly, in the middle of a weekday afternoon, when I needed them most."[8]

Winner's story suggests that our ideals about congregational attention underestimate how God can use worship words. Certainly we should all, leaders and congregants, make an effort to give full attention to all the words we say, hear, or sing in worship, whether those words are familiar or fresh. To use the helpful phrase developed by Roman Catholics during the Vatican II reforms, we should aim for *full, conscious, active participation.* We should find ways to encourage mindful repetition of worthy words, so that we might all grow into them more and more. At the same time, however, we have to recognize that the Spirit may be storing up words in our hearts even without our noticing so that when we need them, they will be there.

## Using Repetition Well

How might worship leaders and pastors encourage mindful repetition of worthy words? Strategies will vary according to the worship style in question, of course. Here are some suggestions.

1. Use appropriate words of Scripture at the same point in the service over the course of many weeks. This is the "grass withers" principle Paul Walther discovered. For example, the many greetings and blessings from the New Testament epistles provide excellent words for opening a worship service:

> May the grace of the Lord Jesus Christ,
> and the love of God,
> and the fellowship of the Holy Spirit be with you all. (2 Cor. 13:14)

Other points in the service where scriptural words might be repeated:

- to open or close a prayer;
- to open or close a time of singing;
- to introduce the Scripture reading;
- to respond to the Scripture reading;
- to invite the people to confession;
- to provide assurance after confession;
- to respond to the sermon or message;
- to bless and dismiss the congregation.

In order to avoid the meaningless repetition trap, it is very helpful to have a rotation of scriptural words (as well as other repeated words) suitable for each purpose. These words can then be varied from time to time.

My home church—which grew from that start-up group that first tried to reinvent the wheel every week—eventually discovered a very effective strategy for combining the benefits of repetition with the freshness we all need. We follow the ancient tradition of observing the seasons of the church year: Advent, Christmas, Epiphany, Lent, Easter, Pentecost. Each season has its own liturgy, made of elements taken from various ancient sources as well as words composed by members of the

### The Worship Sourcebook

An excellent source for finding appropriate Scripture passages to speak at various points in the service is *The Worship Sourcebook*, edited by Emily R. Brink and John D. Witvliet (Grand Rapids: Calvin Institute of Christian Worship/Faith Alive Christian Resources/Baker Books, 2004). This ecumenical resource combines the wisdom of liturgical traditions with the creativity of new resources. The resources are both classical and contemporary at the same time and draw on a wide range of traditions and sensibilities, including globally inclusive materials and materials sensitive to children in worship.

Resources in the first major section are organized helpfully according to different parts of a worship service. The second major section is organized around themes in ecumenical creeds and special services for different seasons of the church year. The book offers theological insight in its introductory sections and, in the remainder of the book, hundreds of suggestions for worthy words for almost every moment in worship, including the opening call to worship, prayers of confession, closing benedictions, and extemporaneous intercessory prayers.

congregation who have the gifts to do that well. Each liturgy is full of scriptural words appropriate to that season. So we repeat the same liturgy for several weeks; then with the change in season, we get a fresh liturgical start. (Each liturgy has room for variation week to week as well, particularly in the song choices.) As the seasons and years pass, the words of the various liturgies come back to us like old friends. They are familiar, but also feel new each season.

2. Use repeated phrases to highlight key words in a sermon. This is the strategy Dr. Martin Luther King Jr. employed in his unforgettable "I Have a Dream" speech. King used the rhetorical strategy of *anaphora*, which means using the same phrase to open a series of sentences. The phrase should be at the heart of the text's message. So, for example, a sermon on the call of Samuel (1 Sam. 3:1–21) might ask the key question: *Are you listening?* Or a sermon on Jesus's lament over Jerusalem could repeat the refrain: *Oh that we knew the ways that made for peace.* Another way to use repetition for impact and participation is to use a refrain that invites a congregational response. After each section of the sermon, the preacher concludes with a phrase like "Give to Caesar what is Caesar's . . . and to God what is God's." After a few repetitions, the congregation knows to join in on "and to God what is God's."

The virtue of this strategy is that, if done well, each time the preacher returns to the repeated sentence or phrase, the phrase has gathered additional meaning from the preacher's words between the repetitions. In this way, the repeated words accumulate richness as well as memorability. The words become, as one of my students put it, a "concentrated vitamin pill" of meaning.[9]

---

**Sermon Refrains and Stickiness**

Several of the sermons I remember most clearly over the years have used this strategy of repetition. For example, I once heard Dr. Tom Long preach a sermon on John 14:1–7. This is the passage in which Jesus assures his disciples with the words: "Do not let your hearts be troubled." To bring us to an understanding of the full power of Jesus's words, Dr. Long first pointed us to many instances of the world's suffering, each time convicting us of our apathy with a refrain: "'Let not your hearts be troubled,' Jesus says. But I fear we are *insufficiently* troubled." Once reminded, both intellectually and emotionally, of the depth and breadth of the trouble in this world, we were then prepared to receive Jesus's peace with a full understanding of what that peace can overcome. I will never hear that passage again without remembering that sermon.

---

3. Use Dr. Suzuki's "one focus" principle. My son's violin teacher, Cassandra Kroondyk, has taught me many wise things as I've observed her over the years. For instance, she often instructs my son to concentrate on only one "focus" at a time. "Play your new piece this week with an intonation focus," she will say. Or "Play your review pieces this week focusing on a bent thumb in your bow hand." This is a teaching principle she learned from her own Suzuki trainers, and it is effective because it encourages patient teaching and learning. By focusing on one thing at a time, we give it time to sink in and become secure, even second nature. When we move on to something else, what we learned is still there even though we are no longer focusing on it. This same principle can be applied to worship. One way to encourage mindful attention to words is to give congregants just a few words to focus on in a service, a sermon, or even a particular prayer.

One way to give a congregation "one focus" is to invite attention to particular words in a song, either before or after singing it. This can be done in a prayer or in words used to invite the congregation to sing. For instance, before singing "Cry of My Heart," a worship leader might pray,

> Dear Jesus, teach us what it means to follow you. Teach us how to obey your words. Teach us to imitate your compassion to the poor. Teach us to serve your world, even when that means carrying a cross. Teach us to follow you in your suffering so that we might also follow you in your peace and joy.

The repetitions of the word *follow* in this prayer have expanded the meaning of that word, drawing the congregation's attention to the word's richness when it appears in the song:

> It is the cry of my heart to follow you.
> It is the cry of my heart to be close to you.*

---

*Terry Butler, "Cry of My Heart," © 1991 Mercy/Vineyard Publishing (ASCAP) admin. in North America by Music Services o/b/o Vineyard Music USA. All rights reserved. Used by permission.

> ### Psalm Refrains
>
> One way that the church has used a "focusing" technique in its use of the Psalms is through *responsorial psalmody*. In this technique, a particular phrase is lifted from the psalm (some psalms have obvious refrains: Ps. 42, 46, 59, 80, 107, 136) and is used as a repeated refrain, sung by the congregation, while the remainder of the psalm is read by the congregation, or sung by a cantor, soloist, or choir.
>
> So, for example, the congregation might speak the words of Psalm 103, two verses at a time, punctuated by a choir singing the first melodic phrase of the André Crouch refrain "Bless the Lord, O My Soul." Refrains like these help the congregation see the whole psalm in the light of one particular truth (e.g., "God is holy" or "God's love endures forever"). They also help the congregation memorize scriptural words.
>
> Best of all, psalm refrains are possible in any musical style from chant to jazz to grunge. In fact, they are a great way to invite the creativity of a congregation's composing musicians, since it's not as intimidating as writing an entire song—just one good phrase is needed.[10]

There are many other ways to help worshipers focus on particular words. One of my students once recalled a Good Friday service for which the bulletin featured key words from the service, beautifully rendered by a calligrapher. Each word or phrase was drawn or depicted to convey something of its meaning. The words "man of sorrows," for instance, looked as if they were bleeding. The emphasis on key words in the bulletin helped the congregation listen for and focus on those same words in the service.

4. Turn off the PowerPoint and put away the hymnals once in a while. One of our students, John Dudich, recalled an occasion when he was serving as the worship leader and . . . disaster struck: the PowerPoint setup crashed. While the tech people scrambled to fix the problem, John was faced with an expectant and uncomfortable congregation. So, thinking fast, he decided to ask people to sing from memory. He chose songs he thought they probably knew and—wonder of wonders—they *did* know them. Not every person knew every word to every song, but they helped each other along and ended up singing with more attentiveness and feeling than ever. John recalls this as one of the most meaningful times of worship he has led.

As my mother-in-law likes to say, the phrase "to know by heart" aptly describes what happens when we memorize. The words sink into our hearts. It's striking that at Christmastime when we are singing the old chestnuts many of us have sung all our lives—"Hark! The Herald Angels Sing," "Silent Night! Holy Night!" "Joy to the World! The Lord Is Come"—everyone's noses are stuck in their hymnals or their eyes are fixed on the screen. After all these years, can't we manage without the printed words? I've taken to deliberately refusing to look at printed or projected words for the old Christmas favorites, and after a few years of this practice I can sing most verses of all the songs with nary a dropped word. This is not a testament to my amazing powers of memory. All of us have powers of memorization we hardly exercise because we are not often called upon to use them.

5. Speaking of songs, since almost all Christians sing in worship, and since we all repeat songs no matter what our stylistic preferences, the words we sing deserve careful attention. For many worshipers, the words they hear repeated most in worship are the words they sing. Not only that, but as we all know, music powerfully enhances our ability to memorize words. This is why our brains are full of advertising jingles and pop songs.

Thus, as we noted in chapter 1, leaders who choose music have an enormous responsibility. They are not only providing words with which members of the congregation *express* themselves to God, they are also *forming* the congregation's spirituality in powerful ways. Therefore, it's worth doing a careful analysis of a congregation's *song diet.*

Five important things to consider:

a.  How are songs chosen? A leader from a famous megachurch explained recently that her musicians used to ask only two questions about a song:

   - Is it heretical?
   - Is it singable?

She remarked wryly that her leaders now realize that while this is a good start, it is not enough.

   Worship music enters churches now in ways far different from only a generation or two ago. In the age of denominations, congregational song was vetted through denominational agencies and tested for doctrinal soundness by theologians as well as for musicality by musicians. Now, however, at a time when the composition of new worship music is exploding across the Christian spectrum, there is also far less pre-assessment of that music before it gets used in local congregations. Popular praise-style worship music especially enters churches through market forces: CDs and concerts by popular artists, musicians at influential churches who record their compositions and disseminate through Internet downloads, and the major worship music publishers such as Maranatha, Vineyard, Integrity, and EMI. Music funnels into these publishers directly from composers. This means that the task of evaluating a song's worth for communal use is left to individual musician/worship leaders or worship teams, who do not necessarily have theological training or even much training as worship leaders. All of this means that every church needs an intentional and informed process for choosing appropriate songs.

---

**The Worship Music Industry**

"Some worry about the control of music production that resides in the hands of a relatively small group of artists, producers, and executives who are not accountable to any church or denomination. It is no secret that a record company's production values—the artistic decisions about repertoire and presentation—are often defined by the needs of the recording and marketing process (projected revenue and expenses, available musical talent, advertising, and so on) instead of the needs of the congregation for worship music people can sing with theological integrity."[11]

—*Robb Redman*

---

b. What is the function of each song? The current situation requires greater savvy than ever in the selection of songs for worship. As we noted in chapter 2, worship leaders should pay attention, for example, to a song's function in the service. In recent years, some Protestants have emphasized the expressive mode in worship songs: in song we express our praise and perhaps our intimate love for God. These are of course worthy things for songs to do. But songs can serve many functions well. Along with analyzing the "direction" of a song's lyrics as noted in chapter 2, worship leaders must also be aware of the worship action the song helps worshipers perform. Is it a song of praise? encouragement? thanksgiving? repentance? Attending to the song's function helps leaders place it meaningfully in the service order and invite worshipers thoughtfully into the particular worship action the song helps enable.

c. Are the words worth repeating? At a bilingual church we know in California, this song was a favorite:

> Thank you, Lord.
> I just want to thank you, Lord.
> Thank you, Lord.
> Thank you, Lord.

The first week we sang it, it felt expressive and simple. We repeated it several times in a meditative way. It translated well into Spanish and we sang it in both languages. It was nice. The next time we sang it, I began to grow tired of it, and each time after that it became more annoying, and soon it was downright distracting from a spirit of thankfulness.

There's certainly nothing heretical about the song. It has a singable melody. And thanksgiving is a crucial function in worship. The only problem with this song, then, is that the words "wear out" too quickly. It might be possible to use it well—perhaps repeating it at different points in the service or using it as a refrain after different parts of a prayer. But it may be that the words simply do not have enough richness of texture to support repeating them over and over at one time.

Simplicity itself is not necessarily an undesirable quality. Certainly we want the lyrics of our songs to assist and not confuse worshipers. As one of my students wrote, one way old hymns can fall short is when they lack the "ease with which a person can latch on to the words and make them their own." On the other hand, words that are too simple or shallow are not interesting or satisfying enough to sustain repetitions over weeks and months.

d. Are we helping the congregation understand and appreciate the purpose of repetition within the song? Newer choruses generally use repetition in order to invite worshipers into the spirit of praise. Sometimes it takes us awhile to enter that spirit and to build community. So the repetitions give us that time, particularly if the musicians play the repetitions with some variations, giving the song an appropriate emotional contour. Other songs use repetition to create a meditative spirit. The songs from the Taizé community in France are particularly effective in setting simple but meaningful words to beautiful melodies. These short songs are meant to be repeated many times, usually with instruments playing varying descants so that each cycle is different. In this way worshipers have the time and space to meditate on the words.

Whatever the purpose of the repetition within a song, worship leaders can enrich the understanding and experience of worshipers with simple words of guidance before singing: "I invite you to meditate on God's goodness to you in the words of . . ."

e. Are we keeping track? It is difficult to analyze the variety and balance of song selection—a congregation's "song diet"—based on vague impressions. Every church should keep a database of songs used in worship in order to analyze over time whether the congregation is being offered a healthy diet of devotional words through song. There is much more on this in chapters 8–11 and in appendix 3.

## Stocking Up on Blessing

Writer Sarah Miller speaks movingly of an occasion on which her family discovered the profound importance of repetition in worship. Her mother had suffered a stroke and had been living in a rest home for five years. Relatives visited regularly, but she never gave a sign that she knew them. Then one New Year's Day, the family was gathered to celebrate, and they decided to get Mom from the rest home to join them. The family began to sing together. As they sang, gathered around the piano, their mother among them, something unbelievable happened: Mom began to sing along. "Her voice was soft," writes Miller, "but she was on key and she knew the words." The family sang "Silent Night," "Amazing Grace," "What a Friend We Have in Jesus," "Holy, Holy, Holy," and others. Miller writes:

> She sang them all. It was a moment of incredible warmth and joy, blessing and almost magical beauty. Even when she couldn't recognize the faces of her own children, even when she seemed incapable of laughter or tears, the songs of faith were still alive. Deep within her spirit, below the frost line of illness and death, the hymns survived.[12]

Every week, we have the opportunity to place words in the souls of God's people, words that could bless them all their lives. What precious treasury of words are we offering our congregations? What blessing will they draw on when illness, loss of memory and alertness, or all manner of weakness come upon them?

## Summary Call to Action

→ Use creative repetition thoughtfully both within and across worship services in order to help worshipers fill their hearts and minds with worthy words.

## Exercises

1. Assess the contents of your own memory. What can you say from memory that you learned in worship? The Lord's Prayer? Some hymn lyrics? What else? Now try to recall as many advertising slogans, television show theme songs, poems, and other song lyrics as you can. What do you discover about the content of your memory?

2. Observe what is repeated in a service you attend. Anything? What words do you bring home with you if any? If you attend this church often, think back over the last several months and recall what is repeated over time at the church. What can you observe about what worshipers here are learning by heart?

3. Find a prayer from a prayer book or worship resource that you like. Repeat it every day for at least two weeks until you have it memorized. Now turn it into a worship resource. You might adapt the words, or you might find words to introduce and frame the prayer. Where might this prayer go in a worship service to make it most meaningful for worshipers?

4. Plan for a service. Begin with the Scripture passage that will be preached on that day. Read it carefully and meditate on it. What words from this passage do you feel the congregation needs to hear and remember? Keep it to a word or phrase of no more than about seven words. How can you help make this word or phrase the "one focus" of the service?

    a. Write a sermon using this phrase as a refrain.

    b. Write a song in which this phrase is repeated or explored or both.

    c. Write a prayer using the phrase to frame the petitions.

5. Make a list of things you wish everyone in your congregation (including yourself and the children of the congregation) had in their hearts, from memory. The Lord's Prayer? The Apostles' Creed? The words to four crucial hymns or songs? Which passages of Scripture? How can you find a way to repeat these things often enough that this will happen, but in creative ways that avoid rote and meaningless repetition?

    a. Plan a sermon series on a particular passage. Sketch out five or so sermons, each focused on a particular word or phrase from the passage.

    b. Consider different ways to use the song you choose in different services. Could it be played more meditatively as a prayer one week and more jubilantly as a praise song another week?

    c. Think of three new ways to present something familiar such as the Lord's Prayer or the Apostles' Creed. Possible strategies:

---

### Thanksgiving for Consecration Sunday at First Baptist Church, Pasadena

In this litany, notice how in each petition, the leader's words begin the sentence and the congregation's response completes that idea. With each petition, the giving of ourselves to God accumulates richness and specificity.

| | |
|---|---|
| *Leader:* | Today in this place, |
| *People:* | *We give ourselves to God.* |
| *Leader:* | Not withholding our time, our talents, or our money, |
| *People:* | *We give ourselves to God.* |
| *Leader:* | Hopeful that our plenty may supply the needs of others, |
| *People:* | *We give ourselves to God.* |
| *Leader:* | Confident that we will reap what we sow, |
| *People:* | *We give ourselves to God.* |
| *Leader:* | In overflowing joy and abounding generosity, |
| *People:* | *We give ourselves to God.* |
| *Leader:* | Thanking God for God's indescribable gift, |
| *People:* | *We give ourselves to God.* |

*—Written by Ryan Bailey, based on 2 Corinthians 8–9*

- dancers interpret each petition of the prayer;
- artists create a series of paintings;
- teenagers write what each petition of the Lord's Prayer means to them, taking turns each week to read their thoughts before the congregation prays the prayer.

# 5

# The Puzzle of Authenticity

In his book *Velvet Elvis*, Pastor Rob Bell of Mars Hill Church in Grand Rapids, Michigan, tells the story of how his ten-thousand-member church got started in the late 1990s. He recalls that he was first inspired by a church in the Los Angeles area while he was attending Fuller Seminary. Sundays after services at this church, he and his wife considered what their dream church might be like, and he thought about what he had learned from playing in alternative rock bands. From this "raw art form," Bell got his ideas about what it means to be authentic:

Do it yourself.
Strip it down.
Bare bones.
Take away all the fluff and the hype.

"This ethos," Bell writes, "heavily shaped my understandings of what a church should be like: strip everything away and get down to the most basic elements. A group of people desperate to experience God." Applying these ideas to a worship service, Bell describes what he and his wife dreamed of as ideal worship: "People would come in, there would be some singing, I would talk about God and Jesus and the Bible and life for about an hour, and then it would be over." Mars Hill Church followed this plan, grew wildly, and Bell and his leadership team discovered that when it came to worship experiences, "The more honest, the more raw, the more stripped down we made it, the more people loved it."[1]

Mars Hill Church and many others like it have tapped into an intense longing for authenticity, particularly among young people. All of us claim we want authenticity in worship. We certainly don't wish to be deceitful, hypocritical, or irrelevant. But what does it mean to be authentic?

### Faking It: The Bane of Leadership

In the introduction to this book, we considered the idea that excellence in worship requires transparency among the leadership, by which we meant that whatever worship leaders do in whatever style, their task is to point worshipers to God, not themselves. Worshipers ought to see and experience God through the words and actions of worship leaders, and leaders should be transparent in that sense. Here we can expand that idea to affirm the integrity of worship leaders, not only in leading truthful, faithful lives in general, but in their acts of leadership as well.

---

**Feel It with Me Now**

As I have taught classes on preaching, I am surprised by how many students are skittish about attending carefully to the emotional contours of their sermons, about deliberately shaping their language in order to solicit an *emotional* response from their congregations. This skittishness is rooted in an appropriate fear of manipulative preaching. But let's think carefully about this for a moment. A preacher will usually have no qualms about wanting the congregation to think her *thoughts* after her. She will work at a logical presentation of material and careful diction so that it is comprehensible and persuasive. In doing so, she is not demanding or manipulating assent—though of course she is leading the congregation in a particular direction. In the same way, it does not seem manipulative or disingenuous for the preacher to preach in such a way that a congregation is led, emotionally, to feel the preacher's *feelings* after her. The preacher does not coerce a particular response, but does try to solicit it. This is no more manipulative than using logic well, provided—and this is crucial—the direction the preacher is headed is one determined by the Scripture and the message of the gospel. In my experience, a great many sermons would be vastly improved if the preacher would create an "emotional" outline of his sermon as well as a logical one. Better still for a preacher to use whatever outline is appropriate to the sermon's content, and then at every point and subpoint of that outline, ask "What should people feel at this point? Remorse? Hope? Anger? Fear? Joy? How can I help my congregation to feel this way?" Inviting them to do so is not a way preachers bring congregants into an encounter with God; but we preachers set the context, we trim the sails, so that our speaking evokes the full presence of our congregations, able then to meet God's presence—in the sermon, and in worship more generally.

**"How Are You in Your Spirit?"**

I was helping to lead a large worship service at a conference. As the band and I were doing tech setup, one of my colleagues and friends, Jorge, noticed that the tech crew had fumbled some details, and that I was distracted and rather peevish. "How are you?" Jorge asked. "Oh, fine," I replied. But Jorge wasn't satisfied: "No, I mean, how are you *in your spirit*?"

Jorge could see that I was not in the right place spiritually to lead others. His words caught me up short. So I excused myself and went off by myself to pray for a little while. When I returned, I was no longer stuck in that self-centered funk, but genuinely ready for worship—and grateful for Jorge's gentle rebuke.

Worship leaders have to combine good practices and skillful techniques with the right attitudes.

Essentially, worship leaders must mean what they say and must themselves be worshiping while they are leading. They must model authenticity in worship in the sense that they are fully, actively, and consciously attentive to what they are doing. Their authenticity naturally invites worshipers to worship authentically themselves.

Any worship leader will testify that this is not always easy. One problem is that the temptation to manipulate the emotions of worshipers is very strong, particularly for leaders with great skill. Song leaders know when to change keys or repeat a chorus to create emotional intensity. Singers know just when to make their voices break so they sound "into it." Preachers know how to make their voices rise and fall and rise to bring people along for that emotional ride. Pray-ers know how to use biblical or heavily metaphorical phrases designed to impress people with their eloquence. Worship leaders with skill and good instincts can develop techniques that reliably "work." These techniques are not necessarily illegitimate. Leaders *should* invite worshipers into the various states of emotion appropriate to worship, just as they invite worshipers into various patterns of thought. Leaders *should* use musical techniques and words skillfully. The problem comes when the technique is prized *because* it displays the leader's skill. In other words, there's a fine line between skillful leadership and showing off.

Then there's the opposite problem: what professional musicians call "mailing it in." This means going through the motions without paying much attention, not being truly present. Like everyone else, worship leaders come to worship with minds full of distractions—*Where is that amp cord? Why was my daughter angry with me this morning? How will I get that report done if I'm here at church all day today?* Life's ordinary worries and tangled emotions are exacerbated for worship leaders by the weight of their responsibilities on Sunday.

Worship leaders, both to avoid manipulation and to be authentically present, must give God time to quiet and heal their own spirits before they can lead others. This can be done in prayer, either alone or with other worship leaders before the service. Perhaps both is the ideal. The spiritual preparation of worship leaders is the first requirement for authenticity, no matter what form the worship itself will take.

Even more, this attitude of preparation for worship must become part of a larger attitude of genuineness about the Christian faith in all of life. Worship leaders often feel the pressure to be perfect and holy and put-together at all times—at least on the outside. But keeping up a good front actually works against leadership effectiveness and good worship. Instead, worship leaders have to allow themselves to be "slammed by life," as one of my students put it. The spiritual life does not always lead us through green pastures and beside still waters. There are valleys of shadows too. Worship leaders have to be open to life—to our own and others' pain, to events in the world, to people who are especially difficult to deal with, to disappointment and frustration. If preachers and pray-ers and musicians can show others how to bring those shadows to God *through worship*, they will demonstrate an authenticity that we all can emulate. Being open to life enables leaders to fill out "empty" technique with solid content, the genuine stuff of real life.

### How *Not* to Be a Transparent Preacher
### by Pastor Grouchy VanMisanthrope

- Make all your examples and illustrations about you and your life; be sure to make yourself look good or expose only those mess-ups that will serve to endear you to the congregation.
- Don't bother to study the Bible passage much to hear what it has to say. When you preach, whatever immediately comes to mind will be fine, so long as it's a bit funny from time to time.
- Don't bother to study the historical context of the Bible passage. Just apply it instinctively to whatever issue you actually want to address that day. Or, alternatively, if you want to show the congregation the results of your seminary education, turn every sermon into a lecture on parallels to the biblical text in other ancient Near Eastern literature.
- Study the slickest, most successful TV preachers, sportscasters, and entertainers. Imitate their styles as best you can.
- Refer to pop culture and technology in every sermon, even if you know nothing about them. Show those young people that you can "relate." Never mind Bible commentaries; read the celebrity blogs and head for the cineplex.
- Keep yourself busy all week administering programs at church. Your congregation expects you to be *doing* something; don't waste time in prayer and study. That's not what they pay you for.

## Insider Terms

Sincere people of impeccable integrity and openness to life, people who prepare thoughtfully and lead attentively, can still lead a worship service that does not *feel* authentic to the worshipers. Right attitude and skilled delivery are essential, but now we turn to further questions of what, exactly, we are delivering. The content of our practices has to be authentic as well.

One common way that worship leaders fail to convey authenticity is in their use of language. As we noted in discussing the expressive dimension of language in chapter 1, it is not always easy to create a common language in worship, one that can be adequately understood and adopted by everyone present in expressing and forming their own devotion. Those of us who have been inside the church for a long time have a large vocabulary of words like *salvation, redemption, atonement, sin*, and so on that we have come to understand through instruction and experience. But children, young people, and newcomers of all ages can stumble over these words. And those of us familiar with them can forget that it is not enough to rehearse our insider vocabulary, no matter how sincerely we mean it. Our crucial code words need explanation for newcomers as well as constant renewal for insiders.

My family visited a very famous megachurch in the Los Angeles area and attended a service that was clearly meant for seekers. After some rousing singing led by a "tight" worship band, a performance by a guest musical group, and a brief prayer for the head pastor of the megachurch (who was absent because of a death in his family), we entered the sermon time. The speaker used engaging, colloquial language, inviting us all to ask questions of Jesus. He assured us that it was all right to have questions. So far, so good. But then he invited people who had not previously made a commitment to Jesus to "examine the evidence" and "make a decision." He invited them to believe that "Jesus is the One," that he died for their sins, rose from the dead, and will give them eternal life.

All this is standard language in the evangelical world, of course. However, even as a lifetime insider who has heard these words all my life, I found myself growing impatient. "But what does all that *mean*?!" I protested in my own thoughts. If I were a seeker confronted with this decision—which the speaker assured us "is a really big deal"—I would want to understand how all these formulaic phrases played out in my life, specifically. What does it *mean* that Jesus is the One? The One *what*? What does it *mean* to have a personal relationship with someone I can't see and who up till now I thought was merely an admirable historical figure? What does it mean to be *saved*? If I make this big-deal decision, then what? And what am I deciding *for*, exactly?

Presumably people who come frequently to this church hear other messages that give a little real-life traction to some of these ideas. I have no doubt at all about the sincerity and integrity of the speaker. But I was stunned at how easily he used these standard phrases, offering almost no specific ideas that would explain them to those for whom they were not already second nature.

How often do we rely on the old formulas without exploring our familiar words anew, both for newcomers and for the refreshment and deepening of insiders' understanding? A glossary in the bulletin wouldn't help much because simple definitions wouldn't be enough anyway. Nor should we abandon complex theological words like *redemption* and *Trinity*. Rather, our worship can be perceived as inauthentic when we use words that have ceased to be fresh and real even to us. We have to explore our names for God, our terms for theological reality, our familiar formulas, over and over again. We have to keep them fresh like a bubbling fountain, not like a stagnant pool.

This principle of vocabulary renewal has the most implication, probably, for preachers. The sermon or message is the best place to do straightforward explaining and to renew our understanding of old or difficult words. *Righteousness, holiness, transgression, justice, prophecy*—in a sermon, a preacher cannot simply give definitions of words like these but, more importantly, needs to use story and metaphor to make these concepts real to people. What does it mean, specifically, for me to pursue righteousness at work? in my home? as a congregation? What is God's holiness like, and how can I strive to be holy?

Authors Kathleen Norris, Frederick Buechner, and Marva Dawn have all written "alphabet" books in the last twenty years, books that serve as a kind of glossary exploring the meanings of difficult words. Each of these authors argues in the preface to his or her book that some people are trying to strip these words out of our worship and devotional lives, but that this is a mistake.

### Exploring a Familiar Word through Song

Marty Haugen's lovely setting of Psalm 23, "Shepherd Me, O God," revives the tired old pastoral trope by reconfiguring our expectations for what the Good Shepherd does for his sheep.

The commonsense notion that the shepherd provides the sheep with what they *need*—food, water, protection—is deepened in an evocative refrain that encapsulates the psalm's three stanzas and expresses how God provides for the flock's good beyond their ability to imagine: "Shepherd me, O God, beyond my wants, beyond my fears, from death into life."*

*Marty Haugen, "Shepherd Me, O God," text and music copyright © 1986 by GIA Publications, Inc., 7404 S. Mason Ave., Chicago, IL 60638 (www.giamusic.com; 800.442.1358). All rights reserved. Used by permission. This song is found in many hymnals and songbooks and is available as a choral folio from GIA, #G-2950.

**Artists—The Enemies of Cliché**

Affirm the artists in your congregation and enlist their help in making basic theological concepts come alive. Artists, often by temperament, dislike clichés and seek fresh ways to see the world. Their perspectives can help startle us into new and deeper understandings of old ideas. Take a risk. Commission the sculptors, poets, painters, textile artists, and others in your congregation to help everyone by using their gifts. Make a list of challenging words and have your artists create works that help congregants understand the spiritual realities these words convey, and then make room for these works of art in the sanctuary space or in worship itself.

For example, I once saw an artistic rendering of the term *discernment*. It was a straight, thick, green line, from one side of the paper to the other. The rest of the paper had a squiggling, convoluted path in purple, also running from one side to the other. The artist commented on it: "I thought discerning God's path for me was choosing the green path. I learned that it was instead accepting the purple one."

We need words like these not only because they are biblical but also because they mean important things and have a valuable history behind them. We need to renew our understanding of them constantly lest we present ourselves as terribly sincere people who live in a reality others cannot seem to enter because our language keeps them out.

## How to Look Inauthentic

Writer and *Christianity Today* columnist Andy Crouch writes in his article "Stonewashed Worship" that "*authenticity* is the watchword of a generation that is suspicious of squeaky-clean, franchise Christianity."[2] Young people have keen noses when it comes to smelling something fake. If the adults in a church are so caught up with making worship beautiful, competent, and theologically correct, or if they are so keen to follow popular formulas for worship that they forget to talk about real things in real language, young people will notice. They will become restless and impatient. Young people are not the only ones who long for authenticity in worship, of course; but they are often quicker with their words and behavior to express what they feel is missing.

Even when the people who plan and lead worship strive to be authentic, mistakes or misunderstandings can create the opposite effect.

*Misused formal language.* Some people assume that formal language is by nature inauthentic. It is not the natural language of the people; therefore, people who recite or read or sing or preach in formal language in worship can't possibly truly mean what they are saying. Of course this is a prejudice. Imagine standing in the

**Spontaneity versus Formality**

"Some of us may so value spontaneity and informality that we are careless of our words and actions, fostering a breezy intimacy that is not worthy of God's worship. Others of us may take our words too seriously, as if a technology of correct words and forms could assure proper approach to God. Then our stuffy reverence may not help people open their lives to God."[3]

—*Ruth C. Duck*

crowd at Gettysburg while President Lincoln delivered the Gettysburg Address. The person standing next to you turns to you and whispers, "What's with all this high-falutin' language? What a big show-off he is!" You would be shocked.

Lincoln chose weighty words for a weighty occasion. Carefully chosen, beautiful, formal words lend a sense of dignity and beauty when used in the right context. Surely beauty and dignity are appropriate to the worship of God, and formal language therefore can have its place in worship.

Good formal language not only fits certain moods and occasions but is also memorable and can be richly expressive. It can compress into a few words ideas and feelings that are difficult to express. For instance, which is the more memorable of these two expressions?

> Pardon for sin and a peace that endureth,
> Thine own dear presence to cheer and to guide,
> strength for today and bright hope for tomorrow—
> blessings all mine, with ten thousand beside!*

or

> God, you bless me in so many ways.

We should not assume too quickly that formal language is inexpressive, even if it is old language. I once did a survey in one of my undergraduate college classes, asking the students to report on their favorite worship song, the one they would not want to live without. The most popular answer by far was "It Is Well with My Soul":

> When peace, like a river, attendeth my way,
> when sorrows like sea billows roll;
> whatever my lot, Thou hast taught me to say,
> "It is well, it is well with my soul."[4]

---

*Thomas O. Chisholm, "Great Is Thy Faithfulness," text copyright © 1923, ren. 1951, Hope Publishing Company, Carol Stream, IL 60188. All rights reserved. Used by permission.

For my students, this hymn is an example of formal language. It uses the archaic forms *thou* and *hast*, it is highly metaphorical, and it was written in the nineteenth century. They would never come up with these words on their own if asked to express what it feels like to be comforted by God. Yet they found the words both deeply expressive of their own sorrow and at the same time deeply comforting.

Formal language is "other" than our everyday speech, but it nevertheless has virtues. It can be used appropriately to draw us out of our everyday experiences and into an awareness of God's otherness, God's majestic presence. Good formal language can also give us words worth remembering because they say a great deal in condensed, memorable phrases. These are ideas about language that some church traditions have always understood and practiced.

We should realize, however, that worshipers must climb a step or two in order to understand formal language and find it expressive for themselves. We have already considered how repetition, if the reasons for doing it are explained, can help worshipers learn to mean good words they are given to say. My students love "It Is Well with My Soul" not only because the words are beautiful and true but because they have sung it many times, often on occasions of great spiritual intensity such as funerals. However, too much formal language can overload worshipers. When every word in a worship service requires the climbing of steps, as it were, then worship can become exhausting. This is especially true for young people and newcomers, for whom those steps feel higher.

So while we should appreciate the usefulness of formal language in worship, worship leaders also have to use it wisely according to their own worship contexts.

### The Hymn Sandwich

At the college where I used to teach, the worship leaders often used a strategy dubbed "the hymn sandwich." This combines the emotional substance of a praise-and-worship-style song with the theological meatiness of a good hymn. The two modes of expression complement each other, inviting worshipers into theological reflection and emotional engagement.

Variations on this include the "hymn lasagna" or the "hymn parfait," in which worshipers move back and forth between two or more songs. In any case, the hymn is performed with popular-music instrumentation—such as guitars, piano, drums—so that even while worshipers are using older, more formal words, the musical language feels natural for them.

For example, one might begin singing the simple Keith Green chorus "O Lord, You're Beautiful." After singing it through twice, without changing key or breaking pace, the accompanying instruments can introduce the classic hymn "Beautiful Savior." (The tune is "Crusader's Hymn/St. Elizabeth." This song is also sometimes known as "Fairest Lord Jesus.") After singing the verses, return to the Keith Green chorus one last time.[5]

Some congregations have a higher tolerance for it than others. Congregations not used to formal language can still happily receive its gifts, but this requires some wise preparation by worship leaders.

*Misused simple language.* Those who avoid the use of formal language in worship sometimes advocate using simple language instead, language that even children understand. The aim in worship, in this way of thinking, is to "purify" the language of all archaisms and fancy terms so that the language of worship is the language of the people.

Unfortunately, this philosophy, taken to the extreme, misrepresents both language and faith. When we aim to reduce our language to entirely understandable, entirely up-to-date words, we suggest that Christianity is graspable, easy, and simple, and that language—in fact, merely our own dialect—is adequate to explain it. This is not true, nor is this what people genuinely desire. Certainly people need language to help them gain some grip on the mysteries of the faith. But they also want to encounter a mystery greater than our understanding. That means our words will always be reaching beyond what they are able to say. Simple, straightforward language is helpful and necessary, but it will never be enough. We should not pretend that it is.

My friend Rev. Norberto Wolf, when discussing this idea, remarked that "simple speaking cannot be done through simple thinking." He was speaking from his experience as a preacher, having learned through many years that making his sermons meaningful and deep, yet understandable, requires much study and great effort. The best simple language in worship is the language that results from much reflection and care. For instance, the acclamation of faith from the ancient communion liturgy is simple enough: "Christ has died, Christ is risen, Christ will come again." But these words come in the context of a sacrament layered with meaning and mystery.

Even children don't want simplicity that is merely simplistic. I know this from reading children's books to my own kids. When our children were little, they much preferred the books with rich, interesting, clever, or beautiful language—even if there were words they didn't understand—to books using only simple words they already knew. This makes sense if you think about it. Children's little minds are designed to hunger after new words. Their whole lives they have gone around in a world of words they don't entirely understand, and they are wired to take pleasure in learning—it's like a game. They are used to grasping things intuitively and figuring out the details later. Children also know immediately when they are being talked down to, and they hate it. In a worship setting, then, it's not that pastors ought to offer children's messages on infralapsarianism versus supralapsarianism. But we do no one any favors by finding some lowest common denominator of simple words. Clear and simple worship words can be good and helpful, but are best used in the context of language that enriches our understanding of the faith and helps us grow toward those mysteries beyond language.

As for those hymns that have archaic or difficult words revised out of them, I think this is often a mistake. There are good reasons to revise hymn words, but making words simpler or completely up-to-date is not necessarily one of those good reasons. I am expressing a personal opinion here, but I say this as a relatively young person and also as a poet. I see no reason to eliminate archaisms such as *thee* and *thou* or the old *-eth* or *-est* endings on verbs. Figuring out what these old forms mean is not difficult even for children, so removing them is not a matter of clearing up confusion. In fact, I see persuasive reasons to keep many archaisms.

The first reason is the sound patterns in these old hymns. Good hymnwriters— the ones whose hymns have lasted this long in the first place—attended to sound and composed their lines so that the sounds created pleasing effects. When we alter these lines, we mess up these sound effects. Unfortunately, for instance, because of the shift to *you* and *your* in English for both singular and plural second person, when we remove the old personal pronouns, we often wind up lingering on *r* sounds or holding out that horrible *oo* vowel rather than gracefully alighting on the more pleasant long *i* or *e* sounds. For example, listen carefully to the sounds in both these versions of the fourth verse of "Ah, Holy Jesus."

> Therefore, dear Jesus, since I cannot pay Thee,
> I do adore Thee and will ever pray Thee,
> think on Thy pity and Thy love unswerving,
> not my deserving.

> Therefore, dear Jesus, since I cannot pay you,
> I do adore you and will ever pray you,
> think on your pity and your love unswerving,
> not my deserving.[6]

Sing both of these versions and your tongue and ear will help you see the wisdom of Robert Bridges's 1899 version compared with the contemporized version. Here's another example from "O Sacred Head, Now Wounded":

> What Thou, my Lord, hast suffered, was all for sinners' gain;
> mine, mine was the transgression, but Thine the deadly pain.

> My Lord, what you did suffer was all for sinners' gain;
> mine, mine was the transgression, but yours the deadly pain.[7]

In this case, when we update the personal pronouns, we lose the beautiful internal rhyme between *mine* and *thine* in the second line, a rhyme that emphasizes the profound exchange of Christ's innocent suffering for our deserved suffering. In the first line, too, we lose the much more harmonious "What Thou" for the phrase

## Updating Hymn Texts

Hymnwriter Brian Wren addresses the question of hymn revision quite thoroughly in his book *Praying Twice*. In chapter 9, he cites the example of "To Me, to All, Thy Bowels Move," a Charles Wesley hymn from the eighteenth century that needed—and has received—some revision. According to Wren, a good reason to change hymn lyrics is when they include words whose meanings have changed over time. So, for instance, the "bowel-moving" phrase mentioned above originally had to do with feelings of yearning and compassion felt deep in the gut (see Phil. 1:8; 2:1), but means something quite different today. Wren also speaks of changing hymn texts because of changing political motivations: it's wise, he notes, to alter references to particular nation-states, or even to the pervasive if implicit imperialism in the mission-related songs of the last few centuries.

When the decision to revise is made, Wren writes, there are two primary aims for the lyric tweaker: First, to preserve the integrity of the congregation's song—so that they might sing the words with understanding and devotion. Second, to preserve the integrity of the author's original work. He insists that this is also the *order* in which these two considerations are to be taken; the congregation's integrity is more important than the hymnwriter's.

Wren's wisdom is teased out with numerous examples and seventeen specific suggestions for those who have decided to revise a hymn (or undertake a significant hymn-revision project). For example, he suggests the reviser look at each text formatted as poetry, respect stress patterns and metaphor integrity, sing each proposed change aloud, and so on.

The bottom line here is that revising the words of an old song requires skill and sensitivity. Not just anyone can do it well.

"What you," which is more difficult to sing and often comes out "whachoo." In order to avoid this problem, one hymnal revises that line to "My Lord, what you did suffer was all for sinners' gain." Even so, much is lost.

Editing hymns when there are good reasons to do so is just fine. But if the hymn is well composed in the first place, removing archaisms simply because they are not in current, colloquial usage tends to exchange poetic qualities for new troubles.

The second reason for caution in changing old hymn words is that some archaisms are worth keeping around. I am one of many people who have a particular fondness, for example, for the word *Ebenezer* in the second verse of "Come, Thou Fount of Every Blessing":

> Here I raise mine Ebenezer;
> hither by Thy help I'm come.[8]

I sang this hymn throughout my childhood and never once felt annoyed by the term *Ebenezer*, even before I knew what it meant. I just thought it was a cool-sounding word and I enjoyed singing it. As poet and essayist Thomas Lynch once said about his own upbringing, listening to Roman Catholic Mass in Latin: "Words made *sound* to me before they made *sense* to me." There's nothing wrong with this. The aesthetic qualities of words often draw us into a desire to understand their meaning as well.

Eventually I learned that the term *Ebenezer* is a richly meaningful word derived from the Hebrew for "stone of help." It is the name Samuel gave to a stone he raised in thankfulness to God after the Israelites subdued their enemies (1 Sam. 7:12). The hymnwriter is taking that story and inviting us to put ourselves into it, to reflect on how far and through how many difficulties God has brought us. We, too, are invited to raise a stone of remembrance for God's help, just by singing a few words.[9] It's a terrifically deep metaphor, and we only need the word explained once in order to benefit from it ever after. This is simply one example to demonstrate that some archaisms may well be treasures, and we expunge them at our own loss. We should recognize that it's fine and natural and even desirable to expect worshipers to grow into rich and important words through instruction or art or study.

*Too much happy-clappy.* This is another authenticity-killer. In an attempt to make worship appealing and comfortable, many churches avoid the darker emotions of the spiritual life and focus only on praise, joy, and thanksgiving. There are good reasons to practice praise and thanksgiving faithfully in worship, of course, but when worship strikes only these tones, worshipers begin to wonder what is being hidden and why. They recognize that a mood of constant happiness does not reflect human reality.

### "Where Is the Lament Team?"

Certain musical ensembles deployed to help lead worship—ensembles made up of amplified guitars and drums and so on—are often called *praise teams*. When these groups lead almost the totality of worship, it makes me wonder whether the naming of this ensemble inadvertently suggests that worship in all its complexity—traversing the contours of our covenant life with the Triune God—can be reduced merely to *praise*.

Given the breadth of human expression fitting for worship (look through the Psalms for a sampling of the emotional breadth Scripture endorses), and given the many liturgical tasks before a congregation on any given Sunday, I sometimes ask my students whether such churches might use other ensembles for other specialized tasks: a confession team, an intercession team, a dedication team, a blessing team, perhaps even a lament team.

I ask tongue in cheek, but in fact I know of a church that *has* a specialized lament team. They call it a *requiem choir* and it is a significant and treasured ministry. This choir prepares songs fitting for use at funerals and then leads the congregation when acute grief makes it difficult for many to sing at exactly the moment when they most need to hear and be part of the church's song.[10]

## Wild Goose Worship Group

The people of the Wild Goose Worship Group in Scotland have a particular gift for creating worship words that combine all the best features of authentic language: they are vital, honest, simple, and fresh, but also pleasing to the ear and easy to speak aloud. As an example, here's a call to worship from *A Wee Worship Book*:

*Leader:*  In the beginning,
            before time, before people,
            before the world began,
*All:*      GOD WAS.
*Leader:*  Here and now
            among us, beside us,
            0enlisting the people of earth
            for the purposes of heaven,
*All:*      GOD IS.
*Leader:*  In the future,
            when we have turned to dust
            and all we know has found its fulfillment,
*All:*      GOD WILL BE.
*Leader:*  Not denying the world, but delighting in it,
            not condemning the world, but redeeming it,
            through Jesus Christ,
            by the power of the Holy Spirit,
*All:*      GOD WAS,
            GOD IS,
            GOD WILL BE.*

*A Wee Worship Book* (Chicago: GIA Publications, 1999), 13–14. Copyright © 1999 Wild Goose Resource Group, Iona Community, Scotland. GIA Publications, Inc., exclusive North American agent, 7404 S. Mason Ave., Chicago, IL 60638 (www.giamusic.com; 800.442.1358). All rights reserved. Used by permission.

In worship, we are invited to bring ourselves to God—our whole selves, including our sadness, brokenness, and hurt. Not only that, but we bring the brokenness of the world before God in prayer. This suggests that in worship, we should be able to express a full range of emotions: not only praise but lament, not only joy but sadness, not only forgiveness but anger, not only faith but doubt. The Bible's prayer book, the Psalms, validates a vast emotional terrain in our worship words.

It's a matter of honesty as well as biblical precedent, then, to show in worship that the spiritual life includes pain, sorrow, weeping, and suffering as well as deep, abiding joy. If one of the things we do in worship is help people learn devotional practices for their individual spiritual walks, then our worship ought to give people permission to express these darker parts of the spiritual life in healthy, biblical ways. We will discuss this further in chapter 11.

### A Read Prayer Is a Dead Prayer

In some parts of the church, the idea that "a read prayer is a dead prayer" is bred in the bone. Not only are precomposed words for prayer perceived as inauthentic, but any kind of preparation suggests a turn away from authenticity and toward performance in its worst sense. Spontaneity is equated with the Spirit's leading and preparation with the Spirit's absence. In other parts of the church, spontaneity is seen as sloppy and dangerous. It puts too much trust in the ability of leaders to feel the Spirit's voice when everyone knows that people are all too susceptible to hearing the voices of their own pride and desire for praise. "If you think the Spirit leads when you pray on Sunday," these folks might retort to their charismatic brothers and sisters, "you should see what the Spirit does Sunday when you prepare on Tuesday."

These two extreme positions are rather bewildering to me. Many worship traditions value both carefully chosen words and the ability to extemporize well. The worship services of my youth followed a predictable order—there was no Spirit-led spontaneity there. We read standard forms from the hymnbook when we celebrated a baptism or the Lord's Supper. But preachers typically preached from notes, extemporizing their sermons based on deep Bible knowledge, heavy-duty theological study, and daily connection with their parishioners, especially the suffering ones. Preachers also were expected to extemporize a lengthy congregational prayer at two services on Sunday, and those who could do this well were deeply cherished by their congregations. So I have a hard time seeing a substantive difference between the Spirit-fill-level of spontaneous words and precomposed words. As we observed in the introduction to this book, the Spirit can be richly present in the composing of a prayer or sermon just as much as in the moment on Sunday. It seems to me that preparation, experience, concentration, and solid content are the necessary ingredients whether the particular words are planned or not.

- Spontaneous words are Spirit-filled if the speaker has prepared through prayer and study, if the speaker has an active, vital spiritual life to draw on in the first place. And of course, the person must be concentrating in the moment as well, not simply rattling off formula phrases gathered from the oral traditions of the worship style.
- Words from older prayer books or words borrowed from newer sources are Spirit-filled if the leader has prepared by studying the words him- or

herself, meditating on them and making them his or her own. And the
leader must also be concentrating in the moment of "performance" on
what the words mean.

- Words composed for a particular worship occasion are Spirit-filled if the
  composer of the words has a vital prayer life and seeks the Spirit's guidance in the composition. And of course there must be follow-through in
  the leading of the words in worship as well.

Any prayer can be a dead prayer, whether it was written in 1549 or last Tuesday
or improvised in the moment. But any prayer can be Spirit-led, too, when writers and leaders call upon the Spirit throughout their process of preparation and
leadership.

### Does Scruffy Equal Authentic?

Striving for authenticity in worship involves many pitfalls, some of which we have
here considered. Perhaps the greatest danger in seeking authenticity is considering
a particular style of worship, and only that style, authentic.

Some churches today, in reaction to both organ-and-hymn worship and slick,
pop-praise worship, have sought authenticity through rawness. Mars Hill Church,
mentioned earlier, would be an example—no "fluff" or "hype." Some churches
today equate scruffiness with authenticity.

Churches seeking authenticity in this way are a healthy challenge to the rest
of the church. They remind us with their emphasis on the comfortable, expressive, and informal that carefully planned and practiced worship can become
too presentational: it can become a show or performance more than a genuine
encounter between God and God's people. But the danger of scruffiness is that
it, too, can become a stylistic imperative. Churches can seek to manufacture
it as a tactic to keep young people around or attract newcomers. In the article
"Stonewashed Worship" mentioned above, Andy Crouch warns that "our longing
for 'authenticity' also bears a suspicious resemblance to the latest plot twist in
the story of consumer culture: the tendency to rapidly replace the squeaky-clean
franchise with the 'authentic' franchise."[11] Crouch compares scruffy worship to
the carefully manufactured authenticity of stonewashed jeans and faux-rustic
Italian restaurants: they are mass-produced, mass-marketed fakes. Indeed, Ron
and I once visited a church the Los Angeles area that left a sour taste in my
mouth with all its carefully designed "authenticity." The stage—and it really
was a stage—was set up to look like a city street corner, very much like the old
*Sesame Street* set. The bulletin featured colorful, trendy graphics. The staff had

innovative job titles like "lead navigator" and "marketplace" and "connection." Everything had a consistent graphic feel, with logos repeated on printed materials and PowerPoint screens. The pastor promoted his own books. I'm not suggesting that these people were anything less than entirely genuine about their faith. But the carefully designed coolness of it all felt to me like authenticity designed by market research. Most troubling to me was our children's reaction. Whenever I wonder about a church's authenticity, before saying anything, I ask my children what they thought about the church. Their response to this place: yuk. They were thoroughly repulsed.

Another danger with some churches who seek to "strip down" in order to be authentic is that the authenticity of worship comes to depend almost entirely on the leader who gives the message. In Rob Bell's description of ideal worship—"People would come in, there would be some singing, I would talk about God and Jesus and the Bible and life for about an hour, and then it would be over"—notice how much of that worship experience depends on him. Bell himself clearly feels the almost crushing weight of that burden. He writes movingly about trying to bear it while remaining honest and open about his own struggles.

Bell's struggle to remain genuine points to another danger: authenticity in worship can end up aggrandizing the leader. For any worship leader trying to be authentic, particularly a preacher, the temptation is to turn authenticity into yet another pose: "Look how authentic I am! Shucks, I'm just being real!" From the point of view of the congregation, this focus on the leader's authenticity can turn in either of two dangerous directions: either it can become too focused on the individual leader, or, in direct contrast, the attention to one personality can become tiresome. "What is so great about you and your authenticity?" a congregant might eventually wonder. "I don't care about you. I want to meet God!" Rob Bell, to his credit and despite his increasing popularity, seems well aware of this problem, but it is a constant and difficult struggle for any prominent leader.

It is possible, in other words, for authenticity (paradoxically) to work against transparency. Worship becomes an admiration session for a particular preacher or music leader's authenticity, an event featuring a brand-name celebrity. This is why in some traditions, those who preside at worship wear chasubles and other vestments. These garments may seem a pointless adherence to tradition and formality, but they do have a purpose. The tradition of vestments arose in order to signal that the person, while presiding, puts himself or herself aside. The leader's individuality and self-expression are not important; instead, the leader is denying self in order to become transparent and serve the people in their worship.

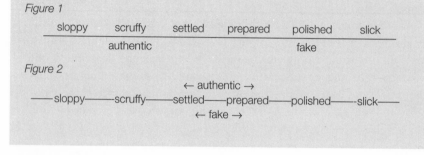

**The Scruff-O-Meter**

What is perceived as authentic varies with context, as demonstrated by the graphic below. No one wants either extreme end of the spectrum: *sloppy* or *slick*. But some people assume that the authentic-to-fake scale runs parallel to the sloppy-to-slick scale. In other words, authentic fits with scruffy while fake fits with polished (figure 1). In fact, however, anywhere on this scale could be authentic for a particular congregation or even a particular individual. "Authentic" and "fake" float freely around the scale (figure 2).

*Figure 1*

| sloppy | scruffy | settled | prepared | polished | slick |
|--------|---------|---------|----------|----------|-------|
| | authentic | | | fake | |

*Figure 2*

← authentic →

——sloppy———scruffy———settled——prepared———polished———slick——

← fake →

## Measures of Piety

It's strange that churches today feel themselves in a kind of authenticity contest, trying to keep up with the scruffy, hip congregations who seem to have a corner on honesty. In fact, however, authenticity is not about scruffiness or about any particular style for that matter. It's not something you can generate through careful design and market research. As Crouch points out, the worn bindings of the hymnals and the peeling floral wallpaper in the ladies' room in the little church on the corner are just as authentic as any raw guitar chord or candlelit prayer meeting.

In the end, worship leaders cannot worry about imitating someone else's version of authenticity. As liturgical historian James F. White observes in his book *Protestant Worship: Traditions in Transition*, "Protestant worship is a vast phenomenon" and very difficult to observe and categorize.[12] White points out that different traditions express piety in worship in different ways, and that those of us used to a particular expression of piety cannot assume that people who do not behave as we do in worship are any more or less authentic. We have different preferences for how we express our devotion, but these preferences in themselves do not make us more or less authentic. For worship leaders, perhaps the most important thing is to understand the worship instincts of their congregants—how their traditions and experiences have shaped their expectations about what worship should be and what authenticity looks and feels like.

We have to be authentic to who we are, each congregation with its own history and cultural context. However, who we are must be continually reshaped by God's vision for who we are *becoming*. We are a people in transition, striving genuinely to die to ourselves and live in Christ. Authenticity in worship, then, is about honoring and also stretching received instincts. Every style has authenticity pitfalls, and for that reason we do well to learn from other styles and even invent new styles in order to enrich and enliven our own.

Whatever songs are sung or instruments played, whether sermons are scripted or extemporized, whether people dance in the aisles or meditate in the pews, the measure of authenticity is born out in who we are becoming. Authenticity is when the leaders and the people mean what they are doing and live it out beyond the parameters of the worship service itself.

## Summary Calls to Action

→ Prepare for worship through prayer and study.

→ Seek ways in worship to explore and explain in terms of everyday life the insider terms and specialized language of the faith.

→ Seek ways to help people receive formal language comfortably.

→ Avoid oversimplifying language for children or anyone else.

→ Help congregants resist the temptation to equate only one particular style with authenticity.

→ Understand your own congregation's instincts for what is authentic; honor and stretch those instincts.

## Exercises

1. Get in touch with your own prejudices. Describe how authentic worship looks to you. Where do those instincts come from for you? Have you ever experienced a different kind of worship that you acknowledge was authentic even though it doesn't fit your paradigm?

2. In a worship service you attend, observe the people carefully. What do they do with their words, their bodies, their faces that shows they are genuinely involved in worship? Then reflect on your own behavior in worship. What do you do that might indicate to others that you are truly worshiping? Are there ever occasions in which you are in fact deeply attentive to worship but your outward behavior would not indicate that to anyone else?

3. Attend a worship service and pretend that you are an outsider, a seeker who does not know anything about the faith. Make a list of words or actions that you find bewildering. Afterward, choose one word or action that you deem most confusing. How might this word or action have been better explained or explored and "made real," without this becoming tiresome for those who already understand?

4. Choose a worship resource that uses formal language, such as a hymn or prayer, and devise a creative way to use it in a worship context not accustomed to formal language. How can you help worshipers climb the step to embrace the lovely otherness of that language?

5. Choose a worship resource, such as a song or prayer, that uses overly simplified language—language that has become vague and bland. Rewrite it so that it has richer, more specific content.

6. Write a sermon or, as an exercise, a short (three-paragraph) sermonette in which you explore a key word in your Scripture text that is so familiar we have stopped noticing it. Through language study, story, and metaphor, create a picture in the minds of your listeners so that they will never forget the richer meaning of that word.

---

### Getting Nefeshed

I once wrote a sermon on Exodus 31:12–17, which is an extended treatment of the commandment concerning rest on the Sabbath. Interwoven with sections on worship and on community (central to the text), the heart of the sermon was a simple word study of the Hebrew term *nefesh*. This term can be translated *soul* or *spirit* or *self* (see Gen. 2:7; Ps. 103:1; Ps. 23:3). *Nefesh* is used as a noun hundreds and hundreds of times in the Old Testament. But it is used only once in a *verb* form—in verse 17 of Exodus 31, when Scripture says that on the seventh day, God rested and was "nefeshed." What would it mean, I asked, for us to model our Sabbath respite on God's, choosing to do or not do based not on cultural blue laws (or the lack thereof) but in Christian freedom on what would "nefesh" us? (As alluded to above, here is where community and worship were folded into the sermon.) Here was a word study that not only illuminated the meaning of the text but hopefully gave the congregation something to take home with them—a biblical filter through which to view the world and to make choices about Sabbath observance.

# 6

## Watch Your Figures

### *Metaphor in Worship*

"Images feed concepts; concepts discipline images; images without concepts
are blind; concepts without images are sterile."

—Sallie McFague[1]

We were visiting a brand-new church, meeting in a brand-new shopping mall in a
brand-new suburb of Los Angeles. In an effort to reach brand-new believers, this
church was employing many familiar techniques: a guitar-led praise band, theater
seating, casual clothes, song sets, and an extended time of theologically abstract
Bible-study preaching (which they called *teaching*). As the final song of the service concluded, we shuffled sideways down the rows and then started inching up
the aisles, heading toward coffee and cookies with the rest of the small but lively
congregation.

Ron, hand to his throat, whispered to me, "I'm parched!"

"There's a drinking fountain in the hallway," I assured him.

"No, no. I'm parched *metaphorically*!" he replied.

I had to laugh, as I knew exactly what he meant. The people in this congregation
had obviously formed a loving, mission-oriented community, and I liked them
very much. But their worship left us dry in the mouth and hungry in the heart.

The problem was not lack of sincerity or effort or even musical skill. The problem was lack of imagination.

We all know that we live in an image-saturated culture. We know that visual images are powerful and that they shape our way of thinking. However, we don't often consider, especially in the church, that apart from any visual devices we may use in our worship spaces, we create images in our minds with words. God is a king, a rock, and a shepherd. The church is a bride. We are sons and daughters of God, we are sheep, we are the Israelites in the desert. The kingdom is a pearl, a vineyard, a banquet feast. Words have the power to create pictures inside our heads, and those pictures profoundly shape our devotion.

Figurative speech is perhaps the most powerfully formative tool we have to shape the beliefs, practices, and passions of the worshiping assembly. As G. B. Caird observes, "Belief in God depends to a small extent on rational argument, and to a larger extent on our ability to frame images to capture, commemorate, and convey our experiences of transcendence."[2] Yet how often do we take stock of the images we present in worship? How often do we consider how those images are forming us as Christians?

I am convinced that we are suffering from a serious illness in many parts of the Christian church today: imaginative malnutrition. Our diet of images—for God, the church, ourselves, sin, the world, and God's intentions for our world—is imbalanced and thin. This imaginative malnutrition is all the more serious because we hardly realize we are suffering from it. It is all the more inexcusable because the Bible and the Christian tradition offer us a banquet feast that we are largely neglecting.

## Why Do We Need Images?

At the time of the Protestant Reformation, the most strident Reformers were iconoclasts in the proper sense of the word: they objected to icons of any sort, meaning that statues, stained-glass windows, paintings, and even decorative architecture were stripped from the churches. Iconoclastic sensibilities became the inheritance of many branches of Protestantism, and one can still see the results in both the black-box, warehouse-design worship spaces of a modern community church and in the clean lines and plain simplicity of many New England churches—bare of any visual representations at all save a cross and perhaps a verse of Scripture carved above the pulpit. In reaction to what the Reformers perceived as the idolatries of the Roman Catholic Church, words alone were to be the medium of faith. Curiously, however (or perhaps consequently), these same iconoclastic Reformers urgently believed in the singing of Psalms, the book of the Bible most crowded with figurative language. So while worshipers could not look with their eyes at

## Image-ination

The insistence on the elevation of word over image during the Reformation was based on an understanding of John 4:24 and a belief that if God was spirit (and not matter), then material means were an unreliable way of connecting God and humans, of receiving God's grace. Here, for instance, is the Reformer Ulrich Zwingli:

> For as grace comes from or is given by the Divine Spirit . . . so this gift pertains to the Spirit alone. Moreover, a channel or vehicle is not necessary to the Spirit, for He Himself is the virtue and energy whereby all things are borne, and has no need of being borne; neither do we read in the Holy Scriptures that visible things, as are the sacraments, carry certainly with them the Spirit, but if visible things have ever been borne with the Spirit, it has been the Spirit, not the visible things that have done the bearing.[3]

Yet lost in the argument over whether words or images are best suited as a means of grace is the recognition that *both* words and visuals have physical properties; they are both material. Likewise, by both words and visuals our *imaginations* are shaped and our spirits opened to the workings of the Holy Spirit.

So it's important to be wary of inappropriate prejudice either for or against words. Words and visual objects can train (or distort) our imaginations. Likewise, we can make idols out of words just as we can out of objects (or people, or just about anything else).

images for God or anything else, they certainly had images on their tongues and in their minds.

During the Enlightenment period, the old iconoclastic impulse was further complicated by philosophical ideas that privileged propositional over figurative language. In other words, the rise of science and reason as the privileged means to knowledge meant that figurative language was seen as imprecise and unreliable. True things were to be said in straightforward language in which one word meant one thing.

Reason and precision of speech are noble values, of course, but this way of thinking about language does not realistically discern how language works. One of the most common and useful ways in which we create meaning is by comparing two unlike things. This comparison creates a bridge from the known to the unknown. For instance, the main screen of one's computer operating system has come to be called the *desktop*. It is not a desktop in the precise, literal sense. But that metaphor allows us to grasp how the computer works, at least enough to be able to use it. Even in science, metaphors are common and necessary. Niels Bohr's model for the atom is only a model; it is extremely useful and accurate as far as it goes, but it does not capture, finally, how the atom *is*, ontologically speaking.

### Figurative Language versus Descriptive Language

Descriptive language simply describes. Good description evokes the senses to create a clear picture in our minds.

She had a fuzzy, pink scarf tossed around her neck.

Figurative language compares one thing to another.

She had a giant, fuzzy, pink caterpillar of a scarf crawling around her neck.

Good writers know that the most vivid language is often figurative because figures evoke a range of sensory input and emotional connotations in a few words.

Within the category of figurative language, English teachers like to distinguish between *metaphor* and *simile*. *Metaphor* is a comparison like the one above, where the scarf was compared to a caterpillar without using the words *like* or *as*. *Simile* is a comparison using the words *like* or *as*.

Her scarf was as fuzzy as a caterpillar.

While a simile does create somewhat more distance between the two unlike things compared, the basic linguistic action is the same.

Metaphors create meaning by helping us understand unfamiliar things in terms of things we already understand. It is a natural component of language, so natural that children learning to speak use metaphor all the time. We place mittens on a small child's hands and she, after considering these bizarre coverings for a moment, says: "Paws!"[4] We are startled into understanding through the comparison of unlike things, and we are even, with good metaphors, delighted by the surprise.

When it comes to the mysteries of the faith, we have no choice but to use metaphor. We like to believe that we can state the truths of the faith in pure, propositional language because we have received the notion that propositional language is the most precise and reliable. So we tend to think that our creeds or summary statements are the most accurate ways in which we convey what we believe. For instance, when we confess that Jesus is the Son of God, we think we mean precisely that. But do we? Jesus is not the *son* of God in the usual sense. A male Father-God did not biologically sire Jesus. Son is a metaphor then. Like all metaphors, it is a comparison that is both true and not true. *Son* means numerous things, some of which apply to the relationship between God the Father and God the Son—and some of which do not. Of course, Son of God is a name for Jesus given in the Bible. It is an inspired, normative metaphor. It has an authority you could not give to a metaphor for Christ that you might devise by yourself. But Son of God is still a metaphor.

All this reminds us that the language we use to describe the mysteries of the faith is always necessarily metaphorical. No human language has ever or will ever have the precise words to describe the full splendor of God. This is a truth about the limits of language that should keep us humble as we try to speak about our faith. As Lutheran liturgical theologian Gail Ramshaw points out, to all the metaphors we use to describe our beliefs, we must always be saying Yes-No-Yes. Yes, this word rightly describes our belief, but no, in these ways it falls short, but yes, we use it, understanding both its revelatory power and its limits.[5]

As we consider worship words, then, we have several tasks. First, while we honor the inspiration and authority of Scripture, we must still understand that the Bible teaches in the supple, beautiful, powerful, but still limited medium of language. However much we rely on the revelatory power of the Bible, even the metaphors in Scripture do not tell the whole story. They are pointers to the truth of God beyond the words of Scripture. This should keep us honest about the challenges of making our worship biblical. We saturate our worship with the words of the Bible, but these words are not always self-explanatory. We need to keep reaching for truth through the words with all the resources we have.

Our second major task in considering figurative language is to recognize that metaphors, when overused, go dead. Nothing particularly vivid or sharp comes to mind when we hear talk about the "cutting edge" in car design, for instance. We've heard that phrase so often we cease to be startled by the like-unlike nature of the metaphor. Language is only active when it is richly evocative or startling or both. This is why writing teachers advise their students to avoid using clichés and dead metaphors. If we use them too much, our words will fail to keep the reader's mind attentive and active. Worn-out figures—such as "love is like a red, red rose"—put our imaginations to sleep.

When it comes to figurative language in worship, then, we have a problem. We have inherited a rich treasury of metaphors from Scripture, and in worship we

### The Limits of Language

"The very first word in theology has to be not about God but about the way we ourselves use words. Specifically, it has to be a firm warning that no words of ours can ever be trusted to mean the same thing when predicated of ourselves and God. Not even the florid ones with Greek and Latin roots. True enough, God is merciful and God is good, and you may make him out to be as omnipresent, immutable, and omniscient as you please. But never think for a minute that you have anything more than the faintest clue to what it's actually like for him to be all those things. You may assume on faith that it is legitimate to use such words, but never forget [the comparison between] the oyster and the ballerina: she can grasp his brand of motion better than he can hers. When you're on the low end of an analogy, be very slow to decide you know what the upper end is all about."[6]

—Robert Farrar Capon

honor and remember and repeat those metaphors (well, some of them anyway). As a result, we have ceased to be particularly startled by them. God is a rock and a fortress, we say, and the words convey a vague impression of strength, but our minds remain blank. No pictures appear, our senses feel nothing, our emotions often remain steady. One of our tasks as worship leaders, then, is to make the old metaphors come alive again—and to find new ones, too, that fit with the old ones but also keep them renewed and fresh.

Third, we need to recognize that metaphors can become distorted. The power of metaphor is that it brings a whole complex of meanings with only a few words. But this is also the danger. God is king, we say, and a whole complex of meanings swarms into view: a crown, a throne, a robe, unlimited power, obeisance, control of resources, perhaps tyranny, egoism, conquering ambitions, court intrigue, and on and on. Biblical metaphors in particular arose out of political systems and cultural practices far distant from modern life. Whenever we evoke any metaphor, biblical or otherwise, we have to sort out the implications we affirm from those we deny. God is not a tyrant. God does not literally wear a crown, except in that Jesus wore a crown of thorns—and that is exactly what undermines our common notions of kingship in connection with God. We fear God as we might fear a mighty king, but we also love God and trust in God's love, like beloved children of a faithful father. When we use metaphors carelessly, we risk allowing ourselves and others to carry around distorted notions. We must always be striving to uncover and correct the distortions.

Finally, we who prepare and lead worship must spread for worshipers a healthy diet of images. It is not enough to make propositional statements about what we believe and urge people to assent, intellectually, to those statements. We are to love God with our hearts, souls, minds, and strength, and one crucial way to engage that full, essential self is through the imagination. Images have power to affect our intellect and emotions at once. Images influence our actions. Filmmakers, television producers, advertisers, visual artists, poets, and novelists all know

### Preaching with Images

In the decades since the 1970s, a school of preaching has emerged called the *New Homiletic*. One of its most influential strands is a homiletical style that attends with special care to the function of the imagination, and in particular to the use of images as the primary tool for constructing sermons. Some critics complain that this type of preaching (or more broadly, the New Homiletic) is limited in the truth it can communicate because it eschews straightforward propositions in favor of polyvalent, metaphorical language. Yet the frequency with which preachers—even well-spoken and straightforward ones—are misunderstood suggests that meaning, whether presented in proposition or image, is not as fixed as we might like it to be.[7]

**Treasures Old and New**

He said to them, "Therefore every teacher of the law who has been instructed about the kingdom of heaven is like the owner of a house who brings out of his storeroom new treasures as well as old."

—*Matthew 13:52*

this. Pastors and worship leaders need to know it too. To engage this power of the imagination, we must mine the storehouse of Scripture and tradition and bring out all its treasures.

Too often, we are satisfied with insufficiently biblical imaginations. We latch on to a few familiar images without letting the rest of Scripture, not to mention our daily experiences, enrich or show the boundaries of particular images. This is how we create malnutrition: we offer only a few of the images available and we do not prepare them well. As a result they deliver only a fraction of the potential nutrients. Paradoxically, a rich spread of images serves both to reveal the limits of any one image and to empower them all, together, to advance our love for God and God's purposes.

## Sin and Salvation

Images and names for God are obviously of paramount importance in worship as in all of Christian life. This is a complex topic, to say the least, and merits its own chapter. Before we tackle that topic, however, we will here consider three other areas of our language in which many people have witnessed and lamented our imaginative poverty as a worshiping community. These areas of our language are those for sin and salvation, for God's purposes, and for human beings.

The term *sin* is a crucial theological category. I would never suggest that we stop using that word. We need it, but we also need to understand fully what it means. It's easy to talk about sin in worship and assume everyone knows what we mean. The trouble is that people don't necessarily know, particularly young people and

**Five Key Challenges of Figurative Language**

1. No human language (even the precious and inspired words of the Bible) can fully describe the splendor and mystery of God (1 Cor. 13:8–12).
2. Even the best metaphors, when overused, go dead.
3. Metaphors can become distorted, bringing misleading implications with them.
4. We need a healthy diet of images for a healthy faith life.
5. To all images, we carefully say yes-no-yes.

newcomers who are immersed in a pluralist culture where what is right and wrong is anything but obvious and agreed-upon. All of us, however old in the faith, may be making incorrect assumptions about sin. It is, after all, a terribly complex idea. It refers both to wrong choices and to our damaged ability to make right choices; to individual fault and systemic corruption; to the smallest thought and the most heinous, world-destroying evils; and to the effects that all these things have on all creation.

With the term *salvation* we have a similar story. What is salvation? Is it going to heaven after we die? Is it belonging to a particular club here and now and following that club's political leanings and purchasing patterns? Is it having all our problems solved? Is it feeling good, or at least not quite so bad?

So often in churches we hear all kinds of talk about sin and salvation, but these are only words. Not only is there little theological explanation of what they mean, but there is also no imaginative power behind the words. How can the gospel be compelling to us, let alone to unbelievers, if we describe the basic dynamic of it in words emptied of meaning?

Another problem common in worship services is a tendency to emphasize one part of this metaphorical system and neglect the other. In some churches worshipers hear many specifics about sin and the need to be forgiven for it, but the word *salvation* is only mentioned and never explored. In other churches, worshipers hear a great deal about healing or justice or new life, but the sin that got us into the situation of needing these things is barely mentioned. The two parts of this metaphor system have to work together to make any sense and draw people into a full understanding of their need for God and God's answer to that need.

In a 1988 article titled "Sin: One Image of Human Limitation," Gail Ramshaw urges us to turn to Scripture and draw out the full range of images for what is wrong with this world and ourselves and how God redeems it. Sin/salvation language is scriptural and traditional, but as it is commonly understood, this linguistic pattern focuses on inward self-examination, individual responsibility, and offense against an angry God. This is not incorrect, of course, but it is incomplete even within the total scriptural witness.

Ramshaw describes four other metaphorical systems taken from Scripture that seem to be more evocative for people in this place and time. These systems are death/life, injustice/justice, disease/wholeness, and chaos/meaning. Here is a summary of these metaphor systems.[8]

1. What is wrong with this world? We die. (Example of supporting Scripture: 1 Cor. 15:20–58.) Everyone can understand that. People can easily dismiss the claim that they are sinful, but no one can seriously imagine that he or she will not die. As essayist and funeral director Thomas Lynch likes to say, "The numbers

**Sin and Salvation Keywords**

These are the dominant words for *sin* used in Scripture's original languages (Hebrew and Greek) and rough translations for each:

Hebrew:
*Hattat* = missing the mark
*Pesa* = breach of relationship
*Awon* = perverseness
*Segagah* = error or mistake
*Resa* = godlessness, injustice, wickedness
*Amal* = mischief or oppression

Greek:
*Hamartia* = offenses against laws, people, God
*Paraptoma* = offenses or lapses
*Adikia* = unjust deeds, unrighteousness
*Parabasis* = transgression of law
*Asebeia* = godlessness, impiety
*Anomia* = lawlessness

These might all be summarized under three broad headings: disobedience of law, violation of relationships, and rebellion against God.

*Salvation* is a term with even greater complexity. Linguistically two words predominate in the Old and New Testaments:

*yasa* in the Hebrew = to save, help in distress, rescue, deliver, set free; and *soteria* in the Greek = health or salvation with spiritual significance.

Yet the use of these words encompasses a vast territory: the physical and the spiritual, individual and communal, eternal and historic, process and event. Furthermore, salvation is always understood in a nexus of relationships between God and humans, humans and other humans, and even humans and nature. Even so, the primary author of salvation in all its meanings is the one true God.[10]

are, after all, convincing on this, hovering as they do around 100 percent."[9] In this light, the Christian witness to the resurrection becomes not just a reward for being good or saying the right prayer but a startling solution to a very real and present problem. Moreover, the powerful metaphor of death and life readily applies to the things that kill our spirits—grief, conflict, abuse, betrayal, failure—and the ways that God redeems these little deaths even in this life.

2. What is wrong with this world? It is plagued by injustice. (Example of supporting Scripture: Matt. 12:15–21.) Liberation theologians have recently emphasized this metaphor system, reminding us that sin is not merely the aggregate sum of individual choices. Injustice infects our governments, our families, our cultures, all our human systems. Connected to this is the truth that God saves us not only

as individuals but as a people. We are called as a holy, set-apart people to repair, in God's name, those broken systems toward the goal of God's perfect justice. In this metaphorical system, God is the perfect judge who knows all truth; God favors those who have been hurt by injustice; and God calls us to examine ourselves and act together as agents of justice in this world.

3. What is wrong with this world? It is diseased; we are diseased. (Example of supporting Scripture: Matt. 9:1–13.) Nothing is healthy or whole. This metaphor draws heavily on Jesus's earthly ministry according to the Gospels. Jesus healed diseases and simultaneously forgave sins, and this helps us understand that the states of our souls and bodies are interrelated. This metaphor rightly reminds us that as with illnesses, some of which we bring on ourselves and some of which we do not, sin is both our fault and something we suffer apart from our fault. Moreover, it pictures God as the Healer, an image that readily encompasses both power and mercy.

4. Finally, what is wrong with this world? It is chaotic, and we long for meaning. (Example of supporting Scripture: Col. 1:15–23.) One of our students reported that when he was working with a church youth group, talking about sin made little sense to them. But when he said, "The world is messed up," they instantly knew what he meant. They recognized the messes in the world and in themselves as something other than how things should be. As Ramshaw rightly points out, the chaos/meaning metaphor system is especially welcome in a postmodern, highly technological, rapidly changing world. Every day, we face a crazy marketplace of competing worldviews, not to mention a thousand forces that could destroy us. We look back on a century of nihilistic philosophies, world wars, and the rise of terrorism. Our popular culture revels in surfaces, illusion, and irony. Nothing seems safe or certain. While the categories of sin and forgiveness may not immediately resonate, either with us or with unbelievers, feelings of fear and confusion surely do.

Our witness, then, is to Christ as the one in whom "all things hold together" (Col. 1:17). Those who follow Christ do much more than assent to a few propositions and say a prayer. They enter a system of meaning that tells them whose they are and why it matters. They enter a set of meaningful practices. Our faith is a way of thought, a way of life, and most important, a relationship with the God who created the world out of nothing, who sustains that world in existence, and who is re-creating that world into a place of dynamic, patterned wholeness.

In worship then, it is not enough to rehearse old habits of speech about sin and salvation. In our songs, prayers, and proclamation, we need to fill out those words with other biblical images, preferably a variety of them, to explain and also engage people in the heart of the gospel message. We need not lose the sense of individual fault and self-examination that comes with the word *sin*; all of these

### Alternative Liturgical Language for Confession and Assurance

Taking a cue from Ramshaw and others who encourage liturgical creativity to recast our language about sin and salvation—what ails us and what God promises us—here are two examples, based on biblical images, of prayers of confession and assurance.

#### Recognition of Exile and Hope of Restoration

God, alone in whom our hearts find their rest, we have awakened to find ourselves far from home. Our paths have led us away from you. We feel lonely and fear we are abandoned. Here, your word seems foreign to us, and we struggle to sing the songs of heaven. In your faithfulness, show us your presence once again, that we, too, may rejoice with all who call upon your name.

We have a Good Shepherd who searches for lost sheep. The Spirit of God still blows through the wilderness and prays for us. The sacred testimony gives us this hope; God delivers us in Christ. Amen.

#### Admission of Bondage and Words of Deliverance

Listening God, hear our cries. We are not free. We have enslaved ourselves and others to debt and despair. We are bound by vain desires, and our liberty to love is curtailed by bad habits. Our emotions hold us hostage to wrongs, real and imagined. In our bondage we are less than what you call us to be. Hear and answer us, we pray, in the name of him who came to set prisoners free.

The God of the Israelites has shown us the way of Exodus. Forsaking what lies behind, we follow our liberating Lord. When we are weak in faith and strength, the Holy Spirit provides daily bread and springs of living water, that we may complete our journey in the land of promise. Thanks be to God. Amen.[11]

metaphor systems bring us back to those essential elements. We simply get there from a slightly different and, for today, more compelling angle.

## The Kingdom

Another crucial part of the gospel message that often languishes in imaginative poverty is the question of what exactly we are being saved *for*. Eternal life after death is a precious and sturdy promise, but what about *now*? If I say a prayer, accept Jesus, and my sins are forgiven, then what? Are we bothering to give people a vision of where we are headed as we walk along that path toward God, and most urgently, what the next few steps might be? Brian McLaren, a leader in the emerging/missional church conversation, remarked once that Christian worship sometimes feels like one of those reunions for those who bought Saturn cars in the 1990s: we all get together and enjoy cashing in on something (atonement) purchased long ago.[12] Do we sometimes present the gospel as only some wise transaction in the past?

In the Gospel accounts, Jesus uses kingdom language to describe where we are headed. We are saved *from* sin, but we also are saved *to* the kingdom. "Repent, for the kingdom of heaven is at hand," says Jesus, and the idea is not to miss it (Matt. 4:17 RSV). Jesus describes the kingdom or "kingdom of heaven" using dozens of metaphors, all of which are worth exploring. In summary, however, the kingdom is a place of right relationship: with God, with each other, with ourselves, and with creation. It's a state of being into which God is drawing us right here and now, in our world, as well as a promise of the perfection God will fulfill in the new creation.

Recently some Christians have been thinking about how to make that kingdom language more understandable and compelling. For some, particularly those who do preach and pray the kingdom often, the term has become somewhat tired. For others, the term *kingdom* simply doesn't have much punch. It refers to a political system of which we have no immediate experience, except perhaps through reading history or fairy tales or tabloid accounts of "the royals." For still others, *kingdom* implies a king and that evokes an oppressively patriarchal system with which God has, for too long, been wrongly associated.

What are some alternative ways to talk about the kingdom? While we can retain *kingdom* as the most correct English word with which to translate the Greek word *basileia* in the New Testament texts, how can we further translate that term for the deeper understanding of worshipers? Some have suggested that we talk about the *reign of God* or the *realm of God*. These suggestions eliminate the gender-specific *king* part of kingdom, so they are helpful for many in that sense. However, they do retain the idea of a monarch and a political system that has lost some real-world traction in the last few centuries. In a recent article in *Sojourners* magazine, Brian McLaren proposes some other possibilities, not claiming that these are the final word but only that these are helpful metaphors that have "special promise."[13] He suggests *dream, revolution, mission, party, network,* and *dance of God*. When I have presented these ideas to others in various workshops, people have added the *project of God* as another good option.

Describing our vision and destination as a people of God requires, as with other important dimensions of the gospel, a variety of metaphors to explain, startle, and compel. The Bible, particularly in the Gospels, offers a rich source of imaginative material. But translating those biblical images and ideas into contemporary images through sermons, songs, and prayers in worship is both permissible and necessary.

## Collocations, the Romance Myth, and the Corn Factor

In composing or selecting figurative worship words, there are some mistakes we can make that may not have serious ramifications in shaping the devotion of the

### Kingdom Alternatives

Here is a summary of the terms Brian McLaren suggested. We have added Scripture passages and additional comments about the possible advantages and disadvantages of each:[14]

*dream* of God (supported by Isa. 35 and Rev. 21, e.g.)
- advantages: positive, personal, about God's desire and not "will" coercively understood
- disadvantages: almost as fairy-taleish as "the wish of God"

*revolution* of God (supported by Luke 14:25–35, e.g.)
- advantages: emphasizes throwing off other "rules" like consumerism, racism, lust; emphasizes change in the real world
- disadvantages: needs a qualifier to disassociate with bad revolutionary tactics including violence (McLaren suggests peace revolution, spiritual revolution, or love, reconciling, or justice revolution)

*mission* of God (supported by Matt. 28:16–20, e.g.)
- advantages: emphasizes our own sending and therefore participation in God's work
- disadvantages: can set up an us-versus-them relational dynamic with those we serve

*party* of God (supported by Luke 14:15–24, e.g.)
- advantages: rooted in several parables of the kingdom as banquet; emphasizes joy and celebration
- disadvantages: *party* as a word has an unhelpfully wide range of connotations, including children's birthdays and fraternity debauchery

*network* of God
- advantages: emphasizes communal interrelation; nonhierarchical
- disadvantages: the term is associated with business, technology, and personal ambition

*dance* of God (Psalms 148–150; Acts 17:28, e.g.)
- advantages: emphasizes dynamic, playful interrelationship; rooted in the doctrine of the Trinity
- disadvantages: lacks the purposefulness of the more justice-related terms

One additional idea from workshop attendees:

*project* of God (Matt. 20:1–16; 28:16–20; Rom. 8:18–21)
- advantages: emphasizes ongoing nature of God's work, our participation; implies positive aspects of building and rebuilding
- disadvantages: some business associations, though not bad ones; a little short on mystery

faithful but that nevertheless diminish our ability to worship fully and attentively. Sometimes, for example, our use of metaphor can fall into distraction or cliché.

Often the problem is one of mixing collocations. A collocation is a set of terms associated with a particular field of knowledge. Law, for instance, has its collocations

> **"World without Walls"**
>
> Here is an excerpt from one of the many new songs being written for the church—songs that embrace the reign of God and depict it with imagination and vibrancy:
>
> > Place my feet on the land where no barriers stand,
> > And its people have sense to reject every fence
> > Till each obstacle falls in a world without walls
> >
> > With God's grace from above fill each heart with such love
> > That we cease from our fights while we prize what unites
> > And we teach in our halls of a world without walls[15]

of words such as *justice, judiciary, client, billable hours, judge, jury, precedent,* and so on. Sometimes in worship we will hear something like this prayer:

> Dear God, please help us to maximize our mission potentials. Bless our objectives and goals and help us to reach them in timely fashion so that we can saturate our region with your gospel.

This prayer expresses worthy desires, but the collocation comes from business-management-speak and seems puzzlingly out of place. The language itself brings with it all sorts of associations about goals, methods, and attitudes from the business world so that the gospel is weirdly transformed into a product and the world into the market to which we are selling it.

Worship has its own collocation, of course. Bringing in other collocations can be useful, serving the purpose of startling us into recognition. But it must be done thoughtfully so that the associations that come along do not undermine or distract from the purpose of the words.

In worship music, the collocation of romantic love, for example—a heavily used metaphor especially in worship songs composed since the 1980s—can bring in some distracting and troubling implications. Comparing the love between God and the soul, or God and the church, to human romantic love has biblical precedent and a long tradition. (Song of Songs; Hosea; Eph. 5:25–32; Rev. 21:2, etc., have all figured large in the Christian tradition of love mysticism.) Since what is sometimes called Contemporary Worship Music (CWM) derives musically from popular music—which has always taken romantic love as a dominant theme—it's no surprise that CWM should frequently take the themes of romantic love and apply them, based on Christian tradition, to God. (See "The 'Fred Test'" later in this chapter.) Romantic love does indeed offer useful experiential comparisons to love for God: the tenderness, the intimacy, the exuberance we associate with being in love with another person is part of what we hope for in our relationship to God.

However, dangers abound in making this comparison. For one thing, romantic love as understood in modern times is ideally between equals, while we and God are not equal at all. Second, the stage of romantic love we call infatuation or being in love is an overwhelming, largely emotive experience. When our worship music draws on that metaphor, it creates an expectation of an emotive experience of faith, a "high" that is difficult to sustain in the long haul of the spiritual life as much as in the long haul of an earthly love relationship. Third, romantic love is well known for its ecstatic highs but also for its terrible lows: it is notoriously volatile, explosive, irrational, and short-lived. How do we gain distance from this part of the metaphor when we apply it to God? Finally, romantic love is between individuals with the result that worship music using this collocation tends to focus solely on the individual and God—a worthy devotional endeavor, but only if our calling to be the worshiping body is not completely left behind.

The song "Your Love Is Extravagant," written by Darrell Evans, serves as an example of how using the romantic love collocation can lead to troubling results.[16] The trouble with this song is that the songwriter borrows the sensuality of popular love songs and applies it to God. Words and phrases such as "intimate," "intoxicating," and "spread wide" draw the romance metaphor into a distracting physicality that in fact undermines the true nature of love between Christ and the church.

Moreover, some women have a hard time singing a song like this, in which yielding to Christ is presented in quasi-sexual terms. For centuries, for women, to love has necessarily meant to yield. Whether the woman submitted her will and her body or only her body, there was no alternative way to describe her role in the relationship. It is still a struggle for women, even in industrialized, "liberated" societies, to create relationships of intimacy characterized by mutual submission (as in Eph. 5:21), the giving of equals to one another in faithfulness, free of an asymmetrical power dynamic. So while women do seek to surrender to Christ as Lord and Master—properly so, as we humans are in no way equal to Christ—we do not want that surrender put in sexual terms in worship. To do so resanctifies unequal power in human relationships. It implies the sanctity of a kind of sexual surrender to the human "lord" that has no place in the Christian imagination.

One of my students, while we were discussing this, passionately reminded us all that the world is full of people who wish not only to make women yield but to violate them. We as the church have the opportunity, she said, to answer that terrible fear by showing how God heals, protects, and shelters women. Therefore, she pleaded, let's not describe God as a seducer. Women deal with far too much of that already. We want God's presence to be a safe place of wholeness and integrity.

In the worshiping assembly, we have to take responsibility for distinguishing human love relationships from our relationships with God. The style, tone, and collocations of pop love songs may help us connect feelings of intimacy and exuberance with God, but such songs cannot take us much deeper into our relationship with the divine. We can say yes to this metaphor, but we also have to help people say no.

Finally, when analyzing a worship resource or composing a new one, watch out for cliché or corny or mixed metaphors. The song "Above All," by Lenny LeBlanc and Paul Baloche, for example, has grown very popular in the past five years. People have worshiped meaningfully with this song.[17] However, it has some problems.

Some people have serious objections to the idea expressed in the song that Christ was thinking of me personally while he suffered on the cross, let alone that he was thinking of me above everyone and everything else. Those who object in this way suggest that Christ was thinking of the Father, or that perhaps we shouldn't presume to speculate what Christ was thinking about.

Leaving that issue aside, though, I object to the image of the rose in the song. Unfortunately, the trampled rose is a terribly cliché image, commonly symbolizing romantic love gone wrong. It's difficult to see how this association helps us acclaim Christ's sacrifice more fully. Moreover, the lyric commits the fault of mixing metaphors by making Christ a rose that takes the fall—with *taking the fall* being a common metaphoric expression that refers to one who suffers punishment on behalf of someone else. This might be fitting to Christ, except that we usually hear this phrase in the context of government corruption, which of course brings confusingly unfitting associations. In a way, the pun on "the Fall"—as in Genesis 3—is rather clever. But the sad little rose combined with that vaguely shady judicial metaphor creates an awkward mix-up in the imagination.

With thousands of great worship songs available to us, we are free to have very high standards. Possible theological trespasses, metaphor troubles, inappropriate

---

### The "Fred Test"

In considering the use of the romance collocation in worship songs, it is helpful to perform the "Fred Test." If you can replace any references to the divine addressee or subject of the song with "Fred" or "Katie," and the song still works as a love song (albeit perhaps a bad one), then it is probably not suitable for the worshiping body. In the song "Your Love Is Extravagant," it's true that in the arms of Fred it is unlikely one would find "a love that covers sin." But the word *sin* and the name *Christ* are the only things about the song that distinguish it from a typical pop love lyric. One of our students remarked that it might be a good idea to perform the "God Test" on romantic songs too. If the singer is praising the beloved in divine terms, perhaps the lyric is bordering on idolatry!

Examples of hymns that use the romantic collocation very well are the old hymns "O Jesus, Joy of Loving Hearts" and "Soul, Adorn Yourself with Gladness."

---

**An Uncomfortably Believable Joke**

*The Christian satire site LarkNews.com pokes fun with this fake news report:*

ANAHEIM—The latest Vineyard Music worship CD, "Intimacy, vol. 2," has raced to the top of the Christian sales charts, but Wal-Mart is refusing to stock the album without slapping on a parental warning sticker. The ground-breaking—some say risqué—album includes edgy worship songs such as "My Lover, My God," "Touch Me All Over," "Naked Before You," "I'll Do Anything You Want," "Deeper," and "You Make Me Hot with Desire."

"We've had concerns about previous Vineyard CDs, but this time they went over-board in their suggestive imagery depicting the church's love affair with Christ," said a Wal-Mart spokesman. "It would be irresponsible to sell this to 13-year-old kids."

A Vineyard Music Group (VMG) spokesman defended the album.

"We felt this was the next logical step in furthering people's intimacy with the Lord, as the title implies," said Sam Haverley, director of VMG public relations. "People aren't content with yesterday's level of closeness. They want something more. We feel this album gives them that."

Wal-Mart represents a third of all CD sales, which has forced VMG to try to negotiate a deal. VMG proposed adding a heart-shaped warning sticker rather than the black-and-white label more often seen on raunchy rap albums, but Wal-Mart refused. VMG is considering issuing a censored version of the album.

"If Christians want to make R- or X-rated music, that's up to them," said a Wal-Mart spokesman, "but we don't have to carry it."[18]

---

collocation mixing—any one of these is reason enough to look elsewhere for better options.

## Inclusive Language for People

Finally, we broach the question of inclusive language. This is a highly charged, highly vexed issue that tends to polarize people and shut down conversations. However, I raise this issue because for many people it is deeply important and meaningful, and also because I hope to offer some insights from my own experience as a writer, poet, and literary scholar that might be different from what you have previously heard. The topic of gendered pronouns falls under the larger topic heading of imagination because how we refer to people in worship affects how we imagine others and ourselves as part of the body of Christ. This is not merely a political issue, therefore, but a deeply theological one.

First, on this question, let me simply give my own testimony. As I was growing up, everyone used the generic masculine. That is, the term *man* was used to refer to humankind in general, and the masculine singular pronoun *he* and reflexive pronoun *himself* were used exclusively to refer to a generic individual. Honestly, I never thought much about this until college. When in college in the early 1980s, I started out using the generic masculine in my own writing because I wanted to be intellectual, and I had learned that this was how intellectuals spoke and wrote. Gradually, the use of inclusive language came more into practice. As I was exposed to words like *humanity* and the use of *she* to accompany *he*, I realized that something was happening to me. The images in my mind began to change. I realized, first of all, that I had been unconsciously associating the intellect, learning, and literature with masculinity. Suddenly I realized that I had to find a way to be both intellectual and feminine. Happily, other women were modeling this for me, both in person and in books I read. As I learned to use inclusive language myself, women and girls suddenly became visible in my mind in a way they never had been before. Strangely enough, so did old people, people of various races and shapes, children, babies. My imagination, in other words, burst into color and widened considerably. I was convinced through imaginative experience that inclusive language makes a positive difference in how we see the world, and I have been using inclusive language for people enthusiastically ever since.

Next, let's examine a couple of objections to inclusive language commonly heard among church people. The first is that inclusive language is part of a "radical feminist" agenda. Unfortunately, many people within the church, including its leaders, know very little about actual feminism beyond the demonizing caricatures they see in religious or secular media. Even granting, however, that some forms of feminism advocate philosophical and moral positions that cannot be harmonized with the gospel, it does not follow that everything every feminist thinker and writer has proposed must be resisted. That would be a logical fallacy. The other objection is the slippery slope argument: if we accept a particular practice (such as inclusive language), we will soon be accepting all the premises upon which that argument can be based and all the political or moral actions that might follow from those premises. This, too, is a logical fallacy. The question of inclusive language cannot be lumped with "the feminist agenda" and dismissed. It must be examined on its own terms.

Here's an analogy that may help: A neighbor walks by your yard and points to one of your trees, saying, "That tree is diseased. You really should cut it down." Even if you heartily dislike this neighbor and object to his politics and lifestyle, he might still be right about your tree. To leave the tree up just because you can't stand him not only hurts you but could also wreck your yard and will certainly cause the other neighbors to snicker at your stubbornness in the face of the truth.·

For Christians, the only important question is this: Does the use of inclusive language follow from gospel principles or not? We have to recognize, first, that the language pattern in which the masculine is taken to mean both masculine and feminine in some contexts—a pattern characteristic of Greek, Hebrew,

English, French, and many but by no means all other languages—is based on the presumption that the male of the species is primary and the female secondary. The female can therefore rightly be subsumed into the male in speech (and in law, government, the household, and so on). Do we believe this? Some Christians believe that men ought to be in authority over women in the home and elsewhere. Others believe that men and women have distinct roles in the home and church, though both are equal before God. Still others believe that men and women may have different qualities in general, but are not confined to particular roles, should share authority as partners in the gospel, and should use their particular gifts in whatever way the Spirit leads. Across this wide spectrum of views, we all believe that women are not invisible to God, but precious to God. In Genesis 1:27, God creates both male and female in God's own image. In Galatians 3:28, Paul claims that in Christ old social barriers break down and

---

### The Asterisk Doesn't Work: A Man's Perspective

I am committed to using inclusive language for people. I am convinced that it is not a small thing—it's a big deal. But I didn't used to think so. When I came to Princeton Theological Seminary as a divinity student in the 1990s, I was accustomed to the widespread practice in academia of using gender-exclusive language for people. But the arguments of those who said that *man* and *men* were exclusive did not persuade me. In my mind, the words had an asterisk after them, telling me to remember that they referred to women too. I didn't really understand what the fuss was about. Then, I attended a chapel service that changed me—first my heart, and then my mind.

Some courageous chapel leaders one day determined to use nothing but feminine references to people throughout an entire service. They were careful to point out that this was an experiment, and a notice at the top of the worship bulletin let everyone know that we should all hear all the references to *women* and *woman* inclusively—that is, with an unspoken asterisk. I rolled my eyes at the lack of subtlety, and resisted this too-heavy-handed attempt at the educational impulse within the community's devotional prayer. But I determined to worship just the same. To my great surprise, I could not. Every *woman* and *her* felt like a slap in the face that said, "You're not welcome here." When the psalm declared "Blessed is the woman who walks not in the counsel of the wicked . . ." I could not imagine myself as that woman, like a tree planted by the waters. When prayers were offered for "women preparing for ministry," I did not feel prayed for. Throughout the service I felt completely shut out. I knew in my head that the inclusivising asterisk was there, but it didn't help any; it was a hurdle I couldn't leap over. I realized how women have felt all along, whether they make a fuss about it or not. And I decided that when I was a worship leader, I would be willing to pay the price of a little extra linguistic consideration in order to help prevent my sisters in Christ from stumbling over that asterisk the way I did. Nowadays, that extra consideration comes to me second nature, and I'm grateful to have been unpleasantly pulled into an important habit of hospitality.

there is "neither . . . male nor female." And in our baptism at the very least, we are equal before God—men and women, both equally dying and rising to new life in Christ. Why then should we make females invisible and secondary, even subtly, in our language?

Therefore, inclusive language for people is not a capitulation to some immoral agenda foisted upon the church by a secular culture. Inclusive language is a matter of saying what we believe. If we believe that God calls people of both sexes—not to mention all ages, races, and tribes—to be redeemed and to live as a holy people, then our language should reflect that belief truly and faithfully. Our language should invite worshipers to imagine their way into a gospel of inclusivity more radical than any merely political agenda could ever arrange.

Today, when preachers go on about how "Christ came to save man from the fall" and make constant references to *him* and *he*, I am not angry and offended so much as terribly sad. After having my imagination opened up to the fullness of human nature, I am back to being forced to translate everything I hear so that it connects to me. Over the years, I have come to recognize keenly how the generic masculine leaves us in the realm of a masculine abstract that fails to evoke in our minds pictures of real women, men, children—people in all their color and variety—struggling with the concrete realities of life. Like many Christians, both male and female, I have come to believe that gender-inclusive pronouns are an important and positive aspect of imaginative redemption.

If you remain skeptical, please try an experiment of your own. Spend a week using only feminine language for people. Replace the generic *men* and *he* with *women* and *she*. Or simply use inclusive language. If, when you do so, the pictures in your mind change, then *men* and *he* do not in fact *mean* both males and females in the most important sense of *meaning*. If females seem to suddenly appear in your mind when you use female or inclusive pronouns, then they were not there before.

When Ron and I discussed this issue with our Fuller Seminary class, we encountered a wide range of initial feeling about it. Some students were skeptical about inclusive language; others were adamant advocates for it. Wherever we stood, we agreed that church people often ignore the issue of inclusive language (as well as God language) because they assume it is a matter for "those liberals." We called this the "relegation problem." As our discussions continued, one student worried that if people hear gender-inclusive language in the culture, and then come to church and hear gender-*exclusive* language, then what does that say about the church? Do we really want to be the place where the female is re-disappeared? What does that say about how we value women and girls? Another student observed that gender-inclusive language opens the door to greater awareness of a multiracial, multicultural church. When we stop thinking about *man* in general, we can begin thinking about all different kinds of people in particular. Still another student wisely put it all in the context of communication. What level of communication do we wish to achieve in worship? he asked. Whom do we want to reach with our words? Are we willing to leave people out?

## How to Use Inclusive Language without Getting into Knots and Tangles

Some people, when faced with the challenge to use inclusive language, respond with helplessness: "I'd like to, but it's so awkward and difficult." This need not be true. Eliminating exclusive language is not that difficult with a little effort and practice. In fact, in my experience, the extra thought involved tends to improve the richness and vividness of the writing. Combining a few standard strategies with some creativity for specific instances will usually do the trick. The more difficult cases ought to be seen not as nuisances but as opportunities for further reflection into the ideas one wishes to convey.

Instances of the generic *man* can easily be changed to *humankind* or *humanity* or *people* or some other even more specific term. Instances of the generic singular pronoun *he* invite numerous possible strategies for improvement. Various subtle things are lost and gained with each possible revision, so that writers and speakers must judge from context which is the best option for each situation.

A solution that is not terribly helpful is the use of the generic *one*, as in "One must give one's money to the poor." Although *one* is non-gender-specific, this is an especially formal usage not often workable even in formal worship. The *ones* tend

---

### Gender-Inclusive Language versus Gender-Neutral Language

In gender-neutral language, words that have a gender inflection are avoided.

*Father* becomes *parent*
*son* becomes *child*
*he* becomes *one*

Gender neutrality is appropriate and usually unobjectionable with occupational words.

*lady doctor* becomes simply *doctor*
*stewardess* becomes *flight attendant*
*chairman* becomes *chair*

However, with relational words, gender neutrality diminishes the relational content of the word. For that reason, earlier experiments in gender *neutrality* have given way to gender *inclusivity*. We can still use *father, mother, brother, sister, son, daughter, he, she*. The goal is to balance the use of masculine and feminine wherever possible.

**Other Common Objections to Inclusive Language**

1. "I'm simply using correct English."

Actually, standard English usage is in the process of a major transition on this point. (Some aspects of the transition, in fact, date back to the sixteenth century.) Authoritative sources now considering inclusive language as standard in North America include

- children's book publishers
- many major newspapers
- many Christian publishers (including this one)
- college rhetoric textbooks
- many churches and Christian colleges

See, for example, this Web site: National Council of Teachers of English
http://www.ncte.org/about/over/positions/category/gram/107647.htm

2. "Everyone knows I mean women too." (This is the asterisk argument.)

Because standard usage is changing, people (especially young people) actually hear *men* and *he* as exclusively masculine. Do these words in fact trigger in our imaginations what we say we "know"?

3. "I wasn't really paying attention. Nobody seems to mind anyway."

Even if no one has complained, we cannot ignore the issue. To ignore it is to disregard as unimportant the people who do care about it and to dismiss their feelings and opinions. Whether our congregants are conscious of the issue or not, we are shaping people's imaginations. How can we do our best by them?

to pile up in a given sentence in awkward ways. And the word *one* is so generic that it tends to distance the idea from the listener.

Another common solution these days is to use the plural pronoun instead of the singular gendered pronoun:

Everyone has their own way of praying.

Grammatical experts are divided on whether or not this is permissible. We do hear this usage more and more, however, even in respected public media such as national magazines and newspapers. It is generally acceptable in more informal speech.

A better solution to the gendered pronoun problem is to eliminate gendered pronouns where possible. Here are some strategies for doing so:

Every Christian must give his money to the poor.

*Strategy 1: Change the singular to plural*
All Christians must give their money to the poor.

*Strategy 2: Change the case to first-person plural or second-person*
We Christians must give our money to the poor.
You must give your money to the poor.

*Strategy 3: Eliminate the pronoun*
Christians must give generously to the poor.

One of the best strategies for retaining the immediacy of the singular while still being inclusive is to alternate *he* and *she* examples. This compels the speaker or writer to come up with additional examples, thereby giving greater richness and specificity to the point being made:

> An insurance rep can tithe his earnings every month. A pediatrician can give her time by working at a free clinic once a week.

This is an especially useful technique in sermons, where there is often call for several examples to give an idea some real-world traction.

## Altering Song Lyrics

When dealing with already written hymn or worship song lyrics, a simple substitution is not always possible because of rhyme and meter. This requires more creative solutions. In his book *Praying Twice,* Brian Wren suggests helpful ways to revise exclusive language in hymns. Wren describes various alterations of a line from the Charles Wesley hymn "Hark! The Herald Angels Sing":

*original*
pleased as man with men to appear

*alterations*
pleased with us in flesh to dwell
pleased on earth with us to dwell

Both these revisions actually improve on the original by strengthening the message of incarnation that the original only lightly implied (although, on that score I think the first alteration is superior).[19]

Alterations to older hymns require an expert touch, as the reviser has to preserve theological as well as artistic integrity. Sometimes, substitutions of a few words are possible. Sometimes the problem requires heavy revision or even the writing of a

**Gender Assumptions**

When you alter pronouns or generate gender-inclusive examples for preaching, be mindful of the gender assumptions you bring to the table, even subconsciously. It's easy to unintentionally reinforce false stereotypes. For example, when offering piquant examples of sinfulness, don't always attribute culpable ambition to men, or backbiting gossip to women. Likewise, don't use alternating examples that match good/bad with male/female. Give men and women equal time in both sin and salvation.

In a similar way, preachers should be careful in their illustrations and examples not to fall into patterns of stereotyping, so that the person doing the ironing at home is always the mom and the person shoveling the snow is always the dad. In fact, for a host of other reasons related to hospitality, a wise preacher will select illustrations over time that connect with the whole church: young and old, active and inactive, white collar and blue, as well as both men and women.

new verse. These situations should be thought of as chances to explore even more deeply what the original hymnwriter was after and to compose even better words. New songs can, of course, be written with inclusive language from the start.

### What about Bible Translations?

Should we use a Bible translation in worship that uses inclusive language? This question plunges us deep into the technical and philosophical issues of translation, not to mention theological issues about the inspiration of Scripture and artistic issues about the beauty and fluidity of various translations. People of intelligence and goodwill disagree on these issues, and the complexity of this discussion is beyond the scope of this book. Let's ask ourselves to do two things.

1. Study the issue and stay informed. The issue is important not only for "those liberals." Every person in your congregation stands to gain from hearing people referred to inclusively, especially young people, especially young women. Please do not ignore the issue of inclusive language and hope it will go away. It won't.
2. At least use inclusive language for people yourself and urge this practice among leaders for songs, prayers, and sermons. Alter worship resources for inclusive language where feasible. Seek worship resources that attend thoughtfully to this matter. There is no theological reason why you should not and every good reason why you should—including our conviction about the value of each individual before God.[20]

Trying to use inclusive language can help develop our sensitivity to language in ways that go beyond just fixing pronouns. Our student Mark Finney, after thinking

> ### Metaphors That Can Hurt
>
> Some language in hymns may also need to be altered (or avoided when writing new hymns or prayers) when it depicts human differences or disabilities in ways that are unfortunate or untrue. For instance, the "dark/light" polarity, used well in the Gospel of John, can become, in careless hands, a "*black/white*" polarity. Then blackness is equated with evil or sin, and whiteness with goodness and purity. This pernicious dichotomy applied to human skin coloration has been the source of a great deal of social evil across the centuries. Likewise, words like *lame* and *blind* must be wielded carefully so that their use does not suggest that our brothers and sisters with visual or mobility impairments are second-class Christians.

over our discussions in class, began evaluating all his sermons with the question: *who is being left out of this message?* He realized that when he preached, he had to think of all his listeners: older women on fixed incomes, teenage boys, divorced men, women suffering from cancer, college students, children, people who felt on the outside for whatever reason. Suddenly the bewildering and beautiful particularity of his congregation became vividly present to him. Mark's question reminds us that in our examples, stories, petitions, and images, in our prayers, sermons, and songs—and not just in our pronouns—we must try to honor, challenge, and represent the whole body of Christ.

### Summary Calls to Action

→ Seek ways in worship to explore and explain in terms of everyday life a variety of biblical metaphors for sin and salvation.

→ Seek ways in worship to explore and explain in terms of everyday life a variety of biblical metaphors for the kingdom.

→ Evaluate worship language for inappropriate or distracting collocations, for confusingly mixed metaphors, and for uncritical use of the romantic love metaphor.

→ Do your best to use inclusive language for people.

→ Ask the question of sermons and all worship resources: who is being left out by this language?

### Exercises

1. What are the most common metaphors you use for sin/salvation? the kingdom? What is your practice on inclusive language? Why?

### Revising Songs—Copyright Issues

When revising songs for congregational use, do be careful about both artistic integrity and legal copyright. You need to get legal permission to reprint, let alone revise, a song written within the past generation. If a revision is desirable, ask first whether you can sing the song and, with integrity, omit the part you want to revise. If not, publishers are sometimes quite quick to respond to requests—use the phone or e-mail and ask for what you'd like.

When the song under consideration is in the public domain, you may, of course, edit it without legal repercussion. But some revisions can gut a song of its artistic integrity. As Christians, we have obligations to authors—both those living and those awaiting the resurrection. Brian Wren suggests that two primary principles of song revision are (1) respect for the integrity of the congregation and its ability to sing a song and mean it, and (2) secondarily, respect for the integrity of the author's original work. The second is not unimportant, but it does not trump the first.

2. During a church service you attend, observe language for sin/salvation. Were any definitions given? Were metaphors used? Keep notes, and after the service summarize what picture of sin/salvation a worshiper might come away with.

3. Do the same for kingdom language. What picture, if any, did worshipers receive of God's purpose and goal for their lives and for the world?

4. Write a song, sermon, or prayer in which you develop one of the alternative metaphor systems for sin/salvation.

5. Write a song, sermon, or prayer in which you develop a kingdom metaphor given in the gospels: the banquet feast, the pearl of great price, the unjust employer, and so on.

6. Write a song or prayer or sermon (or short sermon exercise) in which you develop one of the alternative metaphor systems for kingdom suggested in this chapter. Is it possible to write a song about the "party of God," for example, or are some metaphors better left to the more careful and extensive development (and undevelopment) possible in a sermon? If you write a sermon, be sure you explore the *scriptural* sources of your alternative metaphor system. If you simply explore from the pulpit the idea of "dream," for example, you may give a nice talk that would fall short of being described as a sermon.

7. Take a song or other written resource that you believe has a cliché or mixed metaphor or a misused collocation. Revise to improve it.

8. If you do not generally use inclusive language for people, follow the suggestion  given in the chapter and try it for a week. Carefully monitor your own speech and writing, but also try altering, just in your own mind, generic masculines that you encounter in your reading or listening. How did you experience these changes?

9. Take a sermon, song, or other written resource that does not use inclusive language for people and try to alter it gracefully.

# 7

## Naming God

### *Meeting the One Who Is*

Dr. Lester Ruth, a professor of worship and liturgy at Asbury Theological Seminary, recently presented the results of a research project on trinitarian language in Contemporary Worship Music.[1] His research posed this basic question: Does CWM[2] invite people to worship God as Trinity? In order to answer the question, Ruth obtained from Christian Copyright Licensing International (CCLI) the lists of the top twenty-five songs for the years 1989–2004, as calculated twice each year. Although this sampling might have yielded as many as seven hundred fifty songs if the top songs changed every six months, in fact the total number appearing on all these lists was only seventy-two songs. Since CCLI is the major clearinghouse between churches that use contemporary music and the artists who produce it, their records give a fair account of what is actually happening in churches—some one hundred seventy-six thousand churches now hold CCLI licenses in the United States alone.

When Ruth analyzed the lyrics of his core sample songs, his questions about trinitarian language for God yielded some fascinating answers. How many songs in this core list name the Trinity or reference the triune nature of God? None. How many at least name all three persons? Three. The person of the Trinity most often named specifically was the second person. In virtually all these songs, the triune nature of God was not in any way apparent, either by name or by the actions of

God referred to in the song. In fact, this was another interesting discovery: God has many wonderful adjectives in these songs, but very few verbs. The saving action of God, if described at all, was almost always the crucifixion and resurrection, as appropriated by the individual.

Ruth observes that in the lyrics of these songs, worshipers are invited to worship as functionally unitarian or at best binitarian believers. How did this happen? Ruth, who personally appreciates CWM, offers some helpful explanations. In CWM, the function of the song is primarily to stimulate in worshipers an *affective, personal, intimate* experience of God. The worship song is thought to serve primarily as a heartfelt, genuine, seemingly spontaneous love song from the believer to God. As such, it is functioning almost solely in the expressive mode, and its expression is almost solely emotive. This is the particular style of piety practiced and advocated by the composers, the distributors, and the churches that use CWM.

This engagement of the individual affections is crucial in Christian devotion and also in Christian worship—indeed, whole reform movements (including Methodism, Ruth's own tradition) have come about as a response to the church's neglect of this aspect of worship. At the same time, however, CWM has neglected to take into full account the formative nature of worship, particularly the formative nature of worship songs. As Ruth puts it (in a variation on a famous theological dictum), *lex amandi, lex orandi.* This means, in short, that the rule (or language)

### Trinitarian Language in Top Seventy-two CWM Songs, 1989–2004

| | |
|---|---|
| songs that name the Trinity or triune nature of God: | 0 |
| songs that name all three persons: | 3 |
| songs that name the Holy Spirit: | 0 |
| songs that name the Spirit: | 6 |
| songs that name the Father specifically (incl. 3 above): | 4 |
| songs that name first person by any name (incl. 4 above): (7 known only because second person is also named) | 11 |
| songs that name second person: | 35 |
|     Jesus and/or Christ | 28 |
|     Lord/God/King in clear reference to second person | 7 |

#### Most-Used Titles for God

| | |
|---|---|
| Lord | 44 |
| God | 25 |
| King | 17 |
| Jesus Christ | 27 |

> ### Lex Orandi, Credendi, Amandi, Agendi
>
> Though it has a complicated origin, theologians sometimes use the Latin phrase *lex orandi est lex credendi* (the law of prayer is the law of belief) as shorthand for the notion that the way we pray—the words of our prayers and songs, our ritual actions, and even our church architecture—often reveals much more about the shape and content of our faith than do our creeds or declarations or church mission statements. For example, there is something deeply incongruous about a congregation that says it believes in the Greatest Commandments and the Great Commission, yet in its prayer life hardly ever makes reference to people outside its own walls—the neighbor whom they are to love as self, and the nations to which they are to go with the good news of the gospel. (Whether the church's inherited prayer patterns *should* be seen as determinative for faith is a matter of some dispute.) Some theologians recognize that there are broader connections too—suggesting that action (*agendi*) and affection (*amandi*), prayer (*orandi*) and belief (*credendi*) are all interrelated. How we live, what we love, how we pray, and what we believe—these are part of the dynamic and complex matrix through which our faith is both shaped and expressed.

of love determines the rule (and language) of prayer. But this relationship works the other way, too: as we pray, so we learn to love. The God described in our love songs becomes our picture of the God we love.

Fortunately, contemporary worship musicians and composers have taken note of these oversights in recent years, and in the broader repertoire of contemporary music beyond the core seventy-two songs, Ruth finds an increasing number of songs that deliberately invite adoration of God as Trinity. And of course, worship music is only one part of worship. All worship language, as we noted in chapter 1, has formative power whether we attend to that power or not. Congregations who rarely sing about the Trinity may well preach about God as three-in-one or pray to the Triune God.

Nevertheless, Ruth's enlightening research reminds us of the crucial importance of attending to the ways in which we name God in worship. How we name God, address God, and describe God in worship powerfully forms the imagination of believers. They learn who God is and how they are to relate to God in great part through the words we use in worship.

## The One Who Is

Naming God in worship or any other context is ultimately an impossible task. As we reflected in the last chapter, our language for the mysteries of the faith, most of all the person of God, must necessarily be metaphorical. In the story of Moses and the burning bush, God reveals the divine name as Yahweh, which can be translated many ways: "I am" or "I will be who I will be" or perhaps simply "the One Who Is." God is Being itself, the source of all that exists. Jesus refers to himself by this same name-above-all-names in several instances in the New Testament. To help us understand this ultimate non-name, we reach toward the unnameable across the bridge of other names, all of which are essentially metaphorical.

Some of our metaphors carry the authority that comes from Scripture and from centuries of theological reflection, as distilled in orthodox tradition and doxology. Naming God as Father, Son, and Holy Spirit takes priority over other ways of naming God because it is the result of this kind of rigorous reflection and practice. Other ways of naming God carry the authority of the scriptural text itself: Lord (an English term that translates several Hebrew and Greek terms), El Shaddai, King, Lamb of God, Wonderful Counselor, and Light of the World are all names we can find in the pages of our Bibles. There are also many metaphors for God that are not given as names but still carry biblical authority in creating that bridge from the known to the mystery: rock, fortress, wind, judge, advocate, vineyard owner, eagle. Some of these metaphors are anthropomorphic, others are not. And then there are new names for God that we develop in response to our own spiritual experience, names like "my holy sweetness" (from Augustine's *Confessions*)[3] or "joy-giver" (from the contemporary worship song "As the Deer"). How do we negotiate all these names in our worship language?

Christians disagree on what is the proper way to address God in worship. Some make careful distinctions among names, titles, and metaphors for God, giving strong priority to those terms they discern to be the revealed names. Others permit the use of many biblical names or descriptions, seeking with a variety of names to be faithful to Scripture while also pointing to the plenitude of scriptural revelation about the God we worship. Others also permit names taken from the personal experience of the members of the body of Christ, considering the Bible an authoritative source but not a limiting authority on names for God. Then there's the whole question of gendered pronouns: some insist on using only masculine pronouns for God, others seek to avoid pronouns where possible, and others are experimenting with feminine pronouns or a mixture of masculine and feminine.

These are extremely complex and, in many contexts, explosive arguments. How you deal with naming God in worship will depend on your tradition, your particular congregation, and of course your own conviction on the matter. I would like to address here some broader issues that can be applied all along the spectrum, from those who are most restrictive to those who are most permissive. Later in this chapter, we will consider the question of gendered pronouns. If this question itself is offensive to you, please at least read up to that section and consider the more general issues of imagination at the heart of the reflections here. If you wish to consider the question of pronouns, I hope that the treatment of the topic here

## What Is a *Name*?

Some scholars are careful to distinguish between revealed names for God, titles for God, and metaphors for God, even within biblical texts. Of course, which images/terms fall into which category can be debated. Here are some possible examples:

Names: King, Lord, Father, Son, Holy Spirit
Titles: Lord of Hosts, Son of Man, Wonderful Counselor
Metaphors: Light of the World, mother hen, vineyard owner

Sometimes these distinctions are used to determine how these various images/terms for God might be used in worship. For instance, it is permissible to address God in prayer with a title:

Wonderful Counselor, you bring wisdom to us . . .

However, in this view, it is not permissible to use a metaphor as a form of address—

Mother hen, you draw us to yourself . . .

—although it might be all right in the following formula:

God you are like a mother hen to us, drawing us to yourself . . .

In order to avoid trying to deal with the name/title/metaphor distinction at every turn in this chapter with tortured linguistic formulas, we are using *name* here loosely and informally, as both a noun and a verb, to refer to all the ways we describe God in worship, either by address or description.

While we wish to respect biblical patterns of naming, after very carefully studying the best arguments making these distinctions, we are simply not convinced that these various categories must always remain distinct. In our combined capacities as literary scholar, writer, theologian, and pastor, we find the distinctions impossible to establish or sustain, even apart from any worship practice, without excessive hairsplitting and inconsistency. Moreover, we are not convinced that carefully parsing these categories of names for distinct uses in worship results in significantly distinct effects on imagination or devotion.

will prove helpful and challenging. But the fundamental plea in this chapter is that we all strive to form worshipers in a fully biblical understanding of God, using the fullness of God's revelation as our source.

When we consider how Christians name God, two predominant dangers emerge. The first is that we tend to get stuck on only a few names for God to the neglect of other revealed, scriptural names or descriptions. The result is a distorted picture of God. When we use only a few names for God, we truncate the revealed nature of God and create in our minds an insufficiently biblical picture. One night as my children and I drove home from my son's school choir Christmas concert, I asked them to think over the names for God used in the songs and tell me what pictures of God they had in their minds. "Well," my son said, "it seems like God is either the big old mighty king far away up above, or the nice boyfriend Jesus." We all laughed at his candid summary, but it was sadly accurate. My daughter remarked that when the principal of the school got up to pray after the performance and gave a gentle invitation for people to commit their lives to Christ (which my daughter has already done), she thought to herself, "But *who* am I giving my life to?" The Jesus presented in the music was too bland to be very appealing, and God the king seemed too far away to care. All of this struck me as an enormous waste of an opportunity. Rather than inviting us to reflect on the profound, astonishing, and distinctly Christian doctrine of the incarnation, we were left with a confused and contradictory binity.

Those taking the position that certain names for God as found in the Bible are to take precedence over other names must be especially careful of this distortion problem. "King" is an extremely important name in the Old Testament, for example, and "Father" dominates in importance in the New Testament. Then what precisely does it mean in worship to follow biblical patterns for naming God? Do we use a quota system? If the Bible calls God "King" 17 percent of the time, must we also call God "King" 17 percent of the time in worship? This is not what happens, even among those determined to practice biblical worship. Instead, these two names tend to dominate all others (along with Lord, a distinct though related name). The danger here is that using only those names will result in our imagining God *only* as king and father (both masculine images, a further issue we will discuss later), and becoming so habitual about the names that we don't think much about what they mean. So even among those who wish to follow biblical patterns of naming closely, these names must be explored and explained lest what worshipers hear in them is a thin and distorted picture of God. One way to explore those names, of course, is to explore and use the other names of God or images for God given elsewhere in Scripture.

Unfortunately, human nature is such that we all emphasize names and images for God that reflect who we *wish* God to be, neglecting the less comfortable aspects (for us) of who God *is*. Some of us enjoy the mighty warrior God a little too much; others claim the gentleness of God to the neglect of God's justice. No matter what our positions in the God-language debates, we can end up worshiping an idol. So the second danger is related to the first. We tend to accept names from Scripture or elsewhere (or, conversely, we reject names) without examining the broader metaphorical systems out of which those names come. Plucking a name for God out of Scripture without understanding that name—its history, and how it came to be applied to God, and what aspects of God's nature it names—leaves us in danger of dragging along associations that do not actually apply. The same is true of bringing names for God from sources outside Scripture.

## A Sampling of Names for God in the Psalms

*This list includes one scriptural reference for each term, though several of these forms of address are used multiple times.*[4]

- O God of my right (Ps. 4:1)
- My King and my God (Ps. 5:2)
- O Lord my God (Ps. 7:1)
- O righteous God (Ps. 7:9)
- Lord, the Most High (Ps. 7:17)
- O Lord, our Sovereign (Ps. 8:1)
- My rock (Ps. 28:1)
- God of Israel (Ps. 41:13)
- Lord God of hosts (Ps. 59:5)
- God of our salvation (Ps. 65:5)
- O Holy One of Israel (Ps. 71:22)
- O Shepherd of Israel (Ps. 80:1)
- God of vengeance (Ps. 94:1)
- Judge of the earth (Ps. 94:2)
- Mighty King (Ps. 99:4)
- Lover of justice (Ps. 99:4)
- A shield around me (Ps. 3:3)
- My glory (Ps. 3:3)
- A righteous judge (Ps. 7:10)
- King (Ps. 10:16)
- Rock (Ps. 18:2)
- Fortress (Ps. 18:2)
- Deliverer (Ps. 18:2; 144:2)
- Horn of my salvation (Ps. 18:2)
- Stronghold (Ps. 18:2)
- Redeemer (Ps. 19:14)
- Shepherd (Ps. 23:1)
- God of Jacob (Ps. 24:6)
- King of glory (Ps. 24)
- God of glory (Ps. 29:3)
- Lord of hosts (Ps. 24:10)
- God of my salvation (Ps. 25:5)
- My light (Ps. 27:1)
- My salvation (Ps. 27:1)
- My strength/strength of his people (Ps. 28:7–8)
- Saving refuge of his anointed (Ps. 28:8)
- Help in trouble (Ps. 46:1)
- Helper (Ps. 54:4)
- Mighty one (Ps. 50:1)
- Upholder of my life (Ps. 54:4)
- Refuge (Ps. 62:8)
- God of Sinai (Ps. 68:8)
- Almighty (Ps. 68:14)
- Mighty one of Jacob (Ps. 132:2)
- Hope (Ps. 71:5)
- Trust (Ps. 71:5)
- Portion (Ps. 73:26)
- Father (Ps. 89:26)
- Great God (Ps. 95:3)
- Great King above all gods (Ps. 95:3)
- Maker (Ps. 95:6)
- Lord of all the earth (Ps. 97:5)
- Keeper (Ps. 121:5)
- Shade at your right hand (Ps. 121:5)
- God of gods (Ps. 136:2)
- Lord of lords (Ps. 136:3)
- God of heaven (Ps. 136:26)

## KINGAFAP

In the 1980s, British hymnwriter Brian Wren set out to study the problem of masculine pronouns for God. As we have already acknowledged, for many people masculine pronouns for God are required or at least acceptable. So while Wren's conclusions may not please everyone, his process is still instructive for us all. What we might notice from casual observation about the dominance of certain images for God to the neglect of others, Wren studied and analyzed in helpful ways.

Wren wished to take seriously the challenge of Christian feminist writers who questioned masculine pronouns on the grounds that God is not, in fact, male—a truth about God's nature undisputed in Christian orthodoxy—and that the masculine pronoun was less and less considered to be correct as a generic usage in English. For Wren as a hymnwriter, the pronoun problem was a daily and practical one. He had to address it. What he soon discovered, though, was that pronouns were only the tip of the iceberg. *He* was only a small piece of a large and dominant metaphorical system for God.

As Wren studied hymns from many eras and many parts of the church, he began to notice the dominance of a cluster of names/metaphors for God: King, Lord, Almighty, Father, Protector. No one can dispute that these names are biblical. However, Wren also noticed that, unfortunately, these names for God dominated Christian worship to the point that other attributes of God were fading into the background. The full humanity of Jesus, for instance, was often brushed over in order to get to the *Christus Victor* image of the risen Christ seated at the right hand of God. The dominant picture of God was the all-powerful ruler, merciful though distant, in control, often angry, the conqueror of enemies. This God requires from his subjects submission, obedience, and worship. This God will coerce if necessary. In this scheme, Jesus is depicted as the son of the divine king who comes to earth temporarily to set things right. The incarnation, in other words, is portrayed as an errand on earth that is now completed, the suffering of the Servant merely a temporary measure with no lasting consequences in the nature of God. The term Wren coins to describe this distorted metaphorical system is *KINGAFAP*, an acronym for King-God-Almighty-Father-Protector.

None of these names for God, taken individually, is incorrect. Each is part of the biblical revelation concerning God's nature. The trouble is, taken together, they have a tendency to push out other parts of the biblical witness. As Wren writes:

> Not content with being part of a mosaic of divine metaphors, [KINGAFAP] tries to take over the floor. By nature, it must bid for control. "God *is* King," it whispers. "It says so in the Bible, and in the great Christian creeds. There is no other way laid down by which we can encounter God or God encounter us." To admit that there might be other ways, equally valid, would dethrone the patriarchal idol. Kings can't be one king among many: it goes against their nature.[5]

Gail Ramshaw explains that "the myth of the crown"—her name for this metaphor system—is a residue of the ancient world in which patriarchal, monarchic culture was the rule. (*Myth* here is used in the sense of "meaning-making story," not "false notion.") The Old Testament establishes God as the one true God in opposition to all the idols of polytheistic religions in the ancient Near East. The God of Israel is God above all false gods and King above all earthly kings. In fact, many of the names for God in the Old Testament are actually adapted from names other ancient peoples used for their gods—ours is the true God, the Old Testament writers declare, to which these names truly apply.

The trouble with the myth of the crown, however, is that it suppresses the radical contradictions to this metaphor system already present in the Old Testament and fulfilled in the New Testament. Jesus has "made [God] known" according to John 1:18. In this Jesus, we see that God is not only distant but also with us. God is not only king but also servant. God not only rules but also suffers. We are not only God's servants, but also, as Jesus told his disciples, we are called friends. We are not slaves to the law of the realm, but we enjoy freedom in Christ. We are not the children of the handmaiden but are adopted sons and daughters. While the myth of the crown rightly signals God's power and sovereign care, the gospel witness turns upside down many of our associations with kingship. It shatters the patriarchal, hierarchical system upon which the myth of the crown depends. Instead we become the body of Christ, redeemed through the willing suffering of God, equal in our baptismal renewal and freedom, friends of God, coworkers with God in the new creation.

When we let KINGAFAP language for God dominate in worship, we emphasize some dimensions of God's true character but neglect others. We tend to worship the binity, because in the KINGAFAP system, there is room for an all-powerful sky-god and a heroic, divine son who comes to earth. But where does the Holy Spirit fit in? The Holy Spirit can easily become a "whoosh of vapor" (as Wren puts it) or some other abstraction. We tend to imagine God as a male ruler—the bearded, crowned, king in the sky—even though we know God is neither male nor female and does not, technically, have a beard. We tend to see God as the top of the pyramid with Jesus as second-in-command and the Spirit as a kind of messenger, even though Christian orthodoxy has for centuries declared the nature of God as three coequal persons. So while we acknowledge that the king/crown metaphor system is biblical and in many ways precious to us, we must also admit that it has dangers. Frankly, it can lead us toward heresy.

So why do we hang on so tightly to KINGAFAP in our worship words? Partly we do so out of faithfulness to the Bible and tradition. The Psalms, for instance, draw on this metaphor system more than any other, and our hymnody and liturgy have always tapped into this metaphor and its imaginative power. Partly we call God king out of simple habit. But KINGAFAP also has certain psychic advantages. The king is a powerful archetype across cultures. Humans have a strong desire for a trustworthy person of great power to order and care for their society and exemplify its best values. As Christians we believe this longing is only truly fulfilled in God. Moreover, with good biblical precedent, we understand "worship" to mean submission and bowing down. Though we have never literally done it, we can at least imagine how to do this before a king; it is less natural to imagine how to worship a Father or enjoy a Three-in-One or praise a Servant. Finally, our proper longing for God's sovereignty sometimes devolves into an improper relinquishing of responsibility. If God controls the universe and every detail of our lives—in a fatalistic way—then we can do nothing except bow down. However, if—as the New Testament testifies—we are called to become friends of Jesus, sons and daughters of the King, then we have responsibilities for God's world. We may find this freedom and responsibility difficult, costly, and frightening. Sometimes it's easier to bow down before a King and leave it at that.

There are more trivial, practical reasons for the persistence of *king* language in worship, reasons associated strictly with the English language. When searching for rhymes, for instance, songwriters are very familiar with word groups like *king/sing/bring* and *love/above*. These rhymes are extremely common and very easy to imitate in new songs.

So what do we do about KINGAFAP? It is neither necessary nor wise to eliminate references to God as a powerful sovereign. The biblical witness tells us that this metaphor speaks something fundamentally true about God. We need these images because, after all, it is possible to lose our sense of God's transcendence and power. God can be portrayed as the loving, permissive grandfather who winks at us no matter what we do, or the good fellow in sandals who is the inspiration behind our fashionable causes, or the impersonal Life Force that glows beyond the galaxy. These are idols, too, in their distorted and incomplete portrayal of God's nature.

So we can say yes to the *king* metaphor, but we must also say no. As Gail Ramshaw writes, we must coax every metaphor we use, particularly Old Testament ones, into "speak[ing] the gospel."[6] In the case of the myth of the crown, we must constantly correct it with the shocking contradiction of the King as Suffering Servant. We must portray ourselves not as groveling serfs in a pyramidal system but as adopted sons and daughters in the resurrection community. We must resist the patriarchal residue of this metaphor system that urges us to understand and imagine God in exclusively male terms, thus suggesting that the human feminine is not a reflection of the image of God. We must also recognize, as my students pointed out, that if God is only portrayed as an all-powerful, sovereign king, then how can people explain terrible things that happen in the world? People often respond to evil and suffering by concluding that God is not a king after all, that God is a cruel or neglectful king, or that God doesn't exist. Thus we need correctives to the king metaphor not only for abstract theological reasons but also for urgent pastoral reasons. We need to acknowledge that evil is real, God sometimes seems hidden, and the incarnate Christ shares in our suffering.

Some Christians have been seeking to make these important corrections by not using the word *king* at all. They might use the word *sovereign* instead, for example.

**"Christus Paradox"**

This powerful hymn text explores the paradoxical nature of Christ—the one who is both divine and human. It does so through rich pairings of descriptors that keep us on our metaphorical toes, articulating one truth about Jesus (e.g., Prince) and then another in paradoxical relationship to the first (e.g., Slave). Singing rich hymns like this helps to keep us from believing, even implicitly, that we have captured Christ in our conceptual and linguistic boxes.

> You, Lord, are both Lamb and Shepherd.
> You, Lord, are both prince and slave.
> You, peace-maker and sword-bringer
> of the way you took and gave.
> You, the everlasting instant;
> You, whom we both scorn and crave.
>
> Clothed in light upon the mountain,
> stripped of might upon the cross,
> shining in eternal glory,
> beggar'd by a soldier's toss,
> You, the everlasting instant;
> You, who are both gift and cost.
>
> You, who walk each day beside us,
> sit in power at God's side.
> You, who preach a way that's narrow,
> have a love that reaches wide.
> You, the everlasting instant;
> You, who are our pilgrim guide.
>
> Worthy is our earthly Jesus!
> Worthy is our cosmic Christ!
> Worthy your defeat and victory.
> Worthy still your peace and strife.
> You, the everlasting instant;
> You, who are our death and life.*

This text can be sung to any 878787 tune, but "Picardy" is particularly well-suited, as the word "instant" in the next-to-last line of each verse is sung to a long melisma, expressing paradox at another level.

---

*Sylvia Dunstan, "Christus Paradox/You, Lord, Are Both Lamb and Shepherd," text copyright © 1991 by GIA Publications, Inc., 7404 S. Mason Ave., Chicago, IL 60638 (www.giamusic.com; 800.442.1358). All rights reserved. Used by permission.

Others continue to use the word *king* but are careful to explicate the distinctions between God as king and our common notions of kingship. All of us can use the metaphor well if we supplement and counterbalance the metaphor system based on the myth of the crown with other names for God and other aspects of God's nature.

## Trinity

Happily, the best way to avoid the distortions that can come with the myth of the crown is to secure ourselves in Christian orthodoxy and worship God as Trinity. Simply by naming God as Father, Son, and Holy Spirit in our worship words, we make important first steps toward breaking down the distortions of KINGAFAP. Most of us tend to have a person of the Trinity who most dominates our imagination and to whom we tend to address our prayers. Similarly, various traditions of the faith tend to emphasize one person over the other two. Those in Pentecostal traditions might emphasize the Spirit, those in some evangelical circles might emphasize the Father, and those in social-justice-oriented circles might emphasize Jesus. All of us need to discipline our tendencies to suppress God's triune nature.

Some have argued that the classical names for the persons of the Trinity—Father, Son, and Holy Spirit—need revision because they are predominantly masculine, because they do not clearly show how the Spirit relates to the other two persons, or both. Various alternatives have been suggested:

- Creator, Redeemer, Sustainer
- Creator, Savior, Sanctifier
- King of Glory, Prince of Peace, Spirit of Love
- Abba, Servant, Paraclete
- Lover, Beloved, Mutual Friend
- Parent, Child, Spirit

Even the scholars most in favor of experimentation have had to admit that no one has discovered a fully satisfactory substitute for the classical names. Some of these substitute formulas lose the relationality among the persons or seem to assign each person a particular function (a heresy called *modalism*). Some alternatives retain the relationality but use terms that come from unhelpful collocations or lose all moorings to Scripture. In 2006, the Presbyterian Church (USA) approved a document that "affirms Father, Son and Holy Spirit as the church's anchor language for the Trinity, but lifts up other biblical images of the Trinity for study and use in worship." The document was controversial, as some delegates to the assembly argued that allowing churches to use other terms for the persons of the Trinity would blur the line between revealed names for God and other metaphors for God.[7]

Both sides in this debate have concerns worth heeding. On the one hand, it will not do to lose the ancient trinitarian formula. We need the traditional titles for two crucial reasons: they come from the Bible, and they connect us with Christian tradition. Father, Son, and Holy Spirit are not only biblical but also serve the memorial function we need in worship words. On the other hand, those who voted for the report have legitimate concerns. Simply using the names is not enough. We need also to understand the persons of the Trinity and the inter-relationship of the Godhead. One way to keep our understanding of the Trinity alive and fully biblical is to use alternative names for the persons of the Trinity sometimes or simply to expand on the variety of actions associated with each person of the Godhead.

We need to understand Father, for example, as Jesus did, not as the sky-god who beat out the other pagan sky-gods for rule of the heavens—not the distant, thunder-wielding patriarch—but the *Abba*, creator of the universe, source of all being who also knows us intimately and attentively. We need to understand the Son as the incarnate one, master and servant, healer and sufferer, divine son and brother among adopted children. We need to understand the Spirit as the advocate, the counselor, the shelter in which we dwell, inviting us into the dynamic presence of the Godhead. Moreover, we need to consider the interrelationship among the persons of the Trinity as part of God's nature too. As my colleague Moses Chung pointed out to me, connecting the communal nature of the Trinity to the idea of

### A Trinitarian Prayer

This sending blessing (for the end of a service) was composed by Lauren Mayfield in response to our class discussion about helping worshipers understand the persons of the Trinity. Notice that the prayer does use the king metaphor (in the word *reigns*), as well as both biblical-traditional (Savior) and alternative (inspirer) names for God. The prayer also associates a petition with each person of the Trinity in a way that explains something about the nature of that person.

> May God, who is transcendent, bless you.
> **We will receive God's blessings.**
> May God the Savior heal you.
> **We will receive Christ's touch of well-being.**
> May God the inspirer give you strength.
> **We are strong and will not fall.**
> May God the holy and undivided Trinity
> guard your body, save your soul,
> and bring you safely to the heavenly country,
> where God lives and reigns for ever and ever.
> **We will arrive one day, secure and confident.**
> The grace of our Lord Jesus Christ be with you all.
> **And also with you.**[8]

### Biblical Names for God

*The Worship Sourcebook*[9] offers a helpful listing of names for God from the Bible, along with scriptural references. Below is the list given under the heading *Names of Address for God*. The *Sourcebook* lists other names under the headings *Names of Address for Jesus* and *Names of Address for the Holy Spirit*, and also lists actions and attributes of God. Of course, even these are only partial lists of the rich treasure-house the Bible contains.

- Alpha and Omega (Rev. 1:8; 22:13)
- Almighty and loving God (Gen. 1:1; Ps. 68:1–6)
- Almighty God, giver of strength (Gen. 17:1; Ex. 3:3–8; Ps. 68:4–14)
- Creator (Isa. 43:15; Rom. 1:25; 1 Pet. 4:19)
- Everlasting God (Gen. 21:33; Isa. 40:28)
- Faithful God (Deut. 7:9; 32:4; Ps. 31:5)
- Father of compassion and God of all comfort (2 Cor. 1:3)
- Father of mercies (2 Cor. 1:3)
- God, our healer (Ex. 15:26)
- God, our provider (Gen. 22:14)
- God, our peace, *or* God of peace (Judges 6:24; Heb. 13:20)
- God, our purifier (Ex. 31:13; Lev. 20:8)
- God, our righteousness (Jer. 23:6)
- God, our shepherd (Gen. 49:24; Ps. 23:1; 80:1)
- God and Father of Jesus Christ (Rom. 15:6)
- Gracious God (Jon. 4:2)
- Holy God (Lev. 19:2; Josh. 24:19; Isa. 5:16)
- Living God (Jer. 10:10; 2 Cor. 3:3; 6:16)
- Lord (Gen. 15:2; Ex. 3:14–15; Acts 3:22)
- Lord God (Ps. 68:32; Dan. 9:3)
- Lord of hosts (Josh. 5:14; 1 Sam. 1:3; Ps. 24:10)
- Most High God (Gen. 14:18; Ps. 9:2)
- Our Father (Isa. 64:8; Matt. 6:9; Eph. 1:2)
- Redeemer, covenant God (Ex. 3:14–15; Isa. 49:26)
- Refuge (Ps. 28:8; 46:1; 91:2)
- Rock (2 Sam. 23:3; Hab. 1:12; 1 Cor. 10:4)
- Triune God (derived from 2 Cor. 13:13 and other passages)

harmony, for example, is especially resonant for Asian Christians, as the concept of harmony is very rich and foundational in Asian cultures.

Trinitarian doctrine is not obvious or simple. It requires frequent elucidation in preaching, prayer, and song. If we use the traditional names consistently but also employ a variety of other terms and images to explore those names, we keep people's imaginations active and fill out their theological understandings.

The Trinity, as one of our students wisely observed, is not a feature of God, but God's very essence. Therefore, with the Trinity as our foundational understanding of God's nature, we can look to the Scriptures and find there a wealth of ways in which to fill out our understanding of the trinitarian names and to further meditate on God's divine nature. The chart on the opposite page is only a partial list.

We have a great deal of freedom in invoking these names in worship, even as forms of address in prayer. This conviction is based on the variety of forms of address in the Psalms—our primary biblical model for worship and devotional language. The psalmists freely alternate God's proper name (the Hebrew tetragrammaton rendered in many English texts as LORD) with many titles and names, not to mention images. If we immerse ourselves in Scripture with a trust in its inspiring power, and if we attend to the memorial function of language in worship, we will not need to guard the more dominant names for God with jealous calculations about forms of usage or frequency. These names will emerge, but they will also be enriched by other names, titles, and images. My sense of trust and freedom on this point is also based on my experience with the poetic qualities of language. Through my scholarly study of English devotional poetry of the sixteenth and seventeenth centuries, as well as my interest in contemporary poetry by people of faith, I have come to realize that vivid, startling poetic language about God can pierce the heart in ways that familiar, traditional terms sometimes cannot do precisely because of their familiarity.

The Bible offers us a rich treasury of names for God; when we open that treasury, we are led to expand our understanding of the revealed nature of God. As Ron and I have observed students and workshop participants exploring these names for God, we have noticed something wonderful: *names lead to verbs*. When we name God in a variety of ways, we are led to perceive, expect, and request different facets of God's action in the world. For example:

> Light of the world, illumine us as we read the Scripture today . . .
> Living God, give hope to those who are grieving the death of their
>     grandmother . . .
> Spirit of truth, reveal to us what we are hiding, even from ourselves . . .

These prayers could be expanded to explore these names further. Sermons and songs are also apt places for exploring names for God. This is not an unfamiliar practice. Preachers often enjoy doing sermon series, for example, on the "I AM" statements ("Bread of Life," "Light of the World," "the Way and the Truth and the Life," "True Vine," etc.). This is a wonderful way to open divine names in Scripture for our exploration and meditation.

### The "O" Antiphons

The twelfth-century Latin Advent hymn "O Come, O Come, Emmanuel" gives in its seven verses seven traditional names for Christ. Each verse then explores that name in the form of a petition, longing for Christ to come and fulfill the meaning of each name.

### "O Come, O Come, Emmanuel"

*Sapientia*—O come, Thou Wisdom from on high, / Who orderest all things mightily; / To us the path of knowledge show, / And teach us in her ways to go.

*Adonai*—O come, O come, great Lord of might, / Who to Thy tribes on Sinai's height / In ancient times once gave the law / In cloud and majesty and awe.

*Radix Jesse*—O come, Thou Rod of Jesse's stem, / Unto Thine own and rescue them; / From depths of hell Thy people save, / And give them vict'ry o'er the grave.

*or* (this latter is a more faithful translation of the original Latin antiphon)

O come, Thou Root of Jesse's tree, / An ensign of Thy people be; / Before Thee rulers silent fall; / All peoples on Thy mercy call.

*Clavis David*—O come, Thou Key of David, come, / And open wide our heavenly home; / Make safe the way that leads on high, / And close the path to misery.

*Oriens*—O come, Thou Day-spring, come and cheer / Our spirits by Thine advent here; / Disperse the gloomy clouds of night, / And death's dark shadows put to flight.

*Rex Gentium*—O come, Desire of nations, bind / In one the hearts of humankind; / Bid Thou our sad divisions cease, / And be Thyself our King of Peace.

*Emmanuel*—O come, O come, Emmanuel, / And ransom captive Israel, / That mourns in lonely exile here / Until the Son of God appear.

*—Translated by John M. Neale, with alterations*

As we expand our "diet" of names for God, we have to do more than pluck them out of a verse or from a list and say them. We have to do our best both to understand the context out of which they come and to place them under the scrutiny of the gospel. What does the Old Testament warrior-God name "Lord of Hosts" mean for us today, for example? Some Christians reject all imagery and names for God related to war and aggression. They are right in that these images are exceedingly easy to literalize. We are sorely tempted, when we use such language, to imagine the Lord of Hosts as the divine conqueror at the front of *our* nation, denomination, church, or favorite cause, giving sanction to *our* views and confirming our hatred for our enemies. This approach hardly speaks the gospel of One who came not to conquer in the earthly sense but to die. On the other hand, as Gail Ramshaw writes, "to lay aside battle imagery as too harsh perhaps sentimentalizes the Christian life."[10] Battle imagery has a long history in the Bible and in Christian tradition. It speaks to deep truths

---

### The Collect Form: Names to Verbs

One wonderful way to shape prayers that move naturally from names to verbs is to follow the classic collect form, a prayer in four parts:

**Address**—a name for God
**Acknowledgment**—a theological statement about God's being or activity
**Appeal**—a request
**Aspiration**—a result clause

(This form can also be remembered with a mnemonic shorthand: You/Who/Do/To.)

The collect begins with an *Address*—one of the many possible names for God. The name suggests a trajectory for the entire prayer. For example, naming God as "Merciful One" may suggest a prayer of confession; naming God "Almighty" may begin a plea for rescue; naming God "Creator" may open a prayer of thanks. In any case, the name for God points the way to using a solid verb in the *Acknowledgment*, where the prayer recollects what God has done, as revealed in Scripture or in our own experience of the divine. In this way, rooted in God's past action, the prayer makes its *Appeal*, requesting of God that which is already known to be consistent with God's character. Again, it invites the use of lively verbs. The form then sometimes adds an *Aspiration*, a result clause that articulates the hoped-for outcome.

Examples:

*A prayer of blessing at the conclusion of worship, perhaps during the season of Lent:*

> Tender and compassionate God,
> you long to gather us up in your arms as a hen gathers her chicks.
> Draw us to yourself in love, surround us with your grace,
> and keep us in the shelter of your wings
> so that in our time of testing we may not fall away.[11]

Here is an adaptation of a "classic" collect from the *Book of Common Prayer*:

> Almighty God,
> you alone order the chaotic wills and feelings of sinful people;
> give us the grace to love what you command
> and desire what you promise;
> so that in a world full of change and decay,
> our hearts may be fixed on you, where true joys are found.[12]

Like the chord changes in a jazz song, or the dramatic "beats" of an improv skit, this form can give a stable structure either to written or to spontaneously spoken prayer. It can be used in worship services of any expressive style. And it provides theological strength, rooting our petitions in the character and actions of God in Scripture and history.

of experience in our struggle against illness, addictions, violence, injustice, confusion, hatred, prejudice, lust, greed, and many other forces that tear us away from peace in God. So when we use such names, we have to be careful to adapt them to a gospel context:

> Lord of Hosts, without you to gather and guide us, we are lost and confused. Go before us each day as we resist the powers that destroy your world and your vision of harmony in the new creation. Give strength to those who daily fight depression and addiction. Give wisdom to those who seek to conquer hatred and enmity between nations. Conquer the power within us of greedy desire. . . .

By searching the treasures of Scripture, we begin to correct our natural tendency to get stuck on only a few names, a practice that truncates our understanding of God's nature.


### Bring *Any* Name?

Granted that Scripture gives us a treasury of names, titles, and images for God, what about bringing to worship names or images for God taken from our own experience and imagination? Is this permissible? Where is the line between *many* names and *any* name? Here we put everything we have been observing about figurative language to the test. When evaluating potential ways to name or describe God in worship, we can ask these questions:

- Is the language consistent with the way God is revealed in the Bible?
- Is the language consistent with Christian theology?
- Understanding that to all metaphors we say yes-no-yes, will it be clear to worshipers what is "yes" about this image and also what is "no"?
- Does the language respect pastoral concerns for this congregation; that is, does it assist rather than frustrate our efforts both to bless and to challenge all worshipers?
- If the language is potentially confusing, can it be framed in the service in ways that turn confusion to helpful illumination?

While we may wish to honor and prioritize certain scriptural names for God, we must realize that even those names require explanation, exploration, and the correction of various distortions. When we explore the names for God given in Scripture, grounding those names in our understanding of the triune nature of God and placing them in the light of the gospel, then we open our minds to a fuller view of God's splendor. When we use our powers of introspection and invention to find new language for God, we need to ground that language in revealed names and in respect for the wisdom and experience of the generations. If we can do all this, the idols topple and our love increases for the One Who Is.[13]

### Sample Analyses of God-Language in Worship Resources

In order to demonstrate the kind of careful analysis recommended above, we present the following three examples of worship resources with some sample evaluation.

#### "God the Sculptor of the Mountains," by John Thornburg

God the sculptor of the mountains,
God the miller of the sand,
God the jeweler of the heavens,
God the potter of the land:
You are spark of all creation.
We are formless; shape us now.

God the nuisance to the Pharaoh,
God the cleaver of the sea,
God the pillar in the darkness,
God the beacon of the free:
You are fount of all deliverance.
We are sightless; lead us now.

God the dresser of the vineyard,
God the planter of the wheat,
God the reaper of the harvest,
God the source of all we eat:
You are host at every table.
We are hungry; feed us now.

God the unexpected infant,
God the calm, determined youth,
God the table-turning prophet,
God the resurrected truth:
You are present every moment.
We are searching; meet us now.[14]

This hymn uses twenty different phrases to describe God, sixteen in a grammatical form of address (appositives linked with God and preliminary to the imperatives in the final line of each verse) and four as predicate adjectives (you are . . .). None of these phrases is found, precisely, in the Bible. Yet every one of them is recognizably connected directly to a biblical story, verse, or parable. This is inventive language, but unobjectionably consistent with biblical witness. One small objection to this hymn might be to the word *sightless* in verse 2. Out of respect for vision-impaired people, whose status we ought to avoid equating metaphorically (as it so often is) with slavery or sin, one might change that word to *wandering*. This is more in keeping with the story of the exodus on which that verse is based anyway.

*(continued on next page)*

WORSHIP WORDS

## "Bring Many Names," by Brian Wren

Bring many names,
    beautiful and good,
celebrate, in parable and story,
    holiness in glory,
    living, loving God.
Hail and Hosanna!
Bring many names!

Strong mother God,
    working night and day,
planning all the wonders of
      creation,
    setting each equation,
    genius at play:
Hail and Hosanna,
strong mother God!

Warm father God,
    hugging every child,
feeling all the strains of human
      living,
    caring and forgiving
    till we're reconciled:
Hail and Hosanna,
warm father God!

Old, aching God,
    grey with endless care,
calmly piercing evil's new disguises,
    glad of good surprises,
    wiser than despair:
Hail and Hosanna,
old, aching God!

Young, growing God,
    eager, on the move,
saying no to falsehood and
      unkindness,
    crying out for justice,
    giving all you have:
Hail and Hosanna,
young, growing God!

Great, living God,
    never fully known,
joyful darkness far beyond our
      seeing,
    closer yet than breathing,
    everlasting home:
Hail and Hosanna,
great, living God!*

Here we have five phrases for God, all in the form of direct address. When we presented this hymn to our class of Fuller Seminary students, it was greeted with some skepticism, though it took us awhile to figure out what bothered us about it. "Strong mother God" was startling to some people, but we recognized behind this verse a reference to the figure of Wisdom as presented in Proverbs, a female figure connected to creation. Finally we realized that "Old, aching God" and "Young, growing God" bothered us more. The image of God as old could be connected with the biblical title "Ancient of Days," though the phrase "grey with endless care" doesn't quite sound that note. Instead, it seems to present a weak God not consistent with the church's ancient witness of God's power and glory. Admittedly, the rest of the verse mitigates this somewhat. "Young, growing God" seems to allude distantly to Jesus in the temple and to God's zeal for justice. In the end, the class felt that this hymn has good and defensible motivations behind it. The contrasts in the metaphors do create a yes-no-yes effect on one another. However, we concluded that the hymn

*continued on next page*

was too suggestive of process theology (roughly, the idea that God changes over time) and would therefore cause confusion among worshipers who were otherwise under the impression (based on Scripture) that God is eternal, from age to age the same. The same ideas might have worked better in a different grammatical form and perhaps as part of a sermon or prayer.

Finally, here's a prayer intended to be spoken on Mother's Day:

> O divine source of love, we thank you for the countless ways you make yourself known to us.
>
> O deep lap, we feel supported by your firm strength under us. Yielding yet solid, you are utterly reliable; you will never let us down.
>
> O all-embracing arms, you hold us warmly against your comforting self. In the rhythmic cycles of your body we feel the steady heartbeat of everlasting life.
>
> O sweet breath, you lift our hair and caress our skin. Yours is the breath of kindness; you dry our tears, you whisper solace in the night.
>
> O beautiful, familiar face, your loveliness is constant though your expression changes with climate, age and season. Were we to sleep for a thousand years and awake in an unknown place, still we would know that we are at home in you.
>
> Praise and thanks to you, divine source of comfort, of pleasure, of knowledge and of peace. May we always remember, with every breath and gesture, that we are loved, we are loved, we are loved. Amen.[15]

In class, we acknowledged the intention here to affirm how women and particularly mothers bear the image of God. However, we felt the physicality of the prayer, though intended metaphorically, was overbearing and bordered on inappropriately sensual ("caress our skin"?). We also thought "O deep lap" was downright funny. Here's how one student revised the prayer to make it more biblical and trinitarian and to diminish the excessive physicality of it.

### A Mother's Day Prayer (revised):

> Divine source of love, we thank you for the countless ways you make yourself known to us.
>
> You nurture us, and we are sustained by your grace. We rest in the shelter of your strong and gentle wings. We are safe.
>
> In your all-embracing arms, you hold us close and envelop us in true comfort. Our hearts beat in time with your creation, Creator and giver of everlasting life.
>
> Life-giving breath, Holy Spirit, you move through and around us. You dry our tears; you whisper solace in the night.
>
> Beautiful Savior, your loveliness never diminishes. You are not buffeted by mood, season, and circumstance. Nothing in all creation will ever separate us from your love. In you, we are home.
>
> Praise and thanks to you, God of comfort, of sustenance, of delight, of knowledge, of peace, of salvation. May we always remember, with every breath and gesture, that we are loved.
>
> —Modified by Marla Hyder

### What about Those Pronouns?

In the context of this larger discussion, the problem of pronouns for God, much like the problem of pronouns for people, comes into focus as a problem of the imagination. Those who argue that we must use masculine pronouns for God because the Bible does so must maintain this position against two powerful counterarguments. The first is that gender systems in any two languages do not line up perfectly. It happens that the pronoun systems in Hebrew, Greek, and English are sufficiently similar that one can make the argument for masculine pronouns in English based on the linguistic pronoun gender patterns in the original language—although the numerous exceptions do make the argument complex. With other languages, the transference is not so easy, which raises the question of whether the linguistic gendering of God as masculine is indeed a matter of eternal revelation or a feature of human language that we have to seek to draw our understanding beyond.[16]

The second problem is one of imagination. If we only use masculine pronouns for God, then we come to imagine God as somehow male. We can't help it. Imagining God as male, as feminist theologians have long pointed out, sanctifies the supremacy of the human male over the human female. Those who insist on a masculine presentation of God must be willing to accept the results: exclusively masculine images of God undermine our baptismal equality, reinforcing the notion that while God created females, they are secondary to males, less like God, and perhaps less important to God. Even worse, imagining God as male promotes an unorthodox view of God. Christian orthodoxy insists that God is beyond gender. To worship an exclusively male God is to worship an idol.

How then do we cope in a language that gives us only three choices for pronouns: masculine and feminine pronouns for people, and a neuter pronoun used only for inanimate objects or nonsentient creatures? English simply does not offer us many options.

In recent years, some Christians have experimented with using only feminine pronouns for God, on the grounds that we need some kind of corrective to the centuries of exclusively masculine reference. In our class one day, we decided to try this by singing an old hymn setting of Psalm 103, "O Come, My Soul." We decided to leave in the *thees* and *thous* as well as other male-specific words like *Lord* and *kingdom*, and see what would happen if we changed only the pronouns:

> O come, my soul, bless thou the Lord thy maker,
> And all within me bless her holy name.
> Bless thou the Lord, forget not all her mercies,
> Her pardoning grace and saving love proclaim.

*Crazy! never realized this before*

Things got even more interesting when we got to the last verse:

---

**Pronouns in Hebrew and Greek**

In Hebrew and Greek, masculine pronouns are used when referring to God and Jesus. In Hebrew, the term for the Spirit of God, *ruach*, is a grammatically feminine noun and feminine pronouns are used. The most common term for Spirit in Greek, *pneuma*, is grammatically neuter and neuter pronouns are used. This, even, is an oversimplified summary of the complexities of grammatical gender. How wonderful that God doesn't fit neatly in our linguistic boxes!

---

> High in the heavens her throne is fixed forever,
> Her kingdom rules o'er all from pole to pole.

After finishing the song, we all agreed that the experience was "freaky." Did our images for God change? Yes. Definitely. Would we ask worshipers in our churches to do this? No. They would "freak out," an extreme effect we agreed we should probably not seek in worship. Nevertheless, this simple exercise served to convince us all how very invested we are in our male images of God. When we switch pronouns, we hardly recognize "her."

Using exclusively feminine pronouns for God, of course, has the same problem as using exclusively masculine pronouns. God is not female either. Some Christians use feminine pronouns for the Holy Spirit, or alternate masculine and feminine pronouns for God. These are not ideal solutions simply because they tend to disunite the Trinity in our minds. Faced with these difficulties, we still have to find some way to proceed. In the worshiping assembly we have to consider how our practices declare the true nature of God week after week.

For those who believe that the masculine pronoun must be used because this is how the Bible speaks of God, it is especially important to recognize that this is a metaphor, too, and that we must say yes-no-yes to it. Worshipers must be exposed to passages of Scripture that describe attributes of God we generally associate with femininity: compassion (the Hebrew word is related to the word for *womb*), steadfast love, patience, tender care, the bringing forth of life. Focusing on these attributes in good measure not only tells us true things about God's nature but also helps us to recognize the image of God in our mothers, sisters, daughters, and other women in our lives. This is a matter of theological correctness as well as a pastoral issue. For some women, especially those who have suffered greatly from abuse or prejudice by men, releasing their imaginations from the exclusively male, KINGAFAP God has done nothing less than save their faith.   true

Moreover, the so-called feminine attributes of God must be presented as not "merely" feminine or secondary in any way, but rather as dimensions of God's nature that men must aspire to as well. If men and boys are made in the image of God, then they too should practice compassion, steadfast love, and nurturing

### Relearning How to Pray

Kim (not her real name) was a student at the college where I served as a chaplain. We met one evening when she came along on an inner-city service project I had organized. As we worked side-by-side at the food shelter, I asked her why she had joined "the regulars" this week. She admitted that she was trying to "get some God" back into her life, but she said she couldn't stand going to church. When I admitted that sometimes I couldn't either(!), she let her guard down. By the end of the shift, she had shared with me some painful history: years of abuse at the hands of her father, fights with a codependent mother, and regular struggles with depression and anxiety. When I asked her whether we could pray together, she balked: "I don't pray."

"That's OK," I said. "I'll pray *for* you."

I don't remember what I said, but I do know that given her history, I purposely avoided using any masculine pronouns for God. I asked God to fulfill Jesus's parental promise, and to give Kim the good gifts she was asking for: peace and healing . . . and the ability to pray again.

The next day she stopped by my office. I gave her a book of prayers that very intentionally used a wide range of metaphors and images to address and imagine God—including some prominent feminine ones.

There is more to Kim's story, but the last chapter is this: when she graduated, she gave me a brand-new copy of the book I had loaned her. Her copy (the one I had "loaned" to her) was now worn and dog-eared, marked up and well loved. On a card inside the book she wrote: "God isn't a Guy. Thanks for helping me pray again."

care. At the same time, women and girls need to claim the strength and justice of God as part of their own *imago Dei*. Too often we associate God's feminine attributes only with the female body and reproduction—it's all about wombs and breasts—while masculine attributes are more abstract character qualities such as mercy and conquering power. When we resist these stereotypes, we not only see God better but we also free one another from stereotypes and open our eyes to see the image of God in one another more clearly. This helps us see that justice, power, and authority are also expressed in women and girls, while tenderness, nourishing, and attentive care are also provided by men and boys. So, for example, a statement like the following affirms the "feminine" attributes of God:

> God is like the nursing mother, ever attentive and giving of herself to her child.

However, it's important to resist the usual old feminine/masculine associations when we speak of God's nature:

God is like the fierce mother, judging rightly among her quarreling children.

God is like the wise grandfather, who points us to difficult truths while remaining gentle with us.

God is like the woman who delights in salvaging old things and making them new.

For congregations that do not insist on the masculine pronoun for biblical reasons but simply find feminine pronouns uncomfortable, the best practice is to severely reduce the number of pronouns used for God in worship and carefully attend to broadening our images for God beyond stereotypically masculine ones.[17]

Fortunately in English, neither the second-person address nor verbs are gendered. This means prayer addressed directly to God is free of pronoun trouble; we have only to say "you." However, we do generally use divine names in our addresses to God. By using a variety of names for God in our prayers, we reinforce several important practices at once:

1. We avoid fixating on "Father," "Father-God," and "Lord" as the only ways to address God.
2. We place other names and therefore other images for God in the minds of worshipers: Redeemer, Light, Creator, Holy One, Good Shepherd.
3. These other names and images help direct our petitions. Names lead to verbs. This also reinforces the proper practice that what we ask of God ought always to be grounded in God's nature:

   Redeemer, we look to you in hope as we mourn over our broken world. Redeem the earth from . . . Redeem those in pain from their suffering . . .

4. Naming God in a variety of ways helps us imagine the multiplicity and splendor of God's action in history, in our own times, and in our own lives.

   Holy God, you came as Counselor at Pentecost to renew your people and establish your church. Come today and set our hearts aflame . . . send your power like a wind to sweep away our apathy . . . show us the right paths . . .

When in worship we speak about God in the third person, there are ways to avoid pronouns. One common way is simply to repeat the word *God*:

   Praise God from whom all blessings flow;
   Praise God all creatures here below;
   Praise God above all heavenly hosts:
   Praise Father, Son, and Holy Ghost.

In some instances, the repeated "God" becomes tiresome or feels like an awkward usage. In these situations, the problem can often be solved by using another way to refer to God.

> When God calls us, we want to follow his call, but we face our inner
>     resistances.
> When God calls us, we want to follow God's call, but we face . . .
> When God calls us, we want to follow this divine call, but we face . . .
> When God calls us, we want to follow our Shepherd's voice, but we face . . .

To replace the reflexive pronoun *himself*, many Christians are using *Godself*. This sounds awkward at first, but many have found that after a short time, people get used to it and hardly notice it.

> God reveals himself to us in our prayers and through other Christians.
> God reveals Godself to us in our . . .

## Lord and Other Gender-Specific Names

Those Christians who have thought through the problems of gendered language in worship most thoroughly point out that many of our names for God, especially biblical names, are in themselves gender specific. *Lord* in particular dominates worship across the Christian spectrum. It is central in ancient liturgical texts, central in historic traditions such as that of African Americans, and central (as Lester Ruth's research shows) in pop-style worship music as well.

If we care at all about the memorial function of language in worship and if we value Christian tradition as a whole or almost any part of it, we will retain this name in our worship. Moreover, the term *Lord* has a particular function in English Bibles that is almost impossible to duplicate. In English, the Old Testament name for God, the tetragrammaton YHWH, has been commonly translated LORD, and the Old Testament title *Adonai* as Lord. Meanwhile, the New Testament title for Christ, *kyrios*, has also been translated Lord. By using the same English word, then, we contain in one word our central confession that Jesus of Nazareth *is* God. One more thing: the English word *Lord* comes from the Anglo-Saxon *hlaf-weard*, or loaf-provider. What a lovely metaphor for God, particularly in the context of communion, with its memories of all the ways in which God provides bread, literal and figurative.

It's fair to say that the term *Lord*, while it is vaguely masculine, has become almost completely dissociated with any metaphor system other than Christian worship. British Christians might still have some association between the word *lord* and the aristocracy, but for others the term has little metaphorical content. I suggest that we continue to use *Lord* while being careful to free our imaginations from masculine denotations and any connection to the patriarchal system from which the term originally came.

Once again, using a variety of names for God as triune and for the Second Person of the Trinity helps explain what *Lord* means and destabilize any undesirable residues of this name. In the case of *Lord*, it is often possible to substitute other authoritative, gender-neutral names:

- Master (especially useful as part of a master-apprentice metaphor system)
- Christ
- Living One

The last, Living One, is Gail Ramshaw's favored suggestion since it nicely imitates the way that Lord bridges the Old and New Testaments.[18] The Living One is a suitable translation of the name of God given to Moses in Exodus 3, and it simultaneously names the resurrected Christ. I would add, too, that it refers to the Spirit as well, named in the Nicene Creed as "Lord and Giver of Life."

Other gender-specific names for God can be treated similarly. We can continue to use them so long as we also make an effort to break down their exclusively masculine references by balancing with other names and by directly deconstructing our wrong associations with the masculine names. Sometimes, gender-specific names can be replaced by substitutes. *King* can become *Sovereign*, for example, without serious loss of meaning—except in metrical songs where loss of meter and rhyme causes other problems.

As authors of this book, we personally affirm those who are experimenting with ways to adapt these scriptural terms anew in worship and personal devotion in order to release the gender associations and help us understand the nature of Christ in fresh ways. However, we recognize that many people find substitutions like *Child* for *Son* improper and even offensive. Attempts to erase in biblical translation every gender-specific reference to God or people have resulted in untenable and inaccurate translations. It is probably better to represent the original languages accurately in English (there are different ways to calculate "accuracy," of course), even if that means retaining the androcentric slant of some passages. Our task in the body of the faithful is to consider what the texts meant in their day, and then, by the light of the gospel and the guidance of the Spirit, interpret those texts for today. Sometimes, even when it comes to names for God, this will mean deconstructing gender associations. For instance, the names Father and Son within the trinitarian formulation are meant to speak of the relational nature of the persons in the Trinity. The maleness of the terms is not the point at all. Similarly, the Second Person of the Trinity became a male human being in the incarnation. The maleness was necessary at the time, but hardly the point. Christ became *human*. In that perfect humanity, Christ was able to redeem all of us, male and female.

## Hallowed Be Thy Name

Some of us are more willing to experiment with names for God in worship than many people are. But it's important to understand that people have good reasons for adhering to traditional names for God, even with their gender-specificity. Wherever we stand, we share a wish to be faithful to the Bible, and the memorial function is important, particularly because older people have years of devotion that must not be thoughtlessly swept away. Even within the most conservative restrictions, however, it is entirely possible and urgently necessary to expand people's understanding of God through address and description. We must release our tight grip on patriarchal metaphor systems primarily because they contradict trinitarian orthodoxy and the revealed Word. Moreover, they suggest to outsiders that in church, women and girls can expect to worship a God for whom their sex and nature are secondary. Is that truly what we wish to convey to the worshiping assembly and the world?

Some people regard issues of gender justice as an annoying business that erupted in the 1980s and '90s and has now, thankfully, gone away. This is a terribly parochial view that disregards the importance of these issues for many fellow Christians, in both the West and the rest of the world. The whole world is hungry for healing between the sexes and for more just treatment of women and children. We as the Western church have a responsibility to remain in the vanguard in this process of healing in order to help other parts of the Christian church who are struggling with it in far more dire ways.

As my family and I have visited churches, we have become more and more convinced that the people of God are starving for a richer picture of the One whom we worship. When we ignore the riches of the Scriptures and our tradition, when we subsume our own personal experiences of God in a small set of names that denies our lived experience, we insult the rich outpouring of the Spirit.

When we consider how we name God in worship or in any context, we have to recall that God is the Living One, the ground of all being. Any name we give to God is only partial, only a dim reflection of God's true reality. In fact, every earthly thing is only a metaphor in this sense. A king is only a true king insofar as he reflects the kingliness of God. A father is only a true father insofar as he reflects the fatherhood of God. Likewise, light is only a metaphor for the Light of the World, the Word that said and still says, "Let there be. . . ."

## Summary Calls to Action

→ Analyze the metaphors/images/titles/names for God used in your church's worship.

→ For every name commonly used, find appropriate ways to say yes-no-yes to that name.

→ Name, explain, and worship the Trinity.

→ Expand the repertoire of names/images/titles/metaphors for God in all aspects of worship language. Explore the Bible's treasury.

→ If possible in your context, reduce the number of gendered pronouns for God. Use gendered titles (such as Lord) but seek ways to diminish the gendered aspect of these names and also seek to use alternatives.

## Exercises

1. What are the images for God most common in your imagination? In what ways might the Bible expand or challenge your common images?

2. During a worship service you attend, observe the presence of KINGAFAP. Was this the dominant metaphor system in the service? Were there any elements of the service whose language compellingly challenged the distortions of KINGAFAP, that is, more than a passing reference to God as servant, sufferer, or something other than the distant, masculine ruler? Based on your observations, does this worshiping assembly have a KINGAFAP problem? Now that you are looking for this metaphor system, reflect briefly on the role it plays in your own devotional life. Is it your own dominant image of God?

3. During a worship service you attend, observe whether the congregation is worshiping the Trinity. Are all three persons of the Trinity somewhere named in songs, prayers, liturgical words, sermon? Are the persons of the Trinity related to one another or named separately at different points without reference to the relational nature of God? Which person of the Trinity seems dominant in the worship of this assembly? How might this affect the people's worship and their Christian life as a whole?

4. During a worship service you attend, make a list of all the names and images used to name God as well as the actions God is said to perform. Include some notes about the frequency of each name or action. What picture of God might a newcomer receive after attending this service? What confusions, distortions, insights, or comforts might a newcomer take away? Did this exercise reveal anything to you about your own unconscious images of God?

5. Choose any psalm that you know and love. Explore a name for God in order to shape a prayer. Choose one image from the psalm, and write a prayer in which you name God in terms of the image, then expand the image in praying for the congregation and the world. Remember to speak this image in light of the gospel.

> Psalm 23
>> Example: God, you are a faithful shepherd to us. You know each of us by name, and love us with a fierce, protective love. We ask you to tend the wounds of those who are sick and grieving today, especially . . . We ask you to comfort those who are fearful today, fearful of . . . We ask you to protect those who are in danger today . . . Many people in this world do not know your voice. We pray that you will continue to call to them. Let your Spirit speak to them through the church . . .

6. Let the shape of the psalm as a whole shape the prayer. Write a prayer that names God in terms of the psalm, then follows the contours of the psalm.

> Psalm 1
>> Example: Judge of the nations, Judge of the heart, all things are revealed to you and nothing is hidden from your wisdom. Teach us to walk in the right paths. Lead us away from all the bad counselors of this world: cynicism, fearfulness, despair, prejudice. Lead us instead into the delight of your ways and teach us to meditate on them. Teach us to pray. As a congregation, plant us like healthy trees near the water of your gracious words. We long to yield fruit for you . . .

7. Use an image from the psalm that especially strikes you and explore an action of God through that image.

> Psalm 68:9: You gave abundant showers, O God; you refreshed your weary inheritance.
>> Example: Dear God, we come to you thirsty, like dry ground. We look to you for all that we need and we wait for your gracious care. Send your Spirit to us, nourishing God, like a drenching shower. Work among us so that, like a fertile field, we might grow good deeds that will feed others in this world . . .

Variations on this exercise:

> Tailor the prayer to a particular place in the service: a call to worship, a prayer for illumination, a congregational prayer, a confessional prayer, and so on.

Other passages of Scripture could, of course, form the basis of similar exercises.

8.  Here's a homiletical exercise, fitting even for nonprofessional preachers: Write a short sermonette in which you explore an unusual image for God from Scripture. Start with a text that has a striking image in it. For instance, consider Exodus 13:21–22 and the image of the pillar of cloud and fire. How can that image speak to us today? Or, explore Luke 15:8–10, the image of the woman and the lost coin from Jesus's parable. In what ways is God like a determined housekeeper? To get the most out of the exercise, do the following:

a.  Identify the Scripture text that will be the heart of your mini-sermon.
b.  Pray through the text, and research anything that puzzles you about it.
c.  Write a three-sentence paragraph (at most) that simply restates what the text says, and does so well and beautifully. This is the second paragraph of your three-paragraph sermonette.
d.  Write another three-sentence paragraph, this time in response to asking "So what?" of your second paragraph. This is the third paragraph for your sermon.
e.  Think about your friends, both Christian and non-Christian. What would connect their experience or life to this text? Write another paragraph of no more than three sentences. This is the first paragraph for your sermon.

9.  Compose a three-part prayer structured on the persons of the Trinity. Consider using alternative names for the persons of the Trinity, such as Abba-Servant-Paraclete, Creator-Redeemer-Sustainer, or Lover-Beloved-Mutual Friend. Be careful to avoid modalism! The prayer could be fully written out, or a bidding prayer with petitions alternating with congregational responses and silent prayer, or simply a set of notes that show a planned structure to be improvised on in the moment.

10. Compose a new song acclaiming the Trinity. Can we adore the Triune God with the same intimate love with which we adore Jesus? What images can we employ to draw people into worshipful awe at the beauty and holiness of the Triune God?

# 8

# Something Old

## *Inviting Tradition into Today*

At this point, we have discussed a number of issues that arise when we strive for excellence and authenticity in our worship words. When faced with actually planning worship services week to week, these issues can seem to swarm upon us, nearly paralyzing us. How can we manage everything at once? In an effort to devise a rough-and-ready, practical guideline for planning rich, meaningful, balanced worship language week to week, pastors and those who prepare worship could think about including a few key elements. The other issues we have already discussed—a range of biblical names and images for God, a balanced diet of images, thoughtful use of repetition, context-sensitive authenticity, and a dialogic shape—can be taken as overarching issues that apply to a congregation's overall practice. But when it comes to a particular service, on what basis do we select particular elements?

While trying to avoid a corny Bride-of-Christ joke here, it does seem that the old adage about what a bride should wear on her wedding day might apply rather usefully to this question:

> Something old,
> something new,
> something borrowed,
> something blue.

Every worship service need not have every element. But if, over the course of the weeks and months, a congregation regularly looks back to the past, stays relevant and local, honors the global church, and gives space for grief and lament, it will go a long way toward tapping into the power of language to help the Spirit form the people of God.

## Chronological Connectivity

My uncle Andy, who retired a few years ago after thirty-five years in the ministry, lamented to me once that he now feels disenfranchised when he worships in praise-and-worship congregational settings where his own familiar worship style of only twenty to thirty years ago—organ and chancel choir—is no longer remembered. Andy's feelings are not uncommon these days. Many older people, and even some not-so-old people, feel as if "the old ways" are hardly valued at all, and they feel an understandable sense of loss and disorientation.

Sometimes, it's true, congregations get stuck in the past, and that's not good either. Some churches sanctify a particular worship style as "traditional" (i.e., "correct") and pledge never to deviate from it. They forget that their chancel choirs and organs and hymns were all, at some point in the past, radical innovations. It's historically inaccurate to divide Christian worship into "the way everyone used to do it" and "all those scary innovations of today." The history of the church's worship shows a fairly regular pattern of innovation, equilibrium, stagnation, reform, innovation . . . and in every age, enormous diversity of style.

"Tradition" is not any single thing or style, and old resources are by no means automatically superior to new resources. But in our efforts to be relevant to the moment—a worthy desire—we need to remember that churches can quickly jettison the wisdom of the nearly two thousand years of Christian worship that came before us, here in our place and moment in history.

In fact, we are seeing now in larger congregations a kind of splintering into style groups based on the "native worship language" of each generation represented in the congregation. There's the "traditional" worship for the old folks, the praise-and-worship style for the baby boomers, the gen-X worship for the young adults, and something else for the teenagers. This kind of generational disconnect is a growing problem in the church. Not only does it put a huge burden on worship leaders to run numerous services and keep up with every generation's style; not only does it capitulate rather obviously to consumer culture's tendency toward "brand extension" and "niche marketing"; but most seriously, this practice suggests that we need not attempt to worship with people who are not exactly like us.

Still, style itself is not the problem. We all understand the desire to worship in a style that feels comfortable and real and expressive for us. Designing worship around style, however, can sometimes lead to an obsession with the present to the neglect of the past—or to only one particular past with little regard for the broader history of the church. We can easily forget those who have gone before us, even those who are worshiping earlier in the day than we are; this dishonors them and is unhealthy for us.

We can *remember* in worship in any style. It's not necessary to sing nineteenth-century hymns to do so. We can forget in any style too. As with all things, each congregation has to find ways appropriate to its own context and range of styles.

## For All the Saints

American Protestants are often criticized for being too individualistic and even egocentric in our faith, a criticism with some validity. Perhaps what we need most of all right now in American Protestantism is for the giant of ourselves to recede from the foreground and fit into a wider world and a longer time line. One important thing we can do is place ourselves in a longer story, give ourselves the humbling and ennobling gift of *chronological connectivity*—meaningful links to past and future. We can look back to Christians of ancient times, through our living generations, and on to Christians of the next eras, Christians yet unborn. When we recognize, as the Bible everywhere guides us to do, that God acts in every age of history, we rejoice anew in the greatness and faithfulness of God.

While living in Los Angeles, Ron and I one day visited the Cathedral of Our Lady of the Angels, the Roman Catholic cathedral of the Los Angeles Archdiocese. The cathedral is a gorgeous new building, dedicated in 2002 and designed to reflect the diversity and vibrancy of the city. While it has many striking and meaningful features, our favorites were the majestic, earth-toned tapestries hung along each side of the nave. The twenty-five tapestries designed by artist John Nava compose a single artwork, titled *Communion of Saints*. The tapestries depict 135 saints and holy people, representing every age and region of the world. They are hung so that the figures all stand facing the front of the cathedral, the altar, with hands raised in prayer. There are ancient saints, such as St. Augustine, and recognizable modern saints, such as Mother Teresa of Calcutta. The artist used men, women, and children of all races as models, giving his figures a realism that celebrates the diversity and beauty of all people. Most figures are named, but some are unnamed, suggesting that holy people live anonymously, too, perhaps all around us. The portraits are scaled so that, if you sit in the pews and look along your row, the real people next to you blend with the tapestry saints in a continuous line.

"Therefore, since we are surrounded by such a great cloud of witnesses, let us throw off everything that hinders and the sin that so easily entangles, and let us run with perseverance the race marked out for us. Let us fix our eyes on Jesus, the author and perfecter of our faith."

—*Hebrews 12:1–2*

When I saw these tapestries for the first time, I could not hold back the tears. This powerful depiction of the saints, looking very much like people I might encounter in the streets and stores of LA—or any world city—how could I be anything but overwhelmed? I felt so small next to them, and yet so encouraged. Here was that cloud of witnesses, united in prayer, pointing to the author and perfecter of our faith. I felt part of something so much greater than myself, my little struggles, my tiny perspective.

Few of us have the privilege of seeing a powerful message in art like this, right in our worship spaces, every week. Yet we all desperately need this sense of purpose and story greater than our own lives, and what better place to catch this vision than in worship? We live in an impersonal, competitive, rapidly changing culture. Every day we face the challenge of fitting in, finding our place, seeking meaning in a confusing world. Our extended family networks are often broken or separated by distance. We face the daily challenge of cross-cultural understanding in our neighborhoods, churches, schools, and workplaces. And social institutions that used to knit our communities together have weakened or disintegrated. In this context more than ever, church must be a place where we find our story.

Moreover, we need a longer, wider perspective in order to see beyond the distortions of the consumerist culture, the ocean in which we swim. We need to establish a place of vision from which we can perceive and critique our own blind spots and prejudices.

These are all compelling reasons to let our worship unite us with God's mighty deeds in the past, with God's encounters with generations before us. If we encounter voices from the past in our worship, they can speak to us from their wisdom and enlarge our vision.

### Old Is the New New

As I was discussing the need to remember the past in worship with my friend Rev. Norberto Wolf, he reminded me that old *is* new for so many people. He observed that the people in his own congregation—and we agreed this was a common situation—do not know much history at all, let alone Christian history, let alone their own denomination's or tradition's or congregation's history. Norberto

"Tradition means giving votes to the most obscure of all classes, our ancestors. It is the democracy of the dead. Tradition refuses to submit to the small and arrogant oligarchy of those who merely happen to be walking about."[1]

—G. K. Chesterton

suggested that pastors and worship leaders are the ones who need to know and educate people about the past.

Interestingly, after a few decades during which the praise-and-worship style rose to prominence, the newest worship trends are responding to people's hunger for ancient things, for meditative practices, for ritual and symbol. Many congregations are eagerly exploring worship practices of the past, including worship words from the past, and adapting them for their own use. One important thing we are learning from this exploration is that for many Protestants, since the Reformation we have focused our worship "above the neck"—concerning ourselves with ideas, words, things of the mind. Pentecostals and charismatics have always understood that worship should be emotional and physical as well, but other branches of the church are only now rediscovering that worship teaches us *orthopraxy* and *orthopathy*—right practice and right feeling—as well as *orthodoxy*, or right belief.

### Robert Webber and Ancient-Future Faith

One of the most prominent evangelical voices advocating a reclamation of the church's ancient worship traditions is the late Robert Webber. Webber's landmark book, *Common Roots*, looked at foundational elements of the church's life, worship, spirituality, and mission, and urged evangelicals searching for renewal to return to the classical tradition—the "common roots" of Protestant, Orthodox, and Catholic Christianity. Among those roots were certain theological themes (*Christus Victor*), methods of communication (symbol and ritual), evangelical practices (the catechumenate), and an ecclesial spirituality expressed in baptismal, liturgical, and eucharistic ways.

Some years later, *Common Roots* was revised and republished as *Ancient-Future Faith: Rethinking Evangelicalism for a Postmodern World*.[2] Noting the similarities between postmodern culture and the classical culture in which Christianity was born, Webber argues that ancient expressions of Christianity are not only reliable sources of wisdom; they are particularly well suited to embody the Christian faith in our own age. Webber has been widely influential for these and his other books on worship including *Worship Old and New* and *Worship Is a Verb*.

The term Webber coined, *ancient-future*, has now become something of a catchall, borrowed in homage by others to describe worship (and the faith it expresses and shapes) that embodies ancient values and practices in fresh ways. For some, this has been foreshortened to mean little more than bringing candles into worship. But for Webber, at its heart it is about rooting our faith—as the early church did—in an ancient story, the grand narrative of God's saving work in the world.

While reaching into the ancient past and rediscovering candles, icons, and chanting has a certain vogue about it right now, we can easily neglect the *recent* past. Since generational disconnect even among the living is a vexing problem right now, we only worsen it by disregarding the past few generations. Can we learn from our fathers' and mothers' devotion somehow too?

When we seek to use prayers, hymns, practices, and worship elements from many generations, we offer the people of God, especially young people, a lovely gift. We all need models and mentors. Many people admire their own pastors or someone else wiser in the faith than themselves. Some people admire famous Christians. They say, "I'm a Christian like Rick Warren" or "... like Pastor Gonzalez" or "... like the people in my cell group." But we also need to show people that they can be Christians like St. Thomas Aquinas or St. Francis or Hildegard of Bingen or Dorothy Day or William Wilberforce or any number of others whose examples can inspire and direct us.

## How to Welcome the Old

Every year in January, a couple thousand people from all over the country and the world descend on Grand Rapids, Michigan, for the Calvin Symposium on Worship, sponsored by the Calvin Institute of Christian Worship and the Center for Excellence in Preaching at Calvin Theological Seminary. A few years ago, a group of students from my college led a chapel service during the symposium, leading conferees in the contemporary style of worship that characterizes our Sunday-evening student worship event. Early in the service, congregants sang the recently written song "Good to Me," then, while the instruments continued playing softly in the background, a student spoke a prayer of confession from the Anglican *Book of Common Prayer*—a prayer composed by Thomas Cranmer. She had made a few discreet edits to update the more archaic language, but it was still the same prayer.

After the service concluded, a man came up to the student and told her how meaningful that prayer was for him. He praised her gifts as a pray-er, evidently believing that she had composed the prayer herself or improvised it on the spot!

The moral of this story is that context makes all the difference. When Cranmer's sixteenth-century prayer was removed from any context that might signal "dusty old prayer coming! wizened prayer patriarch alert!" then this man was not distracted by any prejudices he might have had against old things. In the midst of a pop-influenced worship song with the guitars and drums coloring the sonic backdrop, he was able to hear the words and take them as his own.

This story illustrates that whenever we use worship resources from the past, we should follow this basic procedure: explore, adapt, contextualize. Explore the background of the resource so that you are using it respectfully and appropriately; adapt it for your own congregation and worship style; and give it context to help people worship through it.

Some other suggestions:

1. A recognizable worship-service structure helps congregations welcome and understand how an unfamiliar resource or practice might help them worship. Rebecca VerStraten-McSparran, pastor of the alt-worship group Tribe, has adapted the ancient practice of *lectio divina* for her congregation. *Lectio* is a way of reading Scripture primarily intended for private reading. It involves slow, careful reading, listening for the Spirit's guidance, prayerful focus on a few words as the Spirit leads, and silent meditation. During the time when, in other kinds of services, a person reads the lectionary text, Rebecca invites her congregation to practice a kind of

---

### Extending a Psalm

Psalms 78 and 136 are remembering psalms: they recall, in ritual fashion, God's redemptive acts for the people of Israel. For a commemorative occasion in your own congregation, such as a congregational anniversary, try extending one of these psalms.

Someone reads the psalm, teaching the congregation to respond with the refrain "His love endures forever" (or "God's love endures forever"). Once the reader has reached the end of the psalm, members of the congregation (who have prepared ahead of time) can offer further statements of God's faithfulness (beginning with Psalm 136:23–26):

> to the One who remembered us in our low estate
>> *God's love endures forever.*
> and freed us from our enemies,
>> *God's love endures forever.*
> and who gives food to every creature, *refrain*
> Give thanks to the God of heaven, *refrain* [end of Bible text]
> Give thanks to the God who moved John Wesley
>> to preach to the world, *refrain*
> and inspired reform in the church of England, *refrain*
> who sent missionaries to America to renew the faith, *refrain*
> and gave women and men the Spirit of prophesying, *refrain* . . .
> (*etc.*)

This psalm could be extended further, articulating the history of your own congregation—histories many congregations do not usually know very well. In this way we can become familiar with the particular gifts our part of the body of Christ offers to the wider body.

group *lectio*. She reads the passage once, followed by silent meditation, then reads it again, inviting worshipers to listen for what the Spirit is saying to them. She might give other suggestions for an additional time through, including an invitation to people to speak aloud what they are hearing. *Lectio* becomes, for her congregation, a transition between Bible reading and sermon. Their own meditations and responses bridge the private space of listening and the public space of proclamation—largely because of where this practice is placed and how Rebecca guides it.

2. Let the context help lift people past any prejudices or discomfort with old things. As in the example of the Cranmer prayer above, sometimes the current context itself will make a prayer or song come alive. Sometimes, the context alone will allow for minimal, if any, explanations. At the Anglican church my family often attended in the Los Angeles area, the service almost always included a sung psalm. This is an old practice, going back to the early Reformation and before that to Roman Catholic monastic prayer, where simple, unembellished musical reading was seen as the most fitting way to express the elevated character of the Word of God. It could have been a dire moment indeed if, in the context of this small, warm, evangelically minded congregation, we were suddenly subjected to plainchant (which I actually like in its own proper context). Instead, the music leader composed new refrains for each psalm and the pianist played jazzy chords underneath. So while the music leader did chant the psalm verses according to an older style, his easy vocal sound and the music underneath made it all seem perfectly welcome to our ears, and we were able to respond, when our turn came, in a musical idiom we understood. This was always one of our favorite parts of worship at this church; even our older children appreciated it. If you came into the church never having heard medieval chant, you would not have felt disoriented. If you knew anything about European cathedral worship, however, you could appreciate how these musicians were able to combine the spirit of an ancient practice with the here and now.

3. If, unlike this Anglican church, congregants are not accustomed to certain worship words or styles, then it is a good idea to make some gracious and informative introductions. For instance, when using older hymns in a contemporary setting, a worship leader can give a few words noting when the hymn was composed and who might have loved it. Focusing on people from the past rather than the style itself helps people understand that we are trying to learn from those who have gone before by using words that expressed their devotion to God. For example, before singing "Great Is Thy Faithfulness," the leader might say,

> Let us praise God's faithfulness with these words, composed in the early twentieth century. Take courage as we sing words from our mothers and fathers in the faith

### Kevin Twit and the Indelible Grace Project

Campus pastor and musician Kevin Twit knows the power of a good hymn. Twit had been in the habit for years of using treasures like John Newton's letters in his ministry, so he knew the power of well-crafted words, and knew how hymns can serve as mini-meditations on the gospel. Though these texts, despite their depth and power, weren't (and aren't) sung much anymore, Twit's instincts told him to get those words into his students' hearts somehow. He knew they could get past the sometimes archaic language, but the old tunes were a tougher hurdle. Students' hearts would be more easily opened if the texts were matched with settings sung and played in their own musical language. So he, along with others at Belmont University—just outside Music City, USA (Nashville, TN)—set about the task of finding, commissioning, or writing new tunes for those old texts.

After a time, Reformed University Fellowship had amassed a large collection of these musically made-over hymns. Others borrowed them and testified to their power in other contexts. So the record producer in Twit decided to find a way to share these gifts more broadly with the church. He decided to make a recording. He called together some of his very talented musician friends (Derek Webb from Caedmon's Call, Sandra McCracken, and Matthew Smith, to name a few) and went to work. The project, called "Indelible Grace" (after a line in the hymn "A Debtor to Mercy Alone," by Augustus Toplady), and the resulting set of CDs is a remarkable collection of top-flight hymn texts set to professionally performed and produced—but eminently accessible—acoustic folk-rock tunes. The music—including free lead sheets and demo recordings to facilitate use by garden-variety musicians at churches across the country—is available at http://www.igracemusic.com.

"Our goal is not change for change's sake, but to rekindle a love of hymns and to invite many who would never associate rich passion with hymns to actually read the words! We believe that we are impoverished if we cut off our ties with the saints of the past, and that we fail to be faithful to God in our own moment of history if we don't attempt to praise Him in forms that are authentic to who we are."[3]

who lived through World War I and the Depression, and who trusted God's faithfulness in their darkest times.

If spoken words of introduction seem inappropriate, a note in the bulletin or a bit of information on a slide can perform the same function.

4. Among the dangers to consider when using older resources is the possibility of kitsch and thoughtless pastiche. People in the alt-worship and emerging church conversation have already noted the problem of shallow eclecticism and adaptation of historic resources. Throwing together a bunch of candles and old prayers does not create an instant sense of mystery and historical connection. It just feels bewildering—or a little exploitative.

Avoiding the "instant ancient" and the "traditional-*ish*" requires, not surprisingly, study. Study the history of the resource or ritual you are thinking of using.

For instance, understand why and how Christians have used icons in worship before hanging them up all over your sanctuary. The study will enable you to enrich the congregation's understanding and help the historical practice actually instruct the people's devotion—and be to them something more than a matter of trendy surface style.

Also, try not to do too much at once. If your church has never observed the liturgical year before, that might be a big enough hurdle in itself for a few years. Hold off on psalm chanting or labyrinth walking until people have a chance to adjust and adopt the first batch of changes as their own.

5. Be willing to adapt. Sometimes when using older prayers, songs, or practices, foreign elements can't easily be explained. Sometimes we might choose to reject some part of an older practice because a different historical context urges it. For instance, we might want to skip or edit a verse of an old hymn that equates disabilities with a state of sinfulness, or that infuses mission work with Western triumphalism. These might not have been a concern when the words were composed, but our greater sensitivity to certain matters might inspire us, in the name of charity, to adapt.

Also when using older sources, give credit in whatever way is appropriate for your worship setting. This is a matter of respect for authors, artists, and composers as well as a means of informing congregants. Indicate, too, whether a resource has been adapted.

6. Finally, everything olden is not golden. We are looking to recover Christian *wisdom* from the past; age by itself is no guarantee of value. Many Christians will reject some ancient practices, such as the veneration of saintly relics, even though such practices have a distinguished pedigree. Likewise, biblically sanctioned sexism or Christian imperialism, of whatever cultural expression, is not worthy of the One who calls us to serve one another in self-giving love.

**Exercises**

1. What is something precious and beautiful about your own congregation's past, particularly a worship practice? Are congregants aware of it? How do you think most people in your congregation understand their relationship to the history of the church?

2. In a worship service you attend, observe the way in which the past is remembered. Are the works of God in redemptive history celebrated? Are any of the songs, prayers, or other elements taken from other generations of Christian

### Circle Prayer

This prayer, based on "The Breastplate of St. Patrick" (source http://www.prayer foundation.org/st_patricks_breastplate_prayer.htm; adapted by Debra Rienstra), is appropriate as an opening for worship or as a sending. It is meant to be used in a small-group worship setting, or it could be used for a larger congregation with a group of six to ten people leading the prayer. The idea is for each person to speak one line, going around the circle until the prayer concludes.

The original prayer required adaptation for a number of reasons. It is originally in the first-person singular, so here it is placed in the imperative, transforming it into an encouragement to one another in the presence of God. This version also emphasizes the trinitarian dimension of the prayer in the opening and closing. Finally, the original was quite a bit more lengthy and contained a number of lines that would puzzle and distract people rather than help them pray. Lines that request God's protection "against spells of witches and smiths and wizards" or "against poison, against burning, against drowning" may have seemed fitting and urgent in fifth-century Ireland but would take a lot of explaining in, say, twenty-first-century Willmar, Minnesota.

Still, the core of the prayer expresses our enduring need for God's protection in an idiom that connects us with the ancient Celtic church.

Arise today
Through a mighty strength,
Through the Trinity,
the Three in One.

Arise today
Through the strength of heaven;
Light of the sun,
Splendor of fire,
Speed of lightning,
Swiftness of the wind,
Depth of the sea,
Stability of the earth,
Firmness of the rock.

Arise today
God's strength to pilot me;
God's might to uphold me,
God's wisdom to guide me,
God's eye to look before me,
God's ear to hear me,
God's word to speak for me,
God's hand to guard me,
God's way to lie before me,
God's shield to protect me,
God's hosts to save me
From every evil.

Arise today
Christ within me,
Christ before me,
Christ behind me,
Christ beneath me,
Christ above me,
Christ on my right,
Christ on my left,
Christ when I lie down,
Christ when I sit down,
Christ in the heart of everyone
    who thinks of me,
Christ in the mouth of
    everyone who speaks of
    me,
Christ in the eye that sees me,
Christ in the ear that hears
    me.

Arise today
Through a mighty strength,
Through the Loving Father,
the Servant Christ,
the Comforting Spirit,
arise.

history? Does the architecture or interior of the church bring the past into the present? If the past is present, as it were, is it welcomed in some way or just . . . there? Did you feel placed in the larger story of the faith as you worshiped? Why or why not?

3. Take a prayer or song or meditative text or other resource from more than a hundred years ago and adapt it into something you could use in your own worship context. How can you fit it into the worship service so that it helps people confess, praise, adore, meditate, dedicate, or enact some other important part of worship? How can you graciously introduce this element as a way of inviting people to worship with all the saints?

4. Take a prayer or song or symbol or other element from only a generation or two ago and adapt it into something you could use in your own worship context—perhaps your grandmother's favorite hymn. What about this resource was meaningful a generation ago? Can you invite worshipers into the wisdom of that devotional practice too?

> Example: My grandmother's favorite hymn was "By the Sea of Crystal." I think for her it was a comforting reassurance, especially as she neared death, that the struggles and sorrows of her life would be gathered up into the beauty of heavenly worship. It would make a wonderful hymn after a sermon on Revelation, drawing the congregation's attention to the gathering of the saints in God's presence.

---

### Can These Bones Live?

One of my preaching professors spoke of the sermon manuscripts we studied in seminary as dry bones: the record of where a flesh-and-blood preacher, by the power of the Holy Spirit, once spoke the living Word of God. But he did not consider those bones dead and worthless, nor our work studying them merely archaeological. He maintained that these bones could live. And he put this conviction into practice in his home church by periodically selecting outstanding sermons from the church's history to be preached again by him. His congregation knew what he was doing, and in fact was very grateful to hear echoes of some of the church's great preachers: St. Augustine, Calvin, Luther, Jonathan Edwards, Charles Spurgeon, and more. Of course, every sermon is "a word on target"[4] for its own congregation. But there are times when a great sermon beautifully and powerfully articulates a central biblical theme and, when appropriately contextualized, prepared, and delivered, can become again a living Word.

5. Find a classic sermon from a bygone era, and study it to discover what its
salient features are. Is there a startlingly new, yet warmly familiar interpretation
of the Scriptures in it? Is there a dominant metaphor it uses? a single, repeated
question it asks? a structure that builds to a stirring climax? Which of these tools
might you employ—with attribution—in a sermon you might give on the same
text or theme?

# 9

## Something New

### *Incarnating the Gospel Now*

Tod Bolsinger, pastor of San Clemente Presbyterian Church in California, told a story at a worship conference about what is commonly called "the Doxology"—the song "Praise God, from Whom All Blessings Flow." The music director at Tod's church wrote a great new arrangement of this traditional song, and one Sunday during the offering, at the point where they always sang the old version, they taught the congregation the new version instead. After the service, Tod recalled, many people remarked that the new arrangement allowed them to sing the song *as worship* again and not just as "the money song" while the collection was brought forward. Others, however, were not so pleased. One person, on her way out of the service, curtly observed: "You ruined my song."[1]

A telling comment, isn't it? People can become rather attached, even possessive of the familiar in worship—"*my* song." We have already acknowledged the importance of honoring what is familiar and precious to people, the value of repetition, and the wisdom to be received from old things. On the other hand, we are invited, even commanded, to do new things in worship. God has created us in the divine image, and that includes our creativity. God has called us to "sing a new song" of praise, and to delight the Spirit of God with those new songs—and prayers and sermons and dramas and poems. We might offend or annoy people sometimes, and we might make mistakes. But the call to create new words in worship is more than an effort to keep people's attention or stay relevant. It is part of our purpose as creatures who worship their Creator.

> "Sing to the LORD a new song."
> —Psalm 98:1

"Sing a new song" is an exciting permission for us. The gospel is not limited to any generation, to any tribe or nation or tongue. In every age, in every place, the Spirit of Christ comes to offer salvation. The Bible, we believe, can be translated into any language and still be the Word of God. The truth of God is sturdy, enduring, eternal. But the words, words, words in which that truth is expressed and celebrated spread out in every direction. They wash over from the past, and we speak them anew into the future. We sing our new songs, and our voices, too, join the chorus.

Whatever our worship style or tradition, the flow of words in a given service gathers up both old words and new words—the balance varies, but both are always present. We read the Scriptures aloud. We use words from other times and places, perhaps in a traditional liturgy, perhaps in a song or prayer from the last generation, from another continent, or from a composer in the next town. The rest of the words in a service are, shall we say, locally grown. How wonderful, as God welcomes our praises and petitions in every language, even the unspoken language of the heart.

Language is a complex phenomenon, however. Within a single language such as English, there are local dialects and varying registers, collocations taken from different fields of knowledge and discourse, and even generational dialects and individual idiolects, as we have already observed. Of all these sublanguages, are there any that are off-limits in worship? How do we make choices among the local varieties growing in our language gardens? How do we grow these new words well?

## Hip-Hop Church

Crossover Community Church in Tampa, Florida, was founded in the early 1990s specifically to experiment with hip-hop worship.[2] The founders wanted to reach

---

**Worship as Contextual**

"Jesus whom we worship was born into a specific culture of the world. In the mystery of his incarnation are the model and the mandate for the contextualization of Christian worship. God can be and is encountered in the local cultures of our world. A given culture's values and patterns, insofar as they are consonant with the values of the gospel, can be used to express the meaning and purpose of Christian worship. Contextualization is a necessary task for the church's mission in the world, so that the gospel can be ever more deeply rooted in diverse local cultures."[3]

—Nairobi Statement on Worship and Culture

people for whom hip-hop was, in a sense, their native tongue. The lead pastor today, Rev. Tommy Kyllonen, is not only a seminary-trained pastor but also, as part of his ministry, a recording artist and record producer. For this congregation, hip-hop dialect, musical forms, style, and attitude make up the medium in which a biblical gospel is proclaimed. Admittedly, not everything about hip-hop music and culture can be naturalized into church. The

> **Hip-Hop Rock of Ages**
>
> When my strength fades away He makes a way
> So if I fall short
> That's all it is
> God dusts me off
> And has no remembrance
> I'm saved by a grace self-controlled servant
> My works ain't worth His Majesty's earnings
> Big props to the One who Rocks Ages
> And stages I can't rock
> God's Amazing.[4]

language and attitude in some ways need to be baptized, "cleaned up," taken captive for Christ. But Crossover Church is at the forefront of a movement to do precisely that: take the poetry, rhythm, self-performance, media savvy, and dynamism of hip-hop and teach it to speak the gospel. For many people, particularly young people, this is the language that sounds most *real* to them.

Adapting a major subculture like hip-hop into Christian worship requires extraordinary people with great creativity, energy, and pastoral sensitivity. Most congregations are not engaged in quite so clear-cut a stylistic project. Instead, most congregations are trying to "keep it real" for a body of people who bring into church a crisscrossing, confusing array of subdialects. More and more congregations include a good portion of members for whom English is not their first language, further complicating the question of what kinds of words feel real for the gathered body of believers.

For those who are responsible for locally grown worship language—whether that is language prepared ahead of time in prayers, liturgical words, songs, or sermons (or talks or messages) or words that are improvised on the spot in those formats—striking the right tone and balance with "something new" can be a delicate operation. Here are a few issues to reflect on when considering how to develop new words for worship.

### Indigenous but Not Idiosyncratic

Worship words composed locally are by definition indigenous. But even indigenous language needs pruning and trimming in order to become available to assembled worshipers. Novelists and playwrights who write dialect know that they cannot simply record precisely what people actually say. They have to capture the sounds and rhythms and vocabulary of their speakers, but they are still composing the words carefully—so that readers receive the essence of the words. The same is true for worship words. Sloppiness, carelessness, and extraneous words and expressions diminish a congregation's ability to listen, understand, and take words as their own. Carelessness, whether in composition or delivery, dilutes the power of words and reduces the possibility that an individual's words can become the community's words. Every style—formal or informal, planned or improvised, African American vernacular or New England Episcopal—requires some attentive adaptation in order to be effective in worship. The challenge is to use vocabulary and syntax that feel natural but are still offered with more care than casual, personal speech.

For instance, here's how someone from the churches I know best in West Michigan might pray if she were using entirely colloquial language:

"Please, Lord, like, comfort Mrs. Vande Kopple, 'cause she's, like, majorly bumming over this whole leukemia thing."

It will be easier for others to pray along if this is revised to be less casual and more specific:

"Please, Lord, comfort Mrs. Vande Kopple. We know she's feeling very sad because of the leukemia, so we ask you to encourage her."

These words remain colloquial and natural without being sloppy.

### Relevant but Not Tactical

Few things are more embarrassing to people than someone outside their "tribe" trying to adopt their style in order to "relate." Parents of teenagers know all about this. Try to use teenage slang and your son or daughter will laugh at you and may even resent you. They want their own language to themselves, and they expect you to be *you*, the parent, and to behave like it. In a worship context, it's good to expand a congregation's repertoire of language, musical styles, technological tools, and worship actions to connect to groups within and outside the church—but it's useless to adopt any style artificially. People can see immediately that the adoption is being used as a tactic.

### Decorous but Not Fussy

Are there words that should not be used in worship? Sure. We all have an unconscious sense of decorum, which means finding the appropriate word, from among a number of options, for the context. Every congregation has a range of registers that it will comfortably tolerate. Some congregations can appreciate a high language register, but would never abide a pastor using crude language from the pulpit. Other congregations are content with very casual, colloquial, even colorful

**Hip Youth Pastor Now Completely Unintelligible**

*The Christian satire site LarkNews.com had some fun with tactical slang in this fake news report:*

AUSTIN—After immersing himself in popular slang phrases, youth leader Dave Jackson has become completely unintelligible to members of his church, even the youth.

"We stopped understanding him about a month ago," says Tanya Gooden, 17, of his youth group. "It was a slow process. Now when he preaches we have to assume a lot of things by his tone, not his words."

Jackson, tracked down at his church office, told a reporter, "Fo shizzle, my nizzle, it's the big mack tizzle, you trackin'? The get-down was off the hook, bra. Big-time ace. Dey scened until the old folk rolled in and the crew got dot gone. Good Sunday, bra."

Jackson can no longer speak plain English even if he wishes to. At times he desperately tries to cross the chasm of incomprehension he has built. For senior pastor Rich Leonard, that's not good enough.

"He's about to shizzle himself right out of a job," Leonard says.[5]

language and would find a fussy nineteenth-century prayer-book prayer annoying or even laughable. One helpful question to ask about your own congregation is Where is our language-register center? If you have a sense of that, you can more easily judge what might be too high or too low for your congregation.

In general, words between worship elements and words spoken by the congregation should stay at or above a congregation's register center. The same is true for prayers offered by a leader on behalf of the congregation. Announcements and testimonies can range below the center point. And in the sermon or message, the speaker enjoys the greatest range of all. Preachers are able to range from high down to low because they have time to make clear from context or with commentary that they are using language for rhetorical effect. However, preachers should also be aware of what the congregation can comfortably tolerate as the edges of the register range. A visiting preacher steps over this line at his or her peril.

## Inspiration

When faced with the task of composing or improvising worship words for prayers, songs, in-between words, or other liturgical elements, start with the Bible. We mean something very particular and theological when we say that the Bible is *inspired*, but there's plenty of reason to celebrate that the Bible is also *inspiring*—in the more common sense of "prompting our creative responses." One way in which

> ### Language Register
>
> *Language register* is a measure of how words fit context in terms of formality/informality. For example:
>
> > passed away: polite, high register
> > went to be with the Lord: polite, specifically religious register
> > died: neutral, medium register
> > kicked the bucket: slang, casual, low register
>
> *Decorum* is a measure of whether a word is fitting to the context; it depends partly on register. For example:
>
> > she is extremely ill: appropriate for worship
> > she is sicker than a dog: too flippant for worship except perhaps in a sermon as part of a story (not to mention it's a bit cliché)
> > radiance of God's glory: high language register; fitting to express majesty
> > the rain-soaked leaves: neutral register; fitting for description
> > all this resentment crap: low language register; may be fitting to express disgust at petty, undignified behavior (probably only in a sermon)
> > expletives, crude or insulting language, and the like: very low register; not fitting for worship in most contexts, although some congregations might tolerate for particular rhetorical reasons (expressing prophetic anger, perhaps)

we can "Let the word of Christ dwell in [us] richly" is to soak our worship words in Scripture. Those of us who create worship words benefit from our meditation on the Scripture, and the congregation, in turn, receives the results of that meditation. If we respond to the Bible's words with understanding and respect, we are not altering or endangering the Word. The Word of the Lord, after all, endures forever. We are, instead, engaging in an ongoing, communal, locally relevant commentary on our holy book. We are assisting in the larger work of proclamation, which is to connect the ancient words of Scripture with the here and now.

Here are some suggestions for specific strategies when seeking inspiration from Scripture.

1. Explore a name or image for God (especially good for prayers). There are many examples of this technique throughout this book, particularly in chapter 7. Beginning with a name or image for God helps us ground our worship and our prayers in a rich picture of God's revealed nature. To explore the image, consider the different features or qualities that the image suggests.

- Choose a name or image that seems fitting to the occasion and to the place in the service where the prayer will be offered. ("Merciful God," for instance, for a prayer of confession, "Great Physician" for a prayer of healing, and so on.)

- Consider using the more unusual images for God as well as the more familiar. God is not only like a shepherd and a refuge, but also like a householder and an eagle. After a sermon or message on Isaiah 40:

> God, you are like the eagle, protecting us with your fierce love. You are the source of all strength. Many things threaten us, God, and we look to you for our safety and shelter. Teach us also to see with your vision, your perspective. So often we are limited. . . .

2. Place ourselves in a story (especially good for songs and sermon illustrations, even complete sermons). This strategy is an ancient one indeed, coming as it does from the ancient practice of allegorical reading of Scripture. It is the basis of Ignatian meditation exercises as well as a great strategy for developing songs. African American spirituals are often excellent examples of placing ourselves within a biblical story. For instance, "Swing Low, Sweet Chariot" places us in the story of 2 Kings 2, in which Elijah is taken up to heaven. "Were You There" invites us to place ourselves at the foot of the cross and the mouth of the empty tomb.

This is a particularly valuable technique for examining a biblical narrative in a sermon. Rather than analyzing a text from a position outside the text, discern instead how your congregation might identify with each of the major characters in the story. How are we, for example, like the wasteful son in Jesus's parable (Luke 15:11–32)? How are we like the jealous older brother? How are we like the patient father, prodigal in love? Or in the story of Naaman's healing, for example (2 Kings 5:1–19), how are we like the leprous Syrian general? How are we like the Israelite slave girl? Israel's king? Naaman's servants? Elisha? A look at the story through the eyes of each character will uncover surprises and help prevent simplistic interpretations.

---

**The Word of the Lord Does Not Return Empty**

As the rain and the snow
   come down from heaven,
and do not return to it
   without watering the earth
and making it bud and flourish,
   so that it yields seed for the sower and bread for the eater,

so is my word that goes out from my mouth:
   It will not return to me empty,
but will accomplish what I desire
   and achieve the purpose for which I sent it.

—Isaiah 55:10–11

### "Ready My Heart"

Often in songs and prayers and sermons, we are invited to play, imaginatively, the roles of characters in the stories, but we need not be limited to the characters. This wonderful confessional song, appropriate for Advent season, invites us to enter the story in an altogether different role:

> Ready my heart for the birth of Emmanuel
> Ready my soul for the Prince of Peace.
> Heap the straw of my life for His body to lie on.
> Light the candle of hope; let the Child come in.
>
> *Refrain*
> Alleluia! Alleluia! Alleluia!
> Christ the Savior is born!
>
> Mine is the home that is poor and is barren.
> Mine is the stable of cold and stone.
> Break the light to each corner of doubt and of darkness.
> Now the Word is made flesh for the birth of me.[6]
>
> [*alternate ending for second verse:*
> Now the Word is made flesh for his birth in me.]

3. Adapt a psalm (especially good for prayers or songs or planned litanies/ readings). See exercises 5–7 from chapter 7. Here are some further examples:

- The Psalms feature numerous shifts in voice and tone. Study a psalm and turn it into a dramatic reading for several people. Vary between single voices and unison reading to help mark and make sense of those shifts.

- Ask a member of the congregation to paraphrase a psalm in a more contemporary idiom (or use the versions in *The Message* or some other contemporary paraphrase), imagining a particular person or group of people who might pray this psalm. Think about representing various kinds of people within your congregation as well as outside it: older people who have lost a spouse, people suffering from depression, new immigrants seeking to find their place, tenant farmers in Central America, persecuted Christians in China, and so on. This is a terrific way to help the congregation pray and worship with fellow Christians from around the world. Pray a version of Psalm 80, for example, inviting the congregation to pray along with and on behalf of the people of Africa who are devastated by HIV/AIDS.

- Ask young people to write new psalms, specific to the needs and nature of the congregation, and have them lead the congregation in these prayers.

The basic format of the psalm style is to state something and then state it again with slight variation:

> Who can proclaim the mighty acts of the LORD
> or fully declare his praise? (Ps. 106:2)

> But at your rebuke the waters fled,
> at the sound of your thunder they took to flight. (Ps. 104:7)

Psalms also mix together various modes, including praise, lament, complaint, request, remembrance of God's deeds, wisdom statements. And of course, psalms use vivid, figurative language rich with metaphor. The easiest way to inspire new psalms is to invite people to translate freely on the model of a particular biblical psalm.

- Another creative way to adapt a psalm is to create a short film that places verses from a psalm over depictions of contemporary people who might be praying those words in their own way. This would be a helpful focus for meditation before the intercessory prayer, for example.

4. Add local detail (helpful for any aspect of worship). We are accustomed to praying with the words of the Bible and translating its foreign metaphors on the fly. For instance, when we read Psalm 122:1, "I rejoiced with those who said to me, 'Let us go to the house of the LORD,'" we might recognize that the psalm is about the temple in Jerusalem, but we are also thinking of our very own church.

Biblical metaphors and other metaphors are useful because they are porous: each individual worshiper can let the metaphor absorb her or his particular concerns that day. When we sing "When I tread the verge of Jordan, bid my anxious fears subside," we are all thinking of our own specific Jordans. I remember once as a teenager attending worship with a friend and singing this song. She was laughing through her tears as she sang, because she was in fact very anxious about her family's imminent travels. They were going to leave home and spend a year—in Jordan!

Porous metaphors are important in worship. On the other hand, sometimes it is good to make our words very specific to the time and place. What we lose in porousness, we can gain in startling immediacy. Ron and I wrote a Thanksgiving litany years ago that people seem to use and reuse because it allows them to add specific details about their own time and place. When we used it at Fuller Seminary once, we amended the section thanking God for the holiday standards—turkey and mashed potatoes—by giving thanks for favorite campus foods. In particular, we made sure to include a reference to the enormous pots of fabulous Indian food

### An Alternative Worship Psalm Exercise

I visited in 2004 with a community of Christians at South Ealing in London, and they were experimenting with ways to re-pray the Psalms. One week, they assigned everyone to go home and translate or find some way to re-express a psalm in their own words and reflecting their own context. Some people made films, others painted, and one person brought this version of Psalm 113.

#### Psalm 113 [urban remix '04]

God you are heavy!
Followers of Christ give respect to the Boss.
Get on the dance floor and get down.

From the sound of the first tube train before the dawn to the still
    moments of the night when the city pauses for breath
Give God respect.

God is exalted over the many cultures and networks of the city;
His glory is above the financial markets, government and
    businesses.

Who is like our God, the one who sits enthroned on high,
Who stoops down to look on the London Eye, the Tate and the
    Thames.

She raises the poor from the urban areas and the needy from their
    sense of despair and weariness.
He takes them on a shopping spree in Selfridges and pays off
    their mortgages.

From the base of a home the woman whose life has been a fight
    for survival begins to dream and create again—
The joy of life returns.

Respect![7]

prepared by BJ, one of the community's beloved librarians. He served students, staff, and faculty twice a week right on the campus lawn:

> *Leader:* Let us give thanks to God for Thanksgiving turkey and mashed potatoes,
>         for Salvadoran enchiladas, and for BJ's chicken curry.
> *People:* For the abundance of food that sustains our bodies.

## Put Your Artists to Work

We often think of our musicians as "local artists," offering their talents in praise to God and in service of God's people. More and more, church musicians are not only performers of music written by others but composers in their own right. Do we think of those who write words for worship as local artists too? Do we think of those who preach as word artists in their own right?

Every congregation has members who are good with words. Just as we search out and develop our musicians, why not also develop our poets and writers? Some traditions, particularly those for whom extemporaneous prayer and speaking is a high value, identify those who are good at praying and testifying, and regularly give those people opportunity to lead and inspire others, while giving them encouragement and mentoring. For churches who make more use of written worship words, it can be helpful to create a writers group. This allows writers to work together, encouraging and critiquing one another. It also allows writers to produce resources more anonymously, which might protect shy people—and diminish the temptation to self-promotion where that might be a danger. Finally, a writers group more easily enables the church to develop a process of theological oversight for new worship words.

If this is a new or frightening prospect for your congregation, one way to get started is to ask people to write some specific things for a special service or occasion: a brief litany of dedication before the youth go on their annual mission trip, a prayer of thanks at a joint ecumenical worship service, the words of welcome for a newly baptized person, a litany of doubt for the congregation to use on Low Sunday (the week after Easter). A great deal of Bach's music, after all, was written on demand, in the daily grind of his church job. Necessity can be the mother of great worship resources.

### Exercises

1. Who are the farmers of your locally grown worship words? How is the soil? What kinds of fertilizer might you add to that soil? Does your congregation welcome new worship words or is there some resistance?

2. In a worship service you attend, observe the language register used. Is it formal? Casual? Does it reflect a particular region, ethnicity, or Christian subculture? Does it vary within the service? Consider whether you believe the register(s) used was (were) appropriate to the worship acts and the content of the words. Were there any jarring moments when, for example, something that called for reverence was spoken of too casually, or vice versa? What might you have done differently?

A good source of advice and inspiration for individuals interested in developing new worship resources is Ruth C. Duck's *Finding Words for Worship: A Guide for Leaders* (Louisville: Westminster John Knox, 1995).

> **Characteristics of Good Worship Wordsmiths**
>
> - mastery of vocabulary, syntax, grammar
> - sensitivity to the various language styles natural to the congregation's members
> - spiritual maturity
> - passion for the people's worship
> - solid Bible knowledge
> - humility (no need to show off or receive personal praise)
> - willingness to revise
> - ability to work with other worship leaders

3. In a worship service you attend, observe whether any elements in the service were "indigenous" to the local congregation. Was there art or music or drama created by members of the congregation? Did a member of the congregation pray in his or her own words? If there was local word-art, did it serve the worship of the congregation? If there was very little, how did that affect your sense of worshiping in that place with those people?

4. Identify an artist or two in your congregation with whom you would like to work. Identify a special service or occasion and arrange to work on a worship element for that occasion. (Clear this with those in charge if that is appropriate, of course.) How can you make the meaning of the occasion specific to your congregation through your prayer, song, film, drama, sermon, or . . . ?

# 10

## Something Borrowed

### *Worshiping with the Global Church*

Our family used to have a wonderful next-door neighbor from whom we would borrow a cup of brown sugar or a tomato quite often. She borrowed things from us as well, but she was always absolutely conscientious about paying us back, despite our protests that this was not at all necessary. She once borrowed a load's worth of laundry detergent from us, and sure enough, a couple days later, she brought over a little plastic baggie with a cup of powdered detergent in it. As usual, we assured her that this was completely unnecessary. When it came to eggs, though, she agreed to refrain from paying back. "It's bad luck to pay back a borrowed egg," she said.

I had never heard this bit of folk wisdom before, but it reminds us that in the neighborly economy, payment for services rendered is not the point. No one wants to take advantage of others or be taken advantage of, but among neighbors, a little gracious exchange of goods helps build community. You walk over to borrow some ketchup and you catch a glimpse of your neighbor in the middle of supper preparations, you chat about the weather, you say hello to the children and ask how school is going. Nothing dramatic on the surface, but these little moments of connection are deeply important. When you squirt the ketchup on your hamburger later, you think gratefully of your neighbors, acknowledge that you are not self-sufficient all the time, and stand ready to open your own pantry when the occasion arises.

### Embracing Diversity as a Christian Calling

The notion of embracing diversity is a mandate that comes not from the political correctness police but from deeply Christian sensibilities—from patterns of thought and practices of community steeped in the good news of the gospel.

1. First, all Christians belong together to "one body" in Jesus Christ. Our salvation is not primarily a soul-saving individual contract; it is participation in a local and worldwide and diverse body of believers—all united in Christ by the power of the Holy Spirit. We are one with them because we are one in our head, Christ.

2. Second, the unity-in-diversity of this body of believers is patterned on the unity-in-diversity of the trinitarian God whom we worship. Together the Father, Son, and Holy Spirit enjoy a dance of hospitable mutuality, united in work and essence, holding the others at their heart. In the same way, we work together and hold each other so that specialized concerns become mutual concerns.

3. Third, we enjoy deep fellowship with one another—the New Testament calls it *koinonia*, and it means that we share a life in common. Those of us who have the "mind of Christ" are the unreconcilable who have become reconciled, who now think of others before ourselves, whose primary identity is not as Americans or Hispanics or Baptists but as the blessed and baptized children of God.

4. Finally, as alluded to earlier, Scripture paints a picture of the coming kingdom of God in which people from every tribe and nation and people and tongue gather round the throne in praise, bringing their gifts. When we worship expansively, in the accents of the worldwide church, we prepare ourselves for our final destiny when we join in singing a universal song of wonder, love, and praise.

In many North American Protestant churches today, we are waking up to our place in the world neighborhood of churches. We are learning to acknowledge our own need and to borrow songs, art, and other worship elements from fellow Christians in other parts of town or the world, recognizing that doing so can become a way of building community with the whole church.

This is a much more complex phenomenon than neighbors borrowing eggs, of course. The dangers of exploitation, misunderstanding, and unequal exchange are much more serious. Nevertheless, when done in a spirit of respect, gratitude, and humble hospitality, this borrowing witnesses to the unity of the church depicted in Revelation 7:9 and 21:24–26—a unity for which we long and toward which God is working.

### Worship and Culture

Our planet is shrinking, and the relationship among Christian churches in different parts of the world is shifting from a missionary/evangelized relationship—with its uneven power dynamics—to a more complex web of interrelationships and

**Worship Is Expansive**

At its best, our worship makes creative and excellent use of words (and music—and more) from many times, places, peoples, and cultures in order to enlarge our vision of God's kingdom and to situate ourselves properly and humbly within it.

partnerships. For worship, this means that we are becoming more attuned to the challenges of enculturation—that is, to the question of how our worship practices are embodied in or resist the cultures in which they form. Missionaries from America can no longer teach the Tiv people of Nigeria nineteenth-century hymns written by Englishmen, basing their instruction on the unexamined assumption that English hymn-singing is simply what Christians *do*. These days, Christians from all parts of the world are seeking and finding ways that Christ might transform the treasures of their own culture—language, music, art, dance—to enrich their own worship and in turn the devotion of the worldwide church.

In recognition of these trends, the Lutheran World Federation commissioned study teams in the 1990s to conduct research and consultations and to develop statements on the relationship between worship and culture. In 1996, the LWF released the "Nairobi Statement on Worship and Culture: Contemporary Challenges and Opportunities." The Nairobi Statement identifies four principal ways in which worship relates to culture. These four sometimes overlap and sometimes pull in different directions. But the most meaningful worship is found among communities that acknowledge and pursue the truth of all four.

Transcultural: Because Christ transcends all cultures, many things about our worship of Christ also transcend cultures. We share the sacraments of baptism and the Eucharist; we read and preach from the Bible; we seek to learn and live into the biblical narratives of salvation; we share ecumenical creeds, the Lord's Prayer, and the practice of praying and singing—among other things.

Contextual: The mystery of the incarnation, at the same time, means that our worship arises out of particular times and places. Seeking faithfulness to the gospel, we translate the transcultural elements of worship into particular cultural contexts.

Countercultural: Since every particular culture contains elements that are *not* consonant with the gospel, we also seek to avoid mere conformity to the cultural context. Instead, we seek to make worship a place in which culture is both celebrated and intentionally transformed—or even perhaps resisted.

**Resources for Further Study of the Nairobi Statement**

A few excellent resources are available for those who wish to study the Nairobi Statement further:

- The full text itself is titled "Nairobi Statement on Worship and Culture: Contemporary Challenges and Opportunities." It was published in *Ecumenical Review* 48.3 (July 1996): 415–17.
- It can also be found online at: http://www.worship.ca/docs/lwf_ns.html.
- A study guide for congregations was published by the Evangelical Lutheran Church in America: "Getting Ready for Worship in the Twenty-first Century," ed. Karen Ward (Chicago: ELCA, 1996).
- The study papers for the group that produced the Nairobi Statement were published as a special collection titled "Christian Worship: Unity in Cultural Diversity," ed. Anita Stauffer (Geneva: Lutheran World Federation, 1996).
- Finally, a special issue of the academic journal *Studia Liturgica* 27.1 (1997) was devoted to questions raised by the Nairobi Statement.

Cross-cultural: In worship, we live into the truth that in its diversity there remains one church. As the authors of the Nairobi Statement observe: "The sharing of hymns and art and other elements of worship across cultural barriers helps enrich the whole Church and strengthen the sense of the *communio* of the Church" (5.1).

As the Nairobi Statement describes, we must feel that our worship is *ours*, but we must also strive to expand what *ours* means. A particular congregation in a particular cultural context must offer to God authentic worship, in their own language of words, sound, image, and gesture. But they must also connect to other Christians in the body, elsewhere in place as well as time. This emphasis on a larger view of the body becomes increasingly urgent as more and more congregations become multicultural and multilingual. To give worshipers a sense that we are worshiping with others around the world helps make multicultural congregations seem natural rather than aberrations or special challenges. They are pictures of the kingdom coming.

As we move toward embodying that kingdom vision, we will need to let go of the idea that just because we don't agree with every last jot and tittle of some other branch of the church's doctrine or practice, we cannot do anything as they do it. For instance, the Christian Reformed Church (the denomination in which I grew up) split off from the Reformed Church in America (RCA) in 1857 partly because people in the dissenting churches thought it was inappropriate and dangerous that the RCA was using educational materials developed by the Presbyterians.

Perhaps today, with the softening of denominational identities and boundaries, refusal to share is less a problem than unexamined, pragmatic sharing.
Perhaps churches are too ready to borrow an idea from another church simply
because it "works" or "really attracts the young people." So we have to borrow
with the integrity of our own convictions as well as respect for what we appreciate about one another. That takes care, intentionality, and—probably—a
little research.

As with all changes, the key is to begin where you are and take small steps. The
long-term goal is to worship in communion with worldwide Christian neighbors
not just as an exceptional feature of World Wide Communion Sunday or other
special occasions, but as a regular, natural part of your church's devotion.

## Priestly Prayer

The simplest, most basic way to begin is with prayer. Since the earliest days of the
Christian church, one of the church's most important tasks has been to intercede
in prayer for the local congregation, community, church, and world. This is part
of the priestly function of the church—bringing the needs of the world before the
presence of God. Many churches around the world, especially those in liturgical
traditions, carry out this intercessory function in daily prayers, a weekly pastoral
or intercessory prayer, or both. How amazing to think of God's people through
the centuries, each generation entering anew that flowing river of ceaseless prayer
on behalf of the whole world.

Is your congregation entering that flow? This is a matter not only of duty and
church unity but also of witness. After all, a visitor can tell a lot about a congregation from the prayers spoken in worship. Maybe you have experienced services in
which congregations appear to be completely self-centered. They prayed for needs
within their own congregation, but said hardly a word about anything or anyone
outside themselves—unless, perhaps, there had been a hurricane or some other
sort of disaster in the news. Of course it is a beautiful and important part of our

---

**Praying outside Our Walls**

"As we pray for those who are religiously, politically, and economically [and ethnically]
different from us—even at odds with us—we engage in a kind of reprogramming to
exorcise our prejudices. In effect, we petition God to reshape our minds and hearts
so that those whom we might easily regard as enemies may become visible to us
as precious in God's sight."[1]

—Ronald P. Byars

## Point with Power

Many churches use presentation technology—screens and PowerPoint—to project song lyrics or unison prayers or even sermon notes for the congregation to view. This same technology can also be used very effectively to deepen and inform intercessory prayer.

For example, leaders could ask that young people from the congregation (who are increasingly tech-savvy, but often reluctant to pray in public) go to visit an elderly shut-in each week, or a refugee family who participates in the church's ESL program, or any other individual or group that the church ministers to but does not often see or hear from. The young people could bring a camera and take pictures or even a short video of the otherwise invisible and voiceless, asking them what they would like the congregation to pray for on their behalf. The video would then be shown just before the intercessory prayer.

Or better yet, the church could buy a camera and pass it from one small group to another each week. Each week's task: to create a short one-minute film, whether live video or still pictures, to guide the congregation's thanksgiving and intercession. Imagine a one-minute film of scenes: a bustle of people waiting for the subway, a homeless person whose sign offers to work for food, a soldier kissing his family good-bye before he gets on a bus, a family at prayer around someone in a hospital bed, a church-supported missionary standing next to a newly dug well, and so on. As the film is shown in worship, instrumentalists could play a song of prayer underneath (e.g., "Lord, Listen to Your Children Praying," the African song "Mayenziwe [Your Will Be Done]," or the Taizé song "O Lord, Hear Our Prayer"). When the film is finished, the pastor or another leader invites the congregation to pray with him or her for the joys and concerns depicted in the film.

priestly function as a community to pray for needs within the congregation—this is one way we rejoice with those who rejoice and weep with those who weep. But we have to reach beyond our congregational families too.

Bringing the needs of the world before God in the worshiping assembly demonstrates to members and visitors that a given congregation is more than just a nice social club. People long for community, it's true. But people also long for meaning and purpose. Eventually people are likely to become skeptical about and disenchanted with an enterprise that is only caring for and perpetuating itself. People are keenly aware of the world's brokenness, they long to do something about it, and they want to know how. Prayer—earnest, regular prayer—is the most basic and indispensable step.

In the context of North American churches, we need to exercise caution when praying for the world: we need to avoid asking God to be so kind as to make all other parts of the world just like us. Certainly we want the gospel to take root in all nations. But we North American Christians are not the exclusive bringers of light to unenlightened nations. *We* in the West are the mission field, according to churches in the global south! So we need to pray with careful humility, in kinship with other churches and their work in their own nations, as well as for indigenous ministries and missions. We pray *with* the church in the world as much as we pray *for* it, grateful that other Christians are praying also for us—and breaking down the division of *us* and *them* in the process.

Some churches, particularly those that offer daily prayer services, practice a kind of rotation system in their intercessions. They have a pattern of praying, on a rotating basis, for a list of sister churches in their community, sister churches in the world, people in leadership in local and national government, other nations, and then for various categories of need such as those who suffer from disease, the diminishments of aging, mental illness, and so on. Managing the list of the world's needs can seem an overwhelming challenge. But the church's long practice of this kind of prayer has produced many helpful guides and resources.

## Intercessory Prayer Patterns

There are a number of useful patterns one might use in composing or extemporizing an intercessory prayer, in order to be certain that a congregation is praying "outside its walls," and that a balanced range of concerns is part of a congregation's regular prayer life.

1. One common pattern is to pray in concentric circles outward, beginning with the needs of the *congregation*—its members and ministries. The prayer then broadens to include *local* concerns, statewide and *national* concerns, *global* issues, and finally, prayers for the church and the *reign of God*, which reaches across both space and time. The prayer can end on a note of eschatological hope that God's will be done finally and everywhere.

This same pattern can also be used in reverse, beginning with cosmic concerns and narrowing the focus to those of one's own congregation.

2. Another pattern is to identify topics that emerge from a consideration of the Lord's Prayer. So, for example, one might pray in this way:

> Our Father in heaven, hallowed be your name
> [prayers of adoration and thanksgiving]

> Your kingdom come. Your will be done, on earth as it is in heaven
> [prayers of longing for God's shalom]

> Give us this day our daily bread
> [prayers for the needs of the community]

Forgive us our debts, as we also have forgiven our debtors
[prayers for interpersonal reconciliation]

And do not bring us to the time of trial, but rescue us from the evil one
[prayers for the world and for personal struggles with temptation and
    evil]

For the kingdom and the power and the glory are yours forever. Amen.[2]

3. One more option is to structure prayers according to basic human emotions as a way of drawing the people into owning the prayer spoken by someone on their behalf. Thus, one might pray first for those who are *sad and sorrowing*, those grieving fading friendships, broken promises, lost hopes, including details from local and global contexts (a failing marriage, intransigent political corruption, etc.). A next section might include prayers for those who are *fearful or anxious*, for example, someone facing a difficult surgery, or people threatened by poverty or violence.

---

### Praying in Balance

*The Worship Sourcebook* includes a useful list of topics that might serve a congregation as a kind of checklist. Leaders can expand the list as appropriate to their context and encourage those who offer prayers in worship to consult it and try to select a meaningful variety of topics to model, over time, a balanced prayer life for the congregation.

The list includes items under these headings:

For the Creation
For the World
For the Nation
For the Local Community
For the Worldwide Church
For the Local Church
For Those with Special Needs

Under that last heading are several dozen topics, including such needs as:

Those who are orphaned and those who care for them
Those who live as single persons
Those who care for elderly or needy parents
Those who work in government
Those who are persecuted for their faith
Those who are new members of the congregation . . .

. . . and many more. Pray-ers might give these topics additional immediacy by naming people in the congregation (observing appropriate privacy considerations, of course) who fit these categories.[3]

Another section should include prayers for those who know *joy*, for example, those celebrating new births, the signing of peace treaties, and so on.

In all these prayers, leaders should aim to help congregations escape our myopia and include in our prayer lives those in the body of Christ we might otherwise forget.

## Multilingual Worship and Global Song

"Congregational song is one of the greatest areas of liturgical and theological cross-pollination," writes Michael Hawn, a Methodist theologian and musician who has published extensively on cultural diversity in worship.[4] Hawn notes that North American hymnals have for decades been the location of much ecumenical sharing, as German Reformation hymns, Wesleyan hymns, camp revival songs, African American spirituals, and many other styles share space in the same bindings. Hawn sees his own work in understanding and promoting global song-sharing in Christian worship as a natural extension of what the church has always done—intensified in our age, no doubt, by unprecedented cross-cultural communication.

Without minimizing the difficulties of stretching our musical comfort zones, it's still fair to say that worship songs help us connect with other parts of the church in ways that words alone cannot. Music engages our bodies in its rhythms and our emotions in its harmonies and patterns. It carries the spirit of other people's devotion in ways that plumb beneath even the most poetic words. Music also has an infectious quality: it tends to stick with us, in our memories and hearts.

Perhaps this helps explain the explosion of so-called global song in the West, as songs from non-Western churches appear in hymnals and songbooks in Europe and North America. The Wild Goose Resource Group (WGRG), based in Scotland, is one example of those who are intentionally promoting the sharing of worship music across continents. For a long time, European–North American hymnody was exported to mission fields everywhere. Now the flow is reversing. John Bell, one of the founders of the WGRG, advocates for dissolving the categories of "Western" and "global" song. WGRG publications since the late 1990s have intentionally mixed together songs from many continents, including those composed by Bell and others in a specifically Scottish folk idiom.[5] The songs of Scotland or the American South, in other words, are no longer some kind of norm with global song the novel exception; instead, they represent particular regions among many world regions.

Of course, for many churches in North America, there is no need to cross international borders, literally or imaginatively, to share worship songs across cultures. Immigration and demographic shifts continue to urge the creation of

### Resources for Finding Songs from the Global Church

Songs from the global church can be found now in many denominational hymnals and hymnal supplements. Here are a few excellent and concentrated collections:

**Wild Goose Publications**

- *Many and Great*, ed. and arr. John Bell (Chicago: GIA, 1992).
- *Sent by the Lord*, ed. and arr. John Bell (Chicago: GIA, 1992).

**General Board of Global Ministries, United Methodist Church**

- *Global Praise 1*, ed. S. T. Kimbrough and Carlton R. Young (New York: General Board of Global Ministries/The United Methodist Church/GBGMusik, 1996).
- *Global Praise 2*, ed. S. T. Kimbrough and Carlton R. Young (New York: General Board of Global Ministries/The United Methodist Church/GBGMusik, 2000).
- *Global Praise 3*, ed. S. T. Kimbrough and Carlton R. Young (New York: General Board of Global Ministries/The United Methodist Church/GBGMusik, 2004).

**Choristers Guild**

- *Halle, Halle: We Sing the World Round*, ed. C. Michael Hawn (Garland, TX: Choristers Guild, 1999).

Some of these collections and even hymnal supplements offer practical musical tips for those wishing to incorporate global music into their own congregations' worship. Michael Hawn's excellent book *Gather into One* is an academic treatment of this topic, yet it, too, includes invaluable practical guidance.

multicultural congregations, where crossing the boundaries of received language and musical styles is a daily challenge. The particular difficulties of bilingual or multilingual congregations, especially as they struggle with issues of immigration, assimilation, and generational differences among immigrants, are too complex for the scope of this book. Yet it's fair to say that worship practices that routinely invite worshipers to borrow the words of other languages and cultures can serve to ease tensions between language groups. No one gets to "own" all the linguistic or cultural territory in worship.

My family's home church has long sought to place itself in a global context in its ministry programs but also in worship, often in song. These days a given service might include a call to worship from Tanzania, an African American spiritual as a confession song, a sixteenth-century Genevan psalm setting, a Latin Taizé chant, a song composed by a member of the congregation, and a contemporary hymn and an old favorite during communion. Admittedly, sometimes the eclecticism can feel a little jarring. But overall, the variety is a reminder that the church is much bigger than my congregation, my community, and my particular heritage. I am deeply grateful for the gift of insight these songs bring, having been composed in contexts of suffering, struggle, and joy much different from my own.

My family also enjoyed our experiences in Southern California with bilingual worship. We often attended an English-Spanish service and soon got used to singing songs in Spanish even though none of us speak Spanish. I came to enjoy singing in another language. Especially if we are native speakers of English, it's good to remember that English is not *the* language of Christianity in all times and places. I learned to appreciate the feel of Spanish words in my mouth and the defamiliarization effect of singing songs I knew with foreign words. One Christmas Eve service we attended was led in both Spanish and English. All those old Christmas songs seemed wonderfully new to me again as I struggled to fit the beautiful liquid Spanish syllables over the familiar tunes.

Anyone who has studied another language knows that every language has its own unique insights and concepts that can't quite be translated. My Greek teacher in college used to say that the Greeks "divided up the universe" differently than we do. So not only does singing in another language remind us of other Christians and encourage us to step out of the center of our own attention; it also welcomes insights on the faith that other languages offer. For instance, the Puerto Rican song "La Unción" uses the word *unción*, which means, approximately, "anointing." The word has connotations of consecration, healing, and soothing balm. Moreover, it is a beautiful word.

We sing songs from other cultures and traditions weekly at my family's home church, often at least in part in their original language. As with any song we sing, we have to sing a "global" song several times before it's comfortable, and many more times before it feels natural. But that's the great thing about something borrowed: it can legitimately become "something of our own." A worship resource

### Singing in Latin—A Language Not Ours and Thus Ours

Though much of the music from the ecumenical and international community of Taizé is available in English, most of it was written, and meant to be sung, in Latin. This is because Latin is no longer anyone's first language; it therefore "belongs" to no one. Yet by linguistic and cultural heritage, as the formative language of the Western church for a thousand years, it has a pervasive influence on the church today.

This strategy—singing in tongues and styles not our own—is an effective one when worship wars leave various congregational constituencies so embittered that each side counts the number of "their" songs used in a service over against the songs of the other group(s). To continue to use music, but music that no group can claim as "theirs," effectively subverts the dangerous notion that worship is about me, my group, or our preferences.

### The Importance of Visible Diversity

Rev. Norberto Wolf, formerly director of race relations for the Christian Reformed Church, reminds us that "visibility counts." While this chapter is about worshiping with the global church through words, we also wish to echo Norberto's concern that we signal our participation in the global church through the people who lead worship. If our leaders are all one race or ethnicity, that sends a subtle message that "we" are in charge and others must follow. If our leaders show the diversity of our communities and the church, that sends a message that our "we" is a diverse one in which many kinds of people share in guiding the church.

is not like a cup of flour that is finite and consumable; it is more like the widow's oil. Spreading it around does not mean there is less of it to share!

Some people are concerned about Western churches adopting "global" songs because this can be seen as a kind of exploitation: "liturgical ethno-tourism." Considering the history of Western exploitation of other cultural resources, this is a serious danger. Therefore, North American churches must be especially careful to borrow respectfully and in an informed way. Our temptation in a consumer society is to see the world's worship resources as an expansion of our "choice" and to seek endless novelty in the fresh new sounds and colors of the world bazaar—spread out, we assume, for *our* delight. We have to resist this impulse and instead borrow intentionally as a way to honor, welcome, and learn from other Christians and be welcomed in turn.

### Practical Ideas for Worshiping with the Global Church

- Study a new worship element's background before using it. Who created it? What is the context out of which it came? How can you use the resource both to honor the "sending" culture and to make it comprehensible in the "receiving" culture? How can you communicate something about the resource's context to worshipers?

- Introduce and teach new elements, especially songs, joyfully and deliberately. Many churches find that it works well to have a brief teaching time before the service begins. Explain why you are using a particular song or prayer or element. People are not always happy about "foreign stuff" because it doesn't feel expressive for them. Remind the congregation that self-expression is not the only purpose of language in worship. Remind them that we are learning our way into the meaning of the song. With teaching and repetition, the element will become formative and eventually expressive as well.

> **"Siyahamba": A Song of Unity, Defiance, Hope, and Liberation**
>
> The South African song "Siyahamba" has made its way into the worshiping repertoires of many North American Christian communities. Some know it as "We are Marching in the Light of God" and enjoy its joyful syncopation and exuberant melody. Yet it is a song born in the context of oppression and prejudice. It is a song of unity, as the people sing that they act *together*. It is a song of defiance, as the people sing of positive action—marching, and not silent suffering. It is a song of hope and liberation, as South Africans sang in code of their future hope for a world of God's light and peace.[6]
>
> All of this suggests that when North Americans sing this song, they can resist being exploitative when leaders help the congregation remain mindful of the song's original use, perhaps through a short note printed in a bulletin or an explanation by the song leader.

- Connect prayers, songs, and other elements with people. Have a visiting missionary tell the story of a particular Brazilian Christian before singing a Brazilian "Gloria." Or have a missionary write a letter in which Ghanaian Christians share their concerns, and read the letter before singing the Ghanaian Kyrie. Ask a Mexican person in your congregation to explain what a Spanish-language prayer means to her, either by giving testimony in person or by writing a few sentences for the bulletin or projection screen. Tell stories. Relate the resource to a testimony. Provide information. This can be done with a few spoken words, printed words in a bulletin, or with brief text and visuals on projected slides.

- Once a song or prayer or other element is very familiar, it can be done without comment or introduction most of the time. Occasionally, remember the element's origin again for the sake of new people, children, or those of us of all ages who tend to forget.

- Evaluate elements from other cultures as you would worship resources from your own. Just because a song is in another language and sounds exotic doesn't mean it's worth singing. On the other hand, some worthy words can't be translated well, especially if they are song lyrics and the tune limits translation possibilities. The song may wind up sounding thin or just dopey. How can you know if foreign lyrics or prayers or other resources are worthy? Ask someone qualified to make that assessment if you can't do so yourself.

- Make decisions about whether to use the original language or the English translation based on your assessment of the resource and your congregation's readiness. Be creative. Perhaps two readers could lead a prayer, alternating the original language and English line by line. Perhaps you

### "Yesu Azali Awa"

Sometimes too much is lost in translation and it's well worth singing a song in the original language. For instance, the Congolese folk hymn "Yesu azali awa" is a delightful song that can easily be sung by English speakers in the original Ngala language. The verses of the song repeat the same line three times, add a short phrase, then go on to repeat the word *alleluia* three times, like this:

1. Yesu azali awa (3x), na biso.
   Alleluia (3x), na Yesu.
2. Biso tokomona ye (3x), na lola.
   Alleluia (3x), na Yesu.
3. Biso tokosepela na lola. (etc.)
4. Biso tokokutana na Yesu. (etc.)
5. Biso tokolingana na lola. (etc.)

Notice how verses 2–5 repeat the same four opening syllables. In the translation, this delightful sound pattern is completely lost:

1. Jesus Christ is with us (3x), he is here.
2. We will see him on his throne, on his throne.
3. We'll bring praises to him, on his throne.
4. There'll be joy evermore, with the Lord.
5. For his love makes us one, with the Lord.[7]

For a song like this, the original language is the better choice. The English translation can easily be printed alongside or projected on a screen. The repeated lines allow singers plenty of time to meditate worshipfully on the meaning while still enjoying the delightful beauty of the original-language sounds. (In other words, we should not forget the importance of the aesthetic dimension of language in a foreign language either!)

can sing English on the verses, but Spanish on the chorus. Perhaps you can sing the English, then the Korean, then the English again. Alternating in creative ways allows the resource to translate itself, as it were, but also allows the congregation to perceive the original form.

- When using songs from other cultures, the musicians face the challenge of musical authenticity. Do we use the same instruments the sending culture would use? What if we don't have or know how to play those instruments? What if we are not well prepared to play these kinds of rhythms or if we are not trained to sing in this style? And what if the musicians can do it, but the congregation—not so much? What about some kinds of African music that, in the African way of thinking, by definition include dance?

Well, people disagree on this point. Some say that to adapt music from other cultures by translating it into North American idioms is always a kind of exploitation: a way of suggesting that we'll only accept these "gifts" if we can fit them into our predetermined molds. Others say it's better to do our best with other styles of music than not to try at all.

I am very glad for the musicians who are introducing me—raised on Western classical music, English hymnody, and rock and roll—to new kinds of music in worship. I would rather struggle to learn than avoid other styles because I can't do them "right" at first. I'm glad for the musicians who make it a little easier for me, but also stretch me. After all, we do learn. Our congregation has been doing African songs for a long time. Now some of us are learning African drumming techniques, and our liturgical dancers have a few African moves too. Within ten years, who knows? Maybe we'll all be dancing.

So as long as we realize that we are doing other styles "badly" at first, and avoid assumptions that Western styles are somehow superior and thus we have to adapt other styles to make them "better," then I think it's fine that we do other styles "badly" in order to meet congregations where they are and help them learn.

- Avoid kitsch and pastiche. Everything we discussed in chapter 8 concerning the use of historical resources applies here, and even more so as we are borrowing from living people and cultures. The most important ways to avoid shallow borrowing are (1) do a few things well rather than many things poorly and (2) do background research on each element you are naturalizing into your worship. A good way to test how you're doing is to imagine those for whom this resource is naturally expressive worshiping with you. Would they be pleased with the way you are using the gift they've given, even if you are doing it rather "badly"? Or would they be horrified and offended that you have so badly misunderstood?

- Something old and from the Western church is not automatically "ours," even if the congregation is predominantly of European origin. Sometimes it's wonderful to regain a sense of an element's foreignness. Sing "Ein' feste Burg" ("A Mighty Fortress") in German, for example, and invite people to think about Luther and his sense of the earth shaking beneath his feet at the Reformation. Or when saying the Nicene Creed together, remind worshipers that this creed was hammered out in the fourth century in Nicea—a city in what is now Turkey. Affirm what the congregation is already doing in adapting and blending songs and prayers and words from many tributaries into the flow of their familiar worship; defamiliarize what they're used to so they can see that they already know how to blend elements.

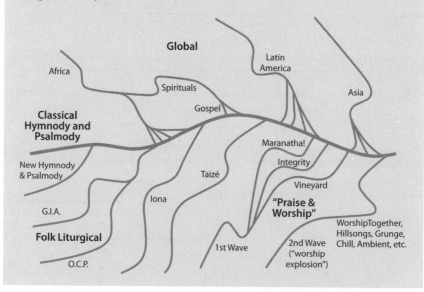

**Worship Flows on the River of Song**

This visual interpretation of the tributaries and sources that flow into the church's song may help congregations see how valuable it may be to explore other parts of the great worship delta.

- Remember sermons. Awareness of our place in the global church does not end with the last song set. Preachers should seek to use ideas, quotations, and illustrations from a variety of races, cultures, and nations as they are able. This means that preachers, as part of their vocation, need to read widely and seek intentionally to be involved in their communities with people outside the dominant culture of their congregations.
- Nonverbal elements are important too. The way people dress, the art hung in the sanctuary or hallways, the images flashed on the PowerPoint—these, too, can indicate that a congregation is mindful that Christ's church spans the generations and the globe.

To sum this up, we can relate Michael Hawn's advice. In encouraging churches to worship with the global church, Hawn recommends that worship leaders think about "centered exploration." In other words, worship leaders should begin by finding the centerpoint of their congregation's comfortable style, then stretch and expand outward from there, slowly and intentionally. It's important not to overload with some kind of sudden global worship frenzy, but to be gracious about people's learning curve. The Revelation vision of the "great multitude that no one could count, from every nation, tribe, people and language, standing before the throne"—this is a glorious reality that God is bringing about. Our task is to strive to see God at work, creating this reality in our world and in our midst.

### Exercises

1. How would you describe your congregation's culture? What historical elements contribute to the language and musical styles at the center of familiarity? How has your congregation experienced globalization? Is there a mix of cultures and languages within your congregation? What does your worship suggest about how local culture relates to the global church? Are Christians from other parts of the world regularly represented somehow in worship? Are they presented as "those whom we help and rescue" or as Christian partners?

2. In a worship service you attend, observe whether the rest of the church is "present" in the language of worship. Does anyone pray for the rest of the church and the rest of the world? Are there any worship elements that come, intentionally welcomed, from other parts of the church? How were you affected as a worshiper by the presence, or lack thereof, of attention to the church beyond the congregation itself?

3. Choose a song or prayer from another nation and research it. Write a few words that could be spoken before singing the song or praying the prayer that would invite the congregation to sing or pray in solidarity with those who originated the element. Think of other ways to invite the congregation into kinship with the Christians who "send" us the song or prayer: Slides? A letter read aloud from a Christian in the sending culture, either actual or fictitious? A visual symbol or artwork that reminds us of our communion with the people originating the element?

4. Write a pastoral prayer in which a leader guides the congregation in prayer for different parts of the church and the world. Find a way for the congregation to respond that reflects our kinship with other Christians. Could we translate "Lord, have mercy" into another language? Could we sing a response using music from another culture?

5. Translate. If you speak more than one language, translate a worship element from one language into another for use in your own worship context. Could you

### Credo Hispano

Creemos en Dios Padre todopoderoso,
    creador de los cielos y de la tierra;
    creador de los pueblos y las culturas;
    creador de los idiomas y de las razas.

Creemos en Jesucristo, su Hijo, nuestro Señor,
    Dios hecho carne en un ser humano para todos los humanos;
    Dios hecho carne en un momento para todas las edades;
    Dios hecho carne en una cultura para todas las culturas;
    Dios hecho carne en amor y gracia para toda la creación.

Creemos en el Espíritu Santo,
    por quien el Dios encarnado en Jesucristo
    se hace presente en nuestro pueblo y nuestra cultura;
    por quien el Dios creador de todo cuanto existe
    nos da poder para ser nuevas criaturas;
    quien con sus infinitos dones, nos hace un solo pueblo:
    el cuerpo de Jesucristo.

Creemos en la Iglesia,
    que es universal porque es señal del reino venidero;
    que es más fiel mientras más se viste de colores;
    donde todos los colores pintan un mismo paisaje;
    donde todos los idiomas cantan una misma alabanza.

Creemos en el reino venidero, día de la gran fiesta,
    cuando todos los colores de la creación
    se unirán en un arco iris de armonía;
    cuando todos los pueblos de la tierra
    se unirán en un banquete de alegría;
    cuando todas la lenguas del universo
    se unirán en un coro de alabanza.

Y porque creemos, nos comprometemos
    a creer por los que no creen,
    a amar por los que no aman,
    a soñar por los que no sueñan
    hasta que lo que esperamos se torne realidad.
    Amen.[8]

*—Justo González, "Credo hispano"*

retain at least some of the original language in a way that worshipers in your context could wrap their tongues around? For instance, translate the verses of a song, but retain the refrain in the original language.

### Credo Hispano (Hispanic Creed), English

We believe in God, the Father Almighty
    Creator of the heavens and the earth;
    Creator of all peoples and all cultures;
    Creator of all tongues and races.

We believe in Jesus Christ, his Son, our Lord,
    God made flesh in a person for all humanity,
    God made flesh in an age for all the ages,
    God made flesh in one culture for all cultures,
    God made flesh in love and grace for all creation.

We believe in the Holy Spirit
    through whom God incarnate in Jesus Christ
    makes his presence known in our peoples and our cultures;
    through whom God, Creator of all that exists,
    gives us power to become new creatures;
    whose infinite gifts make us one people:
    the Body of Christ.

We believe in the Church
    universal because it is a sign of God's Reign,
    whose faithfulness is shown in its many hues
    where all the colors paint a single landscape,
    where all tongues sing the same praise.

We believe in the Reign of God—the day of the Great Fiesta
    when all the colors of creation will form a harmonious rainbow,
    when all peoples will join in joyful banquet,
    when all tongues of the universe will sing the same song.

And because we believe, we commit ourselves:
    to believe for those who do not believe,
    to love for those who do not love,
    to dream for those who do not dream,
    until the day when hope becomes reality.
    Amen.[9]

*—Justo González, trans., "Hispanic Creed"*

### Global Hybridization

Many worship songs no longer travel simple routes from one culture to another, but grow as the products of a rich cross-pollination of many cultures. The song *Eres santo/ You Are Holy*, for example, was translated into Spanish by Raquel Gutiérrez-Achon, but was originally written—in the musical samba form—by Swede Per Harling (a *Swedish* samba?). The recent version of "Soul, Adorn Yourself with Gladness," published in the ELCA's *Renewing Worship* materials, was written originally in German in the seventeenth century, translated into English in the nineteenth century, and then paired with a lilting Puerto Rican melody in the twenty-first century.

Another excellent example is the song *Kwake Yesu nasimama/Here on Jesus Christ I Will Stand*. While in Uganda at a worship conference, church musician Greg Scheer learned a beautiful song of hope and confidence from some visiting Kenyans. It was clearly one of their favorites. Greg's friends translated the original Swahili lyrics sung at their church very literally into English, and then Greg paraphrased them into a more singable version. The lyrics track so closely to the verses of the Toplady hymn "Rock of Ages" that the Swahili may very well be an indigenization of that classic church song, first given as a gift by Western missionaries to Kenyan Christians, and now given back to us.

> *Rock of Ages:*
> Rock of Ages, cleft for me, let me hide myself in thee;
> let the water and the blood, from thy wounded side which flowed,
> be of sin the double cure; save from wrath and make me pure.
>
> *Kwake Yesu nasimama:*
> Here on Jesus Christ I will stand; he's the solid rock of my life.
> There's no other place I can hide 'til the storm that rages subsides.
> My voice cries to God from the flood, and I'm saved because of his
>     blood.
>
> *Rock of Ages (v. 2):*
> Not the labors of my hands can fulfill thy law's commands;
> could my zeal no respite know, could my tears forever flow,
> all for sin could not atone; thou must save, and thou alone.
>
> *Kwake Yesu nasimama (v. 2):*
> It is not the work of my hands that has washed away all my sins.
> I'm redeemed, and all of my days, Jesus Christ will be my heart's
>     praise.
>
> *Rock of Ages (v3 4):*
> While I draw this fleeting breath, when mine eyes shall close in death,
> when I soar to worlds unknown, see thee on thy judgment throne,
> Rock of Ages, cleft for me, let me hide myself in thee.[10]
>
> *Kwake Yesu nasimama (v. 3):*
> When my days on this earth are done, and I stand at God's holy
>     throne,
> my heart will not have any fear—in Christ's righteousness I am here.[11]

# 11

## Something Blue

### *The Ministry of Lament*

My soul is in anguish. How long, O LORD, how long?

Psalm 6:3

While visiting a church in the Los Angeles area one Sunday, our family heard a preacher deal very bravely with the events of the week leading up to that day. He had just received the devastating news that his father was going to die of cancer within a few months. He spoke honestly about not "feeling God's presence" that week.

I appreciated his honesty and vulnerability very much. There are definitely times when what we feel most powerfully is God's absence. These dark places, however unwelcome, are a normal part of our pilgrimage through this valley, where the shadow of death is never far away. We see ample testimony about these valley places in Scripture and throughout the generations.

Still, I hope that on some other day—perhaps when he was feeling a little stronger, not quite so raw—the pastor was able to remind the congregation that it is possible to feel God's presence in our sadness, sorrow, and bewilderment. And that when we don't feel God's presence, we can still cry out to God. That's what

### The Psalms as Models for Lament

Lament is a mode of expression in which we voice our pain to God. It is distinct from requests, praise, wisdom, and other modes.

Request:      God, please help us (or help them) . . .
Praise:       God, you are wonderful . . .
Adoration:    God, we love you . . .
Thanks:       God, thank you for . . .
Wisdom:       God tells us this truth . . .
Confession:   God, we're sorry . . .
Lament:       God, we are in pain . . . we don't understand . . .

The paraphrase below of Psalm 13 from *The Message*, by Eugene Peterson, with its contemporary, colloquial language, helps demonstrate the distinct mode of lament. As we'll see later in this chapter, lament on the biblical model ends with trusting praise.

Long enough, God—
you've ignored me long enough.
I've looked at the back of your head
long enough. Long enough
I've carried this ton of trouble,
lived with a stomach full of pain.
Long enough my arrogant enemies
have looked down their noses at me.

Take a good look at me, GOD, my God:
I want to look life in the eye,
So no enemy can get the best of me
or laugh when I fall on my face.

I've thrown myself headlong into your arms—
I'm celebrating your rescue.
I'm singing at the top of my lungs,
I'm so full of answered prayers.

it means to follow Jesus, the Man of Sorrows. He knows. He's been there. He sits beside us on the mourning bench.

The question for our purposes, though, is how can we teach people this truth in worship? How can we teach people that sorrow and lament are part of Christian devotion, part of Christian life? The Psalms are full of longing, desperation, pain, brokenness—voices crying out from dark places in which God seems far away. The Psalms and many other places in Scripture teach us that God can handle our anger, pain, and doubt; the Bible gives us not only permission but invitation to lament.

Making a place for lament in worship is an often-neglected matter of pastoral care. Every Sunday, every single Sunday, someone in your church will come to worship in grief, confusion, distress. Someone will have heard the diagnosis "cancer" in a doctor's office. Someone will have lost a job. Someone will have wrestled all week with discouragement and depression. What does worship teach these people to do with their grief? Will they feel that they are supposed to "leave their worries at the door" because their pain is unworshipful? Or will they be invited to express it honestly before God? Too many Christians already mistakenly believe that doubt, grief, confusion, and anger are always wrong or sinful. The Bible, by contrast, shows us how to be authentic in our distress and still remain engaged with God.

Even more, every Sunday, every single Sunday, the world around us aches with terrible suffering. God's good creation is choked with pollution. Millions struggle for enough food for themselves and their children. Ethnic hatred simmers in systematic oppression and flares up in violent outbursts. How does our worship teach us to respond to all this? By ignoring it and focusing on our own feelings of religious fervor? By a quick and cursory mention in intercessory prayer? Or are we willing to spend some time and some words on lament, bringing the world's suffering before God on behalf of those who suffer?

Making a place for lament is not only a matter of spiritual formation and pastoral care, but—just as we discussed in the previous chapter—it is also a matter of Christian witness. After the tsunami in the Indian Ocean in 2004, newspapers, magazines, and Web sites were full of interviews with prominent Christians. "How could your God let this happen?!" reporters asked, in anger and bewilderment, while Christians struggled to offer faithful responses. In the face of disaster, tragedy, sorrow, and evil, people look to us and wonder whether Christians have some way of making sense of it all. How do we invite seekers and believers, in our worship, to wrestle with their most difficult questions?

One important way is to admit truthfully that answers in such times are not easy. Sometimes we have to live with the questions, the grief, and the pain. When people come to the church in pain, we have a crucial opportunity to demonstrate

### An Opportunity Missed

On the morning after September 11, 2001, some of my colleagues at another Christian college attended daily worship on their campus and found that the people in charge of chapel that day had decided to disregard the horror of the previous morning's events. Instead of offering a service of lament or prayer or even silence, they went ahead with their previously planned worship, covering over the fear and horror of the community with songs about dancing and singing before the Lord. Feeling disoriented and somehow betrayed, my friends had to leave the chapel service.

In many other contexts, however, congregations across the country offered services of lament, and discovered the significance of bringing our deepest questions and complaints and fears to God.

the distinctiveness of our faith. We Christians do not always need to give pat answers or pretend all is well. Instead, we can see the world's pain straight on because we see it through the eyes of Christ, who knows the pain more fully and completely than we do, having suffered it himself.

By learning to lament in worship, we teach the faithful and witness to seekers. For both, we offer healing balm when we show that there is a way to respond to the world's brokenness that is biblical and honestly expressive, a way that lets us be broken vessels, cracked open enough to receive the life waters of redemption.

## The Biblical Pattern of Lament

For many of us, lament is an unfamiliar mode either in worship or in our personal spiritual walk. We know about praise and adoration; we know about confession; we know about prayer for ourselves and others (petition and intercession). But what is lament?

Lament is bringing before God our recognition that this world is full of pain, sorrow, grief, and despair. Perhaps the most similar mode of engagement with God is confession, so it may be useful to distinguish lament from confession more carefully. In confession, we seek to be honest about our own sin—we own up to all the ways in which our failures cause pain and trouble for ourselves and others. Confession is the taking of responsibility for our part in sin's ravages. In lament, we are seeking not to place blame or locate guilt but to share in God's sorrow over the brokenness of a good creation. In lament, we don't say "I'm sorry"; we may be lamenting things that are simply not our fault or anyone's fault. Instead, in lament, we admit that some things are beyond our understanding. We ask questions: Why? How long? How can this be?

Lament is not the same as despair either. Lament teaches us to bring our despair to God. It reaches out. "To you I lift up my soul," the psalmist often says, amid much trouble and sorrow (Ps. 143:8, for example). The Psalms give us a reliable, inspired pattern for prayer that incorporates lament into the larger context of a fulsome prayer life.

According to liturgical scholar John Witvliet, the biblical pattern shapes our lament in four main movements: invocation, the lament itself, petition, and hope.[1]

> Invocation: We do not throw our doubts, questions, and protests outward to an uncaring universe; we address our lament to God.
>
> Lament: We ask why; we express the pain; we allow bewilderment and frustration their reality as part of our experience. We share God's sorrow and give our sorrow over to God.

"Lament and praise are incomplete without the other, lest praise, particularly general or descriptive praise, be misunderstood as smug satisfaction or lament be understood as a denial or refusal of grace."[2]

—*John D. Witvliet*

Petition: We ask God to act. We know God's character, and so we expect God to judge, to heal, to repair, to redeem. With the psalmist we say, "In your faithfulness and righteousness come to my relief" (Ps. 143:1).

Hope: We express hope, even when we don't feel especially hopeful. The most strenuous lamentations of the Bible are embedded in expressions of trust, in remembrances of God's past faithfulness, and in praise, both given and promised.

So we learn from the biblical model that lament has its place in our worship, but it does not stand alone. It comes in a context that neither dismisses nor overwhelms it, but places it within a larger witness to God's faithfulness.

## Practical Suggestions for Making a Place for Lament in Worship

When introducing lament into the worship practice of a congregation, a crucial consideration is where to place it. Positioning lament thoughtfully will help worshipers understand its purpose and participate more fully and meaningfully. Normally, the most appropriate places for lament are (1) connected to a time of confession, (2) as part of the congregation's regular reading or singing of a psalm, (3) before the pastoral or intercessory prayer, and (4) in the sermon. Probably one place of lament is enough in a regular weekly service. If a congregation is experiencing a particular crisis, worship leaders might wish to respond with a more extensive time of lament or perhaps a whole service of lament.[3]

### Confession

Lament may be connected with confession but should not be confused with it. Confession says "I'm sorry" or "We're sorry." Lament says "Why?" Words of general lament might come first, followed by a clear transition to words of confession. However, be careful not to imply blame that may not be appropriate.

*Lament*
    *Leader:* Why do these storms come, O God of creation?
       Why do you allow these powers to destroy your creatures?
    *People:* Hear us in our confusion and sorrow!

*Confession*

[the following words imply a too-simple notion of causality]:
*Leader:* Let us now confess the sins that brought this divine wrath upon the
    world . . .

[better]:
*Leader:* Let us now confess our sins and cry out for mercy.
*People:* Forgive us when we are indifferent
    and neglect those who suffer.
Forgive us when we forget
    that all creation is precious to you.
Forgive us when we despair,
    for we know you are merciful.
Have mercy on us, dear God,
    for we are your children.


## Psalms

The simplest way to practice lament in worship is to let the words of the Psalms
guide us. Congregations that regularly read or pray psalms are already doing lament
when they read psalms containing that mode—though they may not realize exactly
what they are engaged in. Congregations that do not regularly pray the Psalms can
find in them a ready and reliable way to give worshipers appropriate words. In
either case, leaders need to help worshipers understand what they are doing and
give these psalms some specific traction by using appropriate contextual words.

Another way to pray the Psalms is by composing new prayers based on their
models, localizing the metaphors to contemporary references for particular concerns or occasions. For example (from Psalm 22):

Our God, why have you forsaken those who suffer from AIDS?
    Why do you seem so far from saving them,

### All Is Messed Up, All Will Be Well

The appropriate response to lament follows the pattern of confession/assurance. After
a confession, we long to hear words of God's forgiveness: "As far as the east is from
the west, so far has [God] removed our transgressions from us" (Ps. 103:12). These
words express forgiveness for individual transgressions and seem inappropriate to
address ongoing, systemic sins like racism, pervasive results of sin like environmental
degradation, and miseries of a fallen world such as cancer. But in response to lament, a declaration of God's ultimate sovereignty is exactly right. It assures us (just
as an assurance of pardon does) that however messed up the world is now, in the
end, as Julian of Norwich wrote, "All will be well, and all will be well, and all manner
of things will be well."

so far from the words of their groaning?
O God, the people of Africa cry out for healing by day,
    but you do not seem to answer,
    by night, but the disease continues to ravage lives,
       to orphan children, to devastate whole communities.
Yet you are enthroned as the Holy One of all the earth,
    You are the praise of all nations. [etc.]

### *Pastoral or Intercessory Prayer*

Since the pastoral or intercessory prayer is the main place in many worship traditions where we bring our requests before God on behalf of others, this is an especially natural place to incorporate some sentences of lament. The lament prepares us to pray earnestly and also leads readily into petitions, just as our biblical examples model for us.

The person leading the pastoral prayer can simply alternate some words of lament with the specific petitions:

---

#### Contextualizing Psalm 80

This litany gives context to the words of Psalm 80, connecting the text to contemporary concerns. The reading requires a Scripture reader and a prayer leader as well as the congregation.[4]

*Scripture Reader:* [read Ps. 80:1–2]
*Congregation:* [Ps. 80:3]
*Prayer Leader:* Lord God, we profess before the nations that you are a God of power,
    a God who created the world and all that is in it,
    a God who provides a way of hope and salvation,
    a God who calls together a community of faith to proclaim your goodness to the nations.

    We especially praise you for signs of your work among us, signs of your coming kingdom . . . [name specific reasons for praise].

*Scripture Reader:* [Ps. 80:4–6]
*Congregation:* [Ps. 80:7]
*Prayer Leader:* Lord God, so often you seem distant from us. Despite our fierce prayers, our community and our world are filled with pain and brokenness . . . [name specific reasons for lament].
*Scripture Reader:* [Ps. 80:8–18]
*Prayer Leader:* Lord God, we praise you for the Son of Man you have raised up and the kingdom of shalom that he has ushered in. As we long for the coming kingdom, we still pray:
*Congregation:* [Ps. 80:19]

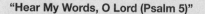

This version of Psalm 5 combines invocation, lament, petition, and hope. The congregation sings a refrain while a reader offers the words of the psalm, sensitive to the shifting emotional landscape the psalm traverses.

—"Hear My Words, O Lord (Psalm 5)," words and music by Greg Scheer.
Copyright © 2007 Greg Scheer. http://www.gregscheer.com. Used by permission.

Judge of the universe, we look on with frustration and horror as the people of Darfur continue to suffer. Why does the evil persist? Where is the solution to this crisis? O Jesus, you are the Prince of Peace. Bring justice and peace to this place. Remove evil ones from power, and have mercy on the helpless.

Another option is to alternate between spoken words and congregational responses taken from the lamenting words of a psalm. The brief setting above of words from Psalm 5, for example, might be sung before and after the prayer as well as during one or two pauses between petitions. When the congregation is not singing, musicians might continue playing quietly as the pray-er continues with the petitions.

Incorporating lament into worship as a regular practice helps make real and practical for worshipers the kinds of assurance the Bible gives: It's all right to ask why, to feel angry, to feel sad, and to wonder why God seems far away. It's all right *not* to have a ready discursive answer or explanation for every bad thing that happens. Instead, the biblical model of prayer teaches us to acknowledge the dark places as part of our experience while simultaneously giving them over to God. We learn to cling to God, even amid the darker mysteries.

**Exercises**

1. Think of a time in your life when you came to worship in a state of doubt, grief, anger at God, or terrible sorrow. How did the worship speak to you in your state, if at all? Recall how you experienced worship at that time and try to think

---

**Lament and Preaching**

Preachers give their listeners a great gift when they are honest about doubt, questions, sorrow, grief, and anger at God as a normal part of the Christian life. Don't be too quick to move to resolution in a sermon. This is not always easy; people expect you to be the one with all the answers. I remember once preaching on Luke 19:41–44, where Jesus weeps over Jerusalem ("if you had only known the things that made for peace . . ."). I followed the contours of the text, inviting listeners to weep with Jesus in helplessness at the violence so prevalent in our world. A politically active congregant complained after the service, telling me, "but we *do* know the ways that make for peace!"

I could only respond, "Do we really? I know there are things we can do to make a difference, but in the text, Jesus doesn't give a five-point plan. He simply weeps. I think it's OK for us to do that once in a while. You've been working all your life pursuing peace; don't you feel tired and frustrated sometimes?"

### "Your Kingdom Come"

The Brazilian lament "Um pouco além do presente/A Little beyond This Our Time" combines lament and holy longing. This combination makes this song wonderfully fitting as a lament on its own or as a way to conclude a time of lament offered in some other mode.

The verses vividly depict the new creation for which we long, while the refrain prays that God will transform our present sorrow into future joy. The refrain concludes in an extended cry of sorrow and longing—a longing that is too deep for words, and so no words are used, but sobbing syllables: Ai-eh, ei-ah, ai-eh, a-eh, a-eh.

> A little beyond this our time
> the future announces with gladness
> no war, no disaster, no crime,
> no more desolation, no sadness.
>
> *Refrain*
> Your Kingdom come, Jesus Christ, the joy of our world recreate,
> our hope and our many longings transform in the fullness of life.
> Ai-eh, ei-ah, ai-eh, a-eh, a-eh. Ai-eh, ei-ah, ai-eh, a-eh, a-eh.
>
> We hope to cast out all our hate,
> we long for a world of pure beauty,
> in which peace will never abate
> and justice will be, then, our duty.
>
> We hope for a new world of trust:
> no one will be feeble nor strong.
> The systems we have are unjust:
> they always divisions prolong.
>
> The seeds of your Kingdom we bear,
> your future is drawing so near:
> the earth with your help we prepare
> until you in fullness appear.[5]

specifically about how the worship words affected you. From this experience, what advice would you give yourself (and others) about lament in worship?

2. Make a list of five people, real or imagined, who might attend worship at your church in various states of grief. For example:

- a woman in her fifties who has just lost her husband after a long battle with cancer
- a young athlete who has just sustained a serious injury that will probably end his career
- a woman who has lost a baby at twenty weeks of pregnancy

- a young man struggling with his growing understanding that he is homosexual
- a family who has just arrived in your church from a refugee camp overseas, having escaped their country's civil war

Attend worship and listen to the words with the ears of one of these people. Perhaps you can enlist others to listen with the ears of the others on your list. What does each person hear? Are the worship words they hear reaching out and answering their struggles? Will they feel the presence of Christ in the words?

3. Choose a psalm that contains elements of lament. Compose a prayer or song or litany that enables the congregation to pray with the psalm in a way fitting to your congregation's worship practice. Don't feel you have to use the entire psalm, but try to include elements of invocation, lament, petition, and hope.

4. Write a sermon, or a short three-paragraph meditation (a sermon-writing exercise) about a passage you do not understand. Be as honest as you can about the questions it raises for you. Try to avoid coming up with the "right answers" to the questions. Instead, concentrate on coming up with the right questions. How might the Scripture's model of lament help you guide listeners in bringing the questions to God, appropriately contextualized, rather than shutting them down?

---

### A Brief Service of Lament—Prayer in the Interrogative Mood

One simple way to encourage folks to pray prayers of lament (whether publicly or privately) is to prompt the prayers with an interrogative word, like *why* or *where* or *when* or *how long*. (The phrase *how long*, in fact, is used more than twenty times in Psalms alone.) This way, our prayers for peace in the Middle East, for example, are not merely petitions for wise leadership; they become expressions of our own helplessness: "When, O Lord, will your children in the Middle East stop firing rockets at one another?"

Here is a short devotional service based on this idea. It embeds the prayer of lament within both a sung *Kyrie* and a concluding *Alleluia*. It also contextualizes the prayer—both the lament and the declaration of God's ultimate sovereignty—as continuous with the "words of the faithful in all times and places."

The service was used with a small group of worshipers who knew each other well enough to feel brave when the time came to offer free prayers of lament. With a larger group, individuals could be asked ahead of time to prepare what they might wish to pray aloud during that part of the service. Having members of the congregation pray aloud from their seats appropriately represents how people come to worship carrying many different types of pain, often in secret.

*(continued on next page)*

The opening words prepare for lament with a context of hope in God's kingdom coming. The words of Psalm 13 are then divided into two main sections. The first section gives us words for lament, while the psalm's conclusion invites us into hope. Both sections are clearly signaled as the testimony of the whole church.

*One:*  The Lord be with you.
*All:*  And also with you.

*One:*  The reign of God is coming.
*All:*  We wait,
we hope,
we believe.

*One:*  The reign of God is here.
*All:*  We see the signs:
in our homes
in the street
among the nations.

*One:*  The reign of God is coming.
*All:*  We cry out in longing
for the day of fulfillment
is not yet here.

*Sing:*  Kyrie eleison

Hear the words of the faithful in all times and places:

How long, O LORD? Will you forget me forever?
How long will you hide your face from me?
How long must I bear pain in my soul,
and have sorrow in my heart all day long?
How long shall my enemy be exalted over me?

Consider and answer me, O LORD my God!
Give light to my eyes, or I will sleep the sleep of death,
and my enemy will say, "I have prevailed";
my foes will rejoice because I am shaken. (Ps. 13:1–4 NRSV)

*Prayers of lament, offered freely.*
*You may wish to begin prayers with the words* why, where, *or* how long.

*Sing: Kyrie eleison*

Hear the words of the faithful in all times and places:

But I trusted in your steadfast love;
my heart shall rejoice in your salvation.
I will sing to the LORD,
because he has dealt bountifully with me. (Ps. 13:5–6 NRSV)

*Sing: Alleluia*

# 12

# The Embedded Word

## *Putting It All Together*

The chapters of this book have explored a broad range of ideas in considerable depth. Any single chapter might give you as a worship leader, pastor, or worship committee member much to think about and might inspire changes large or small. Faced with planning a particular service as a whole, however, you may well feel rather overwhelmed. How do we consider all these issues at once? How do we put it all together?

As suggested in the introduction, the best strategy is to start small and work on one thing at a time. Think about how your congregation might renew the planning process for worship in order to allow more space for reflection on worship and better communication between leaders and congregation. Appendix 2, on the worship planning process, offers some ideas for increasing congregational ownership and maximizing available expertise and vision.

Meanwhile, in this chapter we will consider some basic issues involved when synthesizing all the elements of a service.

### Words and the Bigger Picture

While our family was living in California, we sometimes listened to tapes of services from our home church in Michigan. It was amazing how many people we could recognize simply from their voices as we heard them read Scripture or pray or sing on the tapes. Hearing their voices helped a little with the ache of missing home. Still, listening to the tape was not at all the same as being there. We could hear all the worship words that were spoken or sung in a particular service, but a great deal was still missing.

This experience reminds us that all worship words happen in context, and context can either enhance or diminish words' effectiveness. When we sing words to a suitable melody, for example, we enhance them by making them more beautiful and memorable. When we are stuck with unfortunate acoustics in the worship space, on the other hand, words get diminished: we have to struggle to understand them or to be understood speaking them. Another important variable concerns the positioning of words in the progression of a service. Words of praise at the opening of the service feel different from the same words spoken after a sermon or just before we are sent out to our worship work in the world.

We also need to remember that for some people, words are difficult. They find the linear nature of discourse problematic, they struggle with decoding as readers, they have a hard time paying long attention, or they simply are more responsive to visuals or movement. Many Protestant churches worship in a very plain space and favor a similarly plain worship aesthetic: there is music, but the service is mostly words, words, words. This might be true of a New England congregational choir-and-organ service as much as of a praise-band-driven service.

One of my undergraduate students—she attended a praise-and-worship style megachurch—once wrote favorably about the plainness of her church building and worship style because she felt there were "no distractions." For her, worship was about words, and she felt comfortable with that. But there are many people for whom enduring a long stream of words feels like paddling hard upstream. The pastor of the Tribe congregation in Los Angeles, Rebecca, explained that her congregation, most of whom are artists of some kind, need to see and touch in order to understand and connect. The Bible, if simply read aloud, feels "wooden" and foreign; listening to sermons is a struggle. Rebecca has found that her congregants worship more fully when words are somehow combined with visual art and participatory actions.

Protestants especially have a tendency to consider words and thoughts more spiritual than the body and physical things.[1] But this is a disincarnational attitude. The Word became flesh. *We* are flesh. Words are always embedded in a physical reality, an overall service shape, the sights and sounds and sensory effects of the worshiping assembly, no matter how plain. So it's worth considering how words can work in harmony, and not disharmony, with other forms of meaning-making in worship.

## Structure Itself Has Meaning

Very few things are absolutely *required* for Christian worship, and (naturally) Christians of different persuasions disagree on what these indispensable basics might be. Scholarship on ancient Christian practices reveals that already in the early church there was a broad range of common worship practices. But there is widening consensus that what seem to have been consistent across the range in the early church were these elements: readings, preaching, prayers, a shared meal, and an offering (including the distribution of the meal to those absent).

Over the centuries, the church gathered wisdom about how to create worship practices that in themselves shape Christian devotion over the long haul. Church leaders recognized early on that what we do in worship and the order in which we do it convey messages about God, us, and our relationship. Form has meaning, that is to say. Though recent scholarship has made the picture somewhat more complex, liturgical scholars increasingly agree that by the second, and certainly by the third century, much of the church was worshiping weekly in a recognizable shape that persists in many traditions to this day.[2]

Rooted in Scripture (esp. Acts 2:42, Luke 24, and also the division of Jesus's life into a teaching phase and a sacramental/sacrificial phase), that basic shape is often referred to as the "fourfold *ordo*." (*Ordo* simply means "order.") The *ordo* includes (1) Gathering, (2) Proclamation of the Word, (3) the Eucharist, and (4) Sending. This shape has a particular meaning (see "The Drama of the Liturgy"), and when experienced over and over across many years, it begins to shape a person's soul. We learn that God acts first, that we are part of a larger body, that God communicates with us, cares for us and nourishes us, and gives us a purpose in the world.

Interestingly, these ancient shapes collapsed somewhat in American frontier and free-church worship beginning in the eighteenth century. The Eucharist dropped out, and the basic pattern became singing, preaching, and perhaps an altar call. This shape has meaning as well. The singing serves the function of gathering and is

---

### The Drama of the Liturgy

"This [fourfold] structure is not just an orderly way to organize the service; it actually tells a story that goes something like this: In the midst of our life in the world, we are called into God's presence. There in awe and wonder, praise and confession, we are spoken to by God; called afresh to be God's people; given encouragement, wisdom, forgiveness, and healing; and invited to come to the heavenly banquet where, in the spirit of thanksgiving, we join the saints of all times and places in a great feast of joy. Then, having been fed by God, we are sent back into the world as people renewed, to love and serve in God's name."[3]

—*Thomas G. Long*

generally meant to prepare listeners for the sermon. When an altar call is included, this emphasizes the need to respond decisively to the sermon and therefore tells of a God who seeks and saves the lost and invites a response in the worshiper's will and action. In any case, this service shape gives priority to the worshiper's *experience* of worship, particularly an individual emotional experience that leads to an individual action. The service's goal is to create an emotional state in the worshipers: conviction of sin, persuasion to make a decision for Christ, and so on.

Pentecostal, neo-Pentecostal, and contemporary praise-and-worship services are similar to this frontier model. The goal of worship in these styles, generally speaking, is to bring worshipers into an experience, though that experience may or may not be focused toward a particular decision. Instead, the goal is for worshipers to feel the ecstasy of the Spirit, intimacy with God, the joy of praise. The experience may be aimed more specifically at healing, well-being, attentive listening, or perhaps social action.

These are all broad generalizations, but they reveal a basic dynamic in worship: the structure of worship has both objective and subjective components. The objective component is the meaning conveyed by the shape of the service, and the subjective component is how we experience it, both rationally and emotionally. Whatever your congregation's accustomed pattern and style, it is important to consider both these dimensions. Shaping a service to mean all the right things and disregarding how it feels to people can result in dry, wooden worship. On the other hand, spending all your energy trying to create a particular emotional experience for worshipers risks reducing worship to manipulation and suggesting that the spiritual life is fundamentally about *feeling* a certain way.

Though the Spirit can work through many worship shapes, the ancient fourfold *ordo* has especially great authority and meaning as the basic shape of worship. We can find comfort in its emphasis on God's initiating action in worship. And

---

### Beware a Fixation on Feeling

"The Bible speaks, of course, of times when God is experienced 'in the present moment,' but the Bible also tells the truth about times when the face of God is hidden from human view and God's presence is not immediately felt. In the Old Testament, the hiddenness of God is one of the characteristics that separates Yahwism from the worship of Baal, the Canaanite fertility god. Baal was always present, always ready to provide powerful religious experiences. . . . If one desires an intimate encounter with the holy at every service, then go to the Temple of Baal. Yahweh, the true and living God, sometimes withdraws from present experience. In sum, God does not always move us; and everything that moves us is not God."[4]

—*Thomas G. Long*

those of us who have come to love weekly communion testify that this practice is a life-sustaining and profound uniting of Word and flesh. Moreover, because the fourfold *ordo* is so commonly used in churches around the world in thousands of variations, it has important ecumenical resonances, enabling unity amid great diversity. Finally, when done well, the subjective experience of the *ordo* can be just as rich, emotional, beautiful, comforting, and energizing as the more experientially aimed models—more so, one could argue, because a wider range of emotive responses is expected and allowed.

The important thing is to acknowledge that worship words fit into an overall structure that has meaning in itself, as a structure. As worship planners, the goal is to understand what structure your church is already using, consider why your church is using it, and strive to use words in order to make that shape more transparent and effective for worshipers. Anything we do repeatedly becomes a ritual, and rituals have their effects on us. It's worth thinking about those effects.

## Unity, Flow, and Proportionality

Understanding the overall shape of a service and its purpose and meaning enables us to better create unity, flow, and proportionality in a service. As worship scholar Robert Webber points out, worship is a narrative.[5] It draws us into the grand, cosmic story of redemption by creating a small echo-story every week. Worship musician and author Greg Scheer compares worship to art, noting especially the time-related features characteristic of artfully told stories: "In some ways worship . . . is an art form that unfolds over time; therefore, it uses similar artistic devices—structure, flow, repetition, contrast, and development."[6] Scheer is quick to point out that the "ultimate creator" of this art form is the Holy Spirit. As worship leaders, however, we are welcomed into this creative process. The Spirit uses our skills and creativity to orchestrate this form through which the Spirit nurtures the people of God.

### Unity

Unity in a worship service creates a kind of beauty, but it also helps people understand and recall the main messages of a service. The unifying element might be the Scripture passage or story or the sermon theme as it interprets the passage. In churches that celebrate the liturgical year, a service's theme might be inspired by the particular day in the church year: Christ the King Sunday or Pentecost, for instance.

### Boy Scout Sunday

I remember once guest-preaching a sermon in late November, when both the seasonal changes and the liturgical year suggested a passage from Isaiah 25 about the cyclical return of death into our lives and the promise God makes to one day stop the cycle and put an end to death for good. After the service I was taken to task by an elder in the church for not preaching about "nature" when I must surely have known that this particular Sunday was designated "Boy Scout Sunday." Even though we inserted into the service ten minutes devoted to prayer and thanksgiving for scouts and their leaders, this gentleman felt short-changed when the sermon did not fit the most important theme of the day, from his point of view.

This story suggests the importance of choosing themes for worship services with some theological sensitivity. Weekly worship is one of the most significant ways that Christians mark time—anticipating key events, celebrating them when they come, and exploring their significance afterward. It makes some sense, then, for Christians to locate these key events not in the Hallmark calendar, or the consumer calendar, but in Jesus's story, the narrative told in the church year.[7]

Worship planners give worshipers a lovely gift when they seek ways to weave a particular theme throughout a service—without becoming overbearing or trite. This thematic unity can be created through repeating words, perhaps key words straight from Scripture, and of course by choosing songs that fit the theme. But nonverbal elements are important too. During Pentecost season at our church, for instance, we drape dramatic swaths of red and orange fabric from our exposed ceiling structure. We use a communion set featuring flame images. Our dancers wear red and orange ribbons that trail along in the "wind" they create as they dance. And we surround the sanctuary with the words of Galatians 5:22–23 (the fruit of the Spirit) in dozens of languages.

Seasons like Pentecost and Christmas have obvious symbolic elements to draw out. But any unifying theme can be enhanced with nonverbal elements. A service focused on the story of Jesus stilling the storm in Mark 4, for example, could feature images of stormy seas projected on slides. Another important feature of this passage is the persistence of questions: both the disciples and Jesus ask profound questions of one another. Perhaps the question mark could become an important visual symbol for the service as well, or a face clearly bearing a quizzical expression.

### Don't Overdo It

"The focusing theme should echo through a service, like a musical theme weaves through several movements of a symphony, repeated at key points, but not in every measure."[8]

—Ruth C. Duck

This would honor the questions of the disciples and of our faith life as important and worth pondering. After all, in the passage, Jesus does not give the disciples simple, obvious answers—not in words, anyway. Instead, he challenges them with yet another question and a dramatic miracle.

### Flow

If worship is the enactment of a meaningful narrative, this gives worship leaders a good reason to attend to the details of a service's flow. People need help in understanding where they are in the story. Moments of awkward or abrupt transition can be distracting.

In my composition courses and Ron's preaching courses, we teach students about the importance of "metadiscourse," the signal words that help readers and listeners understand where they are in the overall structure of an essay or sermon. These are words like *therefore, then, as a result, on the other hand*—the signposts for a reader's progress through the flow of ideas. Worship ought to have graceful metadiscourse as well.

Sometimes it seems to worshipers that one element follows another in the worship sequence because . . . well, because that's how we do it. We take an offering next because the offering always comes after the sermon. We play this song next because it's in the same key as the last song. Sometimes we have no good reason to follow one thing with the next, and sometimes we have a good reason that few people ever think about. But each act of worship can gain richer meaning not only when the sequence has a thoughtful purpose but also when that purpose is made transparent for worshipers.

For instance, we pray before reading the Bible in order to ask the Spirit to help us understand what is read. This can be signaled in the words of the prayer, of course, but also in a simple spoken invitation to prayer: "Please join me in praying for the guidance of the Spirit as we open the Scripture together." The offering comes after the sermon in many service orders because it is part of our grateful response to God's revelation: we respond with ministry in the world, and our checks and bills are a symbol of dedication to that ministry. This might be made transparent to the congregation with a few words in the bulletin, on the screen, or spoken aloud: "God has spoken to us. We give thanks and promise our grateful service with these tokens of our lives and work."

Transition points between the elements of worship are wonderful teaching moments for worshipers. When worship planners have thought carefully through the sequence, they can help worshipers see how each act of worship fits into the narrative arc of the service and becomes a richer part of each worshiper's devotion. Even in very loosely structured, more improvisational services, worshipers need

> ### The "In Between Words"—A Few Guidelines
>
> When speaking in worship . . .
>
> - Don't *instruct* people what to do next; instead *invite* them to participate in the act of worship.
> - When introducing a song or reading, give a foretaste of the next text, or refer to the preceding one.
> - Let people know how each act fits into the dialogue of worship and the theme of the service.
> - Attend to the emotional contours of the service—what's happening in your heart and in the hearts of the congregation.[9]

to know why they are doing what, when. A few simple words from the leadership can provide that metadiscourse.

Of course, the emotional ebb and flow of a service is just as important as the theological reasoning behind the sequence of elements. When our family lived in England, we attended services several times at a wonderful Anglican church in central London. We loved many things about worship at this small parish church, especially participating in communion there. But one thing we could never figure out. After we had all been served communion in a circle around the altar, we returned in quiet joy to our pews ready to burst out in praise and gratitude. But instead we were presented with the announcements, or "notices" as they are called in the UK. The church had numerous active ministries and plenty of members who were eager to talk about them, so "notices" could go on for fifteen minutes. By the time the last person finished the last announcement and sat down, all our praise-energy had drained away, and we struggled to stir up enough enthusiasm to make it through the final hymn and recessional.

As Greg Scheer points out, some worship elements are naturally "dynamic" and others are "static."[10] That is to say, some elements have forward energy toward the next thing, while other elements give the feel of closure at the end. An upbeat praise song feels dynamic—we gain emotional energy while singing it and want that energy to lead to the next thing. A sermon, however compelling, is static in most worship traditions in the sense that it comes to a closure, and we instinctively need a pause before beginning another energy cycle. Announcements, important as they are, are definitely static. (See " 'Go in Peace and Be Sure to Buy Raffle Tickets': Dealing with Announcements" on p. 36 for more on the announcement problem.)

Arranging the emotional landscape of a service requires practice, careful observation of worshipers' responses, and no small amount of good instinct. When worship leaders sense a problem with flow in a service, it may have to do with a lack of thoughtful purpose in the worship order. But it may also be a matter of emotional flow. (For more on the emotional landscaping of sermons, see "Feel It with Me Now" on p. 96.)

### Proportionality

What we spend the most time on is likely to be what we value most. This is true in life as well as in worship. Time is another nonverbal element that must be used carefully. Proportionality in worship simply means that we give each element its due amount of time in the overall hour, or hour-and-a-half, or two hours of the service. The problem might be, however, that not all worshipers value various parts of worship as other worshipers do. Some might complain about an overly long children's message or too many praise songs or a skimpy sermon. In my own tradition, some pastors are reluctant to celebrate communion more often—even though the leadership would like to do so—because they are afraid congregants will complain that it "takes too much time" or that "the service is too long now."

Here again, the challenge is to understand what congregants instinctively value when considering how to apportion time to each element. Some churches think nothing of a seventy-five-minute service with a twenty-minute communion sequence because they agree as a congregation on the high value of weekly communion. In other traditions, an hour-long sermon is the norm. In the Orthodox Church, people think nothing of standing up for an entire two-hour service. Some congregations expect a full twenty minutes of singing at the opening of the service and will feel cheated if they don't get it.

Worship leaders need to understand that any long-term change or even temporary shift in the proportions of time allotted to a worship element will feel to congregants like a change in how each thing is valued, and that may indeed be true. Good reasons for the change and clear communication about it will ease these concerns.

## Everything Communicates Something

In worship, everything communicates something: the architecture of the space, the art on the walls, the arrangement of the chairs or pews, the style of music, the skin color of the people up front, and the words. As the story of the young woman reminds us (see "The God of Abundant Grace" on the next page), what is lacking or missing communicates too.

As you think about words in your worship service, think about how what you say might be undermined or supported by other components of the worship experience at your church. We once attended an Easter service at a small church in which the traditional hymns rightly celebrated the glory and joy of the day.

### The God of Abundant Grace

I was preaching on Isaiah 55: "Everyone who thirsts, come . . . eat what is good, and delight yourselves in rich food!" (Isa. 55:1–2 NRSV). The communion table had been prepared to underscore the message of overflowing grace that comes from a God of great abundance. So we did not have small pieces of cubed white bread, or flat wafers; instead we had a large ceramic plate, piled high to overflowing with large loaves of multigrain bread. And instead of individual plastic cups on a sterling silver tray (what a plain-spoken friend of mine calls "shot glasses on a hubcap"), we had a large pitcher filled with good wine and matching common cups to pass around.

After the service, a student came to me, weeping with joy to tell me how much the service had meant to her. "I never really understood before," she said, "about God's overflowing 'steadfast, sure love'; about 'abundant mercy' and what that means—that it's not just barely enough, but way way way more than we could ever need."

"But you've been part of the church your whole life," I said, a little surprised. "You've heard hundreds upon hundreds of sermons . . . have you never heard this before?"

"I'd heard it," she responded. "I've just never *seen* it."

However, the PowerPoint slides with the hymn lyrics and announcements were horribly festooned with little animated GIF files, including a little pink alien creature with big ears carrying a sign saying "Happy Easter." Using nonverbal elements is a good idea. But in this case, the message these elements conveyed was that the Risen Lord is really *cute*!

To give a positive example, a preacher at Fuller Seminary chapel once spoke about being "acquainted with grief." She was a psychologist and spoke of people's griefs and sorrows. But while she spoke, behind her were projected a rotating sequence of medieval paintings of the crucifixion. Jesus's silent companionship in suffering gave context to everything she was saying about human suffering, even before she made the connection directly in words.

What these examples suggest is that not all nonverbal elements are equally fitting or effective. Fortunately, we are seeing a new emphasis on art in worship and new roles for artists. Artists have for a long time been misunderstood and held suspect in many Protestant circles, but that attitude is shifting dramatically. Now we are seeing how much we need people who are gifted in the creative uses of nonverbal forms. Musicians have gained obvious and dramatic importance in Protestant worship in recent decades—almost too much, as now we are seeing concerns about a kind of worship musician celebrity culture. But people are also realizing that we need our sculptors, architects, textile artists, dancers, painters, and designers of all kinds to help us engage our whole selves in worship.

If you haven't done so already, now may be a good time to seek out the artistic talent in your congregation and seek ways to get artists involved in worship preparation and leadership. (For more ideas on how to do so, see "Recommended

> **Pulpit Presence**
>
> I once had a pastor who had a problem with pacing back and forth while he preached. Normally this isn't a problem; a little physical liveliness in a preacher can be a good thing if it doesn't prove too distracting. Alas, in this case it *was* distracting—*meaningfully* distracting. That is to say, his pacing had purpose: when he would stand behind the pulpit, he would usually be speaking about Scripture. He was a good exegete, and he would explain what the Bible said and apply it to our lives. But then he would step from behind the pulpit and its implied authority, and stand to the side or walk back and forth across the chancel area, telling the congregation about the latest insight he gleaned from an Ann Landers column or a prime-time sitcom. Deb and I agreed that he could move from being a good preacher to a great one if he would simply tether himself to the pulpit and, by doing so, keep his focus on the Word.

Resources.") Find time to reflect regularly on your own services to discern competing messages between words and other elements. Find time to visit other churches to see what they say with their words and other things.


## Conclusion

While bringing our best efforts to worship—seeking excellence and authenticity—might seem overwhelming, we have much to comfort and support us. The explosion of worship resources in recent years means that you can find informed, skilled assistance on almost any aspect of worship. Moreover, as Ron and I have seen over and over again in our teaching and observations, small changes make a big difference. And we know that we can rest in the Spirit, knowing that all we do, however imperfect, is perfected by the Spirit, through the faithfulness of Christ.

In this assurance, we can go forward to give our best and even fail. The model of the Psalms gives us confidence that God welcomes our boldness in worship. As theologian Walter Brueggemann writes:

> Israel's prayer—even though stylized and therefore in some ways predictable—is rarely safe, seldom conventional, and never routine. It is characteristically daring, outrageous, and adventuresome. Israel's prayer is indeed limit-language that pushes to the edge of social possibility, of cultural permit, of religious acceptability, and of imaginative experimentation.[11]

As we remembered at the beginning of this book, leading worship is a humbling and thrilling privilege. May the Spirit work through your words and work to bless and transform the sons and daughters of God.

## Exercises

1. Greg Scheer speaks of three basic forms for worship service structure: liturgical, thematic, and experiential. Read pages 87–109 of *The Art of Worship* and think about your own congregation's typical pattern. Which of the three basic forms most closely describes your practice? Why do you do things this way? Tradition? Imitation? A studied decision some time ago or recently? Do you think worshipers have a basic understanding of the reasons behind your worship order?

2. Attend a worship service and consider the nonverbal messages you perceive. What does the space tell you about what this congregation values? What visual elements are present? What do worshipers do with their bodies? Were there particular moments when you noticed that nonverbal elements either intentionally supported or unintentionally undermined what was said?

3. Attend a worship service and consider the way time is allotted. What is given the most time in the service? the next most? the least? Were there moments where you felt that something went too long or got short-changed? What might be some reasons that this happened?

4. Watch a video of yourself preaching and consider how your body helps or hinders your message. Does your body convey authority? friendliness? anxiousness?

# Practical Advice for All Occasions

## *Ten Tips*

The exercises and suggestions in the chapters are mostly concerned with larger issues of imagery and approach. But what about the nitty-gritty, practical matters of which words to put in front of which other words, which words to take out and leave in?

The tips here are meant to help with that practical side of developing worship words. Not only do they apply to words you might prepare or improvise in worship, but they also can be used to choose good words from printed or recorded resources and to edit or adapt where appropriate.

### 1. 'Tis a Gift to Be Simple

Worship words are public speech, offered to all and owned by all. They are not meant to display the eloquence of, or solicit praise for, the speaker. Therefore, particularly in prayers, avoid overworking any one point, idea, or metaphor.

> O God, you refresh us with life-giving rain on a late summer's day, and bless us with a crisp hint of autumn's way. Our alleluias are but an echo of your voice, a ripple upon the waters from your splash, an aroma that lingers from your presence, a satisfying aftertaste from your banquet.[1]

This example comes from a longer, lovely prayer. The vividness and specificity of the whole prayer are admirable, although this particular section might be too much. The idea expressed is that our praise responds to signs of God's revelation in nature as well as worship. If the prayer were spoken by a leader *and* printed or projected *and* the phrases appeared on separate lines, then it might be possible for a congregation to perceive and appreciate the images. If, however, the congregation were asked to speak this, or if they were asked only to hear this without visual help, then the piling on of metaphors—all of which are intriguing—would probably be too much. In public prayer, the people need to grasp the words as their own the first time through. Simpler would be better in this case.

## 2. Reflect Abundance

On the other hand, vivid and specific vocabulary reflects the richness and beauty of creation and of God's revelation to us. Choose words for their appealing sound and for their ability to create pictures in the listener's mind. Less is more, though. A few carefully chosen details help to focus people's attention and keep their imaginations awake while not overwhelming them.

> God, we thank you for nature.
>   (general and bland)

> God, we thank you for autumn leaves and bright sunshine.
>   (specific, telling details that remind us of many more beauties beyond)

## 3. Omit Unnecessary Words

This old writing chestnut should be observed in moderation. Efficiency of expression is not the absolute, highest good, even in public speech. Nevertheless, sloppy language full of fluff and filler weakens our ability to communicate and to let words *mean*. Improvised words are, naturally, more subject to fluff and filler because we need time to think of what to say next. But we can gain time in other, better ways: preparation, speaking more slowly, and allowing a little silence, for instance. Without making language stiffer or more formal, we can still make each word more meaningful and powerful.

> Dear Lord Jesus, we just want to come before you today praising you and thanking you for all your goodness.
>   (the key ideas, praise and thank, are buried amid unnecessary phrases)

Dear Jesus, together we praise and thank you for your goodness.
(the key words emerge and invite appropriate vocal emphasis)

When preparing written prayers, spend time specifically revising to eliminate fluff and filler. Anything spoken or sung by a congregation requires ruthless revision, particularly songs that will be repeated. The dearly loved song "As the Deer," by Martin Nystrom, for example, for all its virtues, still contains this verse:

> You're my friend and You are my brother,
> even though You are a King.
> I love You more than any other,
> so much more than anything!*

The effort to portray Jesus as friend, brother, and King is laudable. This is a nice instance of moderating the KINGAFAP system discussed in chapter 7. If only the rest of the verse had the same heft. The last line, especially, adds nothing either to the concepts presented or to the emotional tone or to the sound pleasures of the verse. Unfortunately, filler lines like this become more tiresome the more we have to sing them.

### 4. Replace Jarring or Tangled Words

Laurence Hull Stookey, in his excellent book on praying in public, presents an example prayer of confession containing this line:

> Have mercy upon us, O Lord, for we lack the quality of magnanimity.

The prayer is supposed to be spoken by the congregation together, but, as Stookey aptly observes: "'Quality of magnanimity' is a phrase no congregation should ever be asked to utter aloud."[2] He notes that while people probably know what *magnanimity* means, they would be unlikely to use the word, so it feels artificial to ask them to pray with it. Worse than that, it's an extremely difficult word to say, especially with a group.

If people are being asked to speak words aloud, those words must have manageable sounds and rhythms. (See #9 below.) Words can be troublesome for other reasons as well. They can be jarring or inappropriate in their register or collocation. For example:

---

*Martin Nystrom, "As the Deer," © 1984 Maranatha Praise, Inc., admin. by Music Services, Inc. All rights reserved. Used by permission.

Dear God, please help us to maximize our mission potentials. Bless our objectives and goals and help us to reach them in timely fashion so that we can saturate our region with your gospel.

This example, taken from chapter 6, borrows language strongly associated with management and business and therefore it feels jarringly out of place in worship.

### 5. Address God Thoughtfully

This applies to prayers as well as liturgical words and songs. In chapter 7, we discussed using a variety of biblical names, titles, and images for God in order to honor the fullness of God's revelation to us.

Grammatically speaking, there are several ways to do this.

a. Address God with a name.
    *Wonderful Counselor, we pray for your wisdom ...*
   This works well with familiar names and titles for God. When using less-familiar titles or images for God, the effect might be rather odd:
    *Farmer, we pray that you ...*
   Though God is depicted as a farmer in several parables, "Farmer" by itself does not have the established status of more-common names for God, and seems to lack reverence.

b. Use a comparison.
   If a direct address to God using the name or image seems weird, use a comparison instead.
    *God, we know that you are like a farmer who plants the seed of your Word in this world ...*

c. Use an adjective or prepositional attribution.
   Another helpful strategy is to use attributes of God as adjectives:
    *Compassionate God, comfort your people today ...*
    *Righteous God, we long for your justice to be revealed ...*
    *God of wisdom, speak into our confusion ...*

### 6. Keep Address Consistent

Because worship is a dialogic encounter between God and God's people, we have to signal the direction of the conversation through forms of address. Sometimes we address God, sometimes (through Scripture) God addresses us, and sometimes we address one another. At any given point in a service, it should be clear who is talking to whom.

Consistency of address has a tendency to fall apart during intercessory prayers when inexperienced leaders forget that they are speaking to God and begin informing the congregation:

> Dear God, please heal Bernard McClellan, who was admitted to the hospital last night for tests on his heart. We expect that he'll be OK, God, but we won't hear the test results until Tuesday.

The news about Mr. McClellan is better conveyed before the prayer, with the leader addressing the congregation. God already knows what has happened to this man, and there's no need to inform God further. Of course, God knows everything we ever pray. But in prayer, we focus on what we are asking God to do, on what we are thanking God for doing, or on acclaiming God's divine qualities—not on rehearsing information.

Every part of the service requires some thought as to who is addressing whom—including every song we sing, as noted in chapter 2. This allows us to signal to the congregation what part they are playing in the dialogue.

### 7. Focus on Verbs

This is good advice about any kind of writing. Writing full of vigorous verbs feels interesting and vital. Writing with a preponderance of bland verbs feels static and boring. For any piece of writing—a sermon, a song, a prayer—a helpful but possibly sobering exercise is to circle all the verbs. If you find a high proportion of to-be verbs (*is, am, are, was, were, be, being, been*) or other bland verbs such as *have, become, let,* then your writing could use a verb makeover. (Distinguish to-be verbs, however, from helping verbs such as *was* in *was squandering.* In this case, the *was* is simply part of the past progressive form of *squander.* If your technical knowledge of grammar is sketchy, ask a friendly local grammarian for help.)

The three verses of "Come, Thou Fount of Every Blessing," for instance, feature twenty different verbs, most of them interesting:

| | | | |
|---|---|---|---|
| come | teach | sought | wander |
| tune | praise | rescue | feel |
| sing | raise | interpose | leave |
| cease | hope | constrain | take |
| call | arrive | bind | seal |

The vivid and varied verbs in this song are, in my opinion, one reason so many people find this song both beautiful and deeply meaningful.

In prayers, pay attention to imperative verbs. Laurence Hull Stookey cites the example of the Lord's Prayer as our model and permission for using direct verbs in prayer:

> Notice what Jesus did not say:
>> Let us today find our daily bread.
>> We hope that we may be forgiven, as we forgive those who sin against us.
>> Be with us in the time of trial.
>> May we escape evil.[3]

Instead, Stookey notes, Jesus used the imperative forms: *give, forgive, save, deliver* (more precisely, the New Testament records the Greek equivalents). Similarly, in our prayers, we might praise God for aspects of God's nature, and we might thank God for many things. But when we are asking God to act, the verb should have a prominent place in the structure of the line:

> God, we ask that you would please make a change in this community with regard
>> to our racist attitudes.
>> ("Make a change" is weak and buried in the sentence.)
> God, drive out the racism in our community.
>> ("Drive out" is much stronger and is given an emphasized position.)

When we emphasize verbs in prayer, we also signal a crucial theological truth about God: God *acts* in our world.

Focusing on verbs also helps weed out excessive *nominalizations*. These are verbs that have been made into nouns, such as *sanctification* from *sanctify*. Writing that contains numerous prepositions and words that end in -*tion* or -*ization* is probably suffering from excessive nominalization. Too much nominalization is very difficult to follow when reading and even more difficult when listening.

> We need to achieve the realization that our state of sinfulness is in direct violation
>> of God's plan of redemption, which is to bring us salvation.
>> *What?!*
> We must understand: although we are sinners, God desires to save us.
>> *Oh, I get it!*

## 8. Think about Structure

In chapter 2, we discussed how to plan and signal the overall structure of a worship service. Structure helps us understand and respond to the theological basis of worship: God's call, our response. Structure also, happily, helps people stay attentive. The same is true of elements within the service.

- Sermons or messages that have a thoughtful structure, gracefully signaled to listeners, help people follow along and remember what they have heard.
- Songs have structure too. Composers of song lyrics should consider how a particular song develops a theme or otherwise progresses from one verse or section to the next.
- Prayers. Even short prayers should have some kind of structure. The collect (see "The Collect Form: Names to Verbs" on p. 159) is the simplest and most flexible. Longer prayers, such as intercessory or pastoral prayers, need careful preparation. Even if such prayers are improvised, the pray-er should prepare ahead of time how she would like to organize the prayer so that the congregation can pray along attentively.[4]

### 9. Limit the Number of Syllables in Words and Phrases

A skilled speaker preaching or praying can use longer phrases and more complex sentence structures, particularly if the congregation is used to complex language. However, when writing words meant to be spoken by the congregation, simplicity and clarity must reign. This does not mean that words must be plain and dull, however.

Stookey recommends actually calculating the average ratio of syllables per word and aiming for a ratio of between 1.3 and 1.5. More simply, when writing words intended to be spoken in unison, stick with one- and two-syllable words most of the time, and use longer words perhaps once per line, if that.

As for line length, people generally speak in phrases of between four and ten syllables. People can speak pretty well in unison if it is clear to them how the words are grouped into phrases. Amazingly, people speaking together will naturally reflect these groupings with matched pauses and inflections. If the phrase groupings are too long or unclear, however, the unison speech will disintegrate into mumbles.

Here's an excerpt from a prayer that would *not* be appropriate for unison:

> Lord, grant us to meet with tranquillity of soul all that may befall us this day.
> Grant that we may obey your holy will every hour of this day;
> guide us and maintain us in all things;
> reveal to us your will for us and those around us.[5]

Besides being generally wordy, the phrases are simply too long. Even breaking them up on the page wouldn't help. Here's an edited version:

Lord, grant us tranquility
to receive the day's gifts.
Teach us to obey your holy will.
Guide us, protect us,
and reveal your purposes
for ourselves and others.

In this version, the phrases are between five and nine syllables. By breaking the lines at the phrases, we enable the congregation to know exactly how to group the words. Only two of twenty-eight words are more than two syllables. Moreover, the whole thing is simpler and more direct than the first version.

### 10. Listen, Listen, Listen

For those who speak extemporaneously, the best way to evaluate the clarity and effectiveness of your words is—however horrifying this might seem—to listen to tapes of yourself. You can't eliminate problems ahead of time this way, but you can learn and improve for the next time.

For those preparing written resources for themselves or others to speak in worship, you can test-drive the prayer or litany ahead of time by reading it aloud or having someone else do it—and listening carefully. If anything is awkward or jarring, revise.

Either way, you are listening for the aesthetic dimension of words especially. Do the words *feel* comfortable, even delightful to say? Do the sounds of the words fit the meaning and tone desired? Are the sentences too complex to be understood on a first hearing? The time required to revise well is service well rendered on behalf of the worshiping people.

APPENDIX 2

# Worship Planning Process

**Efficiency versus Synergy**

Sometimes when I'm asked to be a guest preacher at a church, the worship planning team consists of just two people—the guest preacher (me) and the church secretary.[1] Here's a summary of the typical three-minute worship planning conversation:

> Secretary: "If you just tell me the sermon title and the three songs you want to sing, we'll be done."
> Me: "Uh, OK."

On the other hand, I've experienced highly collaborative worship planning, and I know that involving more people means inviting complications. Here's a summary of forty-five full minutes of discussion that occurred late in the evening when everyone was tired and cranky:

> Sarah: "Can't we please sing [name of undeniably wretched worship song here] this week?"
> Rest of group: "No."
> Bill: "Why can't our Advent services be more upbeat?"
> Rest of group: "We've been over this."

Involving only a couple people in worship planning can be wonderfully efficient. But sometimes efficiency isn't necessarily a virtue—a little team-based diversity of opinion might be welcome, and it might give the congregation greater ownership in worship. However, the synergy of team-based worship planning needs careful management in order to fulfill its promise.

So what is the *best* way to organize the worship planning process? Here I offer a few observations, along with a model to assist in analyzing your own congregation's worship planning routine.

### Flow Charts

A helpful exercise in thinking about worship planning is to draw a flow chart—a diagrammatic representation—of the worship planning process in your church. Use boxes, circles, arrows, and dotted lines. You don't have to know anything about official flow chart protocols or standard function shapes. Just think on paper about each step in your congregation's practice. Is it a fairly simple procedure, involving maybe three people: pastor, musician, and church secretary?

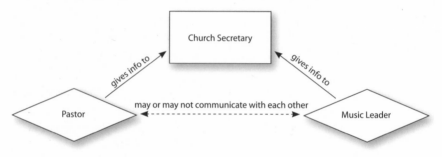

Or is it complex, involving layers of decision making and revision, calling on the skills of preachers, pastoral musicians, multiple worship teams, graphic designers, hospitality professionals, and tech support personnel?

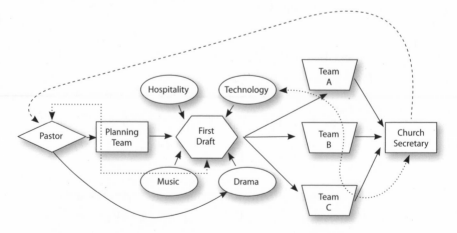

We often think about the *product* that emerges from worship planning and the *personnel* involved in it. Sometimes we reflect on the *principles* that guide our planning. But seldom do we give serious consideration to the *process* by which the Holy Spirit moves through both tradition and innovation to create the worship services enacted by our congregations on Sundays.

## Planning Styles

Whatever your own planning style, it's likely dominated by one of two organizational philosophies: collaborative or centralized. Each has its strengths and weaknesses.

If your church's planning process is primarily *centralized*, decision making is concentrated in one or two people (usually the pastor and/or minister of music). These folks often have the necessary theological and/or musical expertise to make decisions on behalf of the congregation. This creates a very efficient process—a definite benefit, given the relentless recurrence of Sunday morning every seven days. At the same time, the concentration of power can lead to authoritarian attitudes, a humdrum sameness that comes from limited sources of creative input, or both.

On the other hand, if your church's process is primarily *collaborative*, it is characterized by input from a broader congregational constituency. More people feel a part of the process, which increases ownership, expands the range of ministry gifts used, lightens the per-person workload, and increases overall creativity. At the same time, it also increases the likelihood that suggestions, while creative, are unfitting if not downright heterodox. And efficiency goes right out the stained-glass window.

The trick, then, is to find a *process* that incorporates the virtues of these two models while minimizing their drawbacks.

## Caveats

I have been working for many years with various groups to develop worship planning models that combine the virtues of efficiency and collaboration. But before I present what I have learned, a few caveats are in order. First, what I describe here is an idealized rather than an actual model. That is to say, it's the target toward which I've tried to help people aim, fully understanding that we won't always quite get there.

Second, since I've worked a great deal with undergraduates and seminary students, this model incorporates a significant pedagogical component. However, this is an acknowledgment of reality in congregations as well: few people in a congregation are trained in worship. Sometimes even the pastors have very little theological or practical background in worship planning.

Finally, the model I present here may or may not be right for your congregation; your own context may require something altogether different. My hope is that when you analyze your own situation, this model may inspire you to come up with a decidedly *better* worship-planning process. If you do, I'd love to hear about it.

## A Five-Part Planning Process

Whatever your situation, I believe the worship planning process has at least five distinct stages: Previse, Devise, Revise, Realize, and Analyze. Most congregations accomplish all five, even if by accident, but few are intentional about each stage. For example, a congregation may put lots of energy into the second stage (devise) and next to nothing into the fourth and fifth stages (realize and analyze). It may be that a bit of focused tweaking would be all that's needed to greatly improve your congregation's worship planning. I'll describe each stage and then offer some final comments.

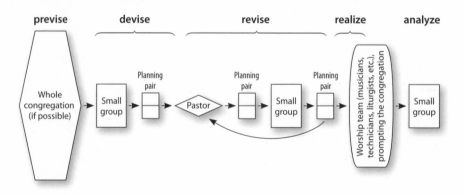

## Previse

This first stage is about soliciting input from as broad a group as possible. You could invite anyone who wishes to participate to a post-service potluck at which you discuss the next season's services. Begin with a bit of education about worship basics (see the above chart) and then brainstorm about themes, songs, drama, art, dance, and so on. Make use of a broad range of resources, including magazines, Web-based material, other worship services, and the like. Don't worry at all about straining out the good ideas from the bad. Write everything down. Use what the Willow Creekers call an "Umbrella of Mercy" (no idea is a bad idea). Use butcher paper as tablecloths, and provide the crayons.

The idea here is to include the maximum number of people to create the maximum amount of synergy, generating the maximum number of good ideas with the maximum amount of congregational ownership. This is a great way to invite participation from gifted and interested people who, for whatever reason, can't be on a more time-intensive planning team. This may also be a way to dissipate budding "worship war" tensions before they gain momentum. Let each congregational constituency be heard. And just as important, let each hear *each other*—so try to arrange for some kind of mixed seating.

A meeting like this is also an excellent opportunity to teach. We often assume our congregations know fundamentals, but that's not always the case; congregations need reminders about the meaning and purpose of worship. They may not be eager to come to an education-hour workshop on this topic, but they'll jump at the chance to voice their opinion about which songs to sing, what themes to address, and how worship should be conducted. A yummy chicken-and-rice dish or pasta salad doesn't hurt either. You might arrange a meeting like this two to six times per year.

### Devise

Here is where a small group of winnowing "experts" begins to separate the wheat from the chaff. When I taught worship at Calvin College, I met weekly with a group of twelve worship apprentices, each of whom was responsible for a different area of expertise. You can use your own small group of gifted (mostly lay) individuals: one person who's gifted with words, another who has an artistic bent, a musician or two, a dramatist, a technician, a pastor or theologian, someone who prays well, someone who naturally thinks about making people feel welcome, and so on. If you're short of specialists, select people who can wear multiple hats. Look at the vast material generated at the previous stage and begin to filter. Once a broad direction is chosen, assign particular services to individuals or pairs of worship planners. They work on their own time and then come back with a first draft of a particular service to show to the key decision-making individual. This draft should include service basics: a sermon theme and text, a focus statement for some important prayers, and some possible songs to use at various points in the service (for confession, for dedication, for praise, etc.). Maybe the draft includes a graphic identity (e.g., a rock) or the main idea for the drama, and so on. Whatever is included here, the pieces should fit into a structure that is recognizable to your congregation. Don't try to do *everything* different every week. (See chapter 4, especially "Creative Burnout" and "The Virtues of Repetition.")

## Revise

Here's where things really heat up. At the revision stage, the decision-making person (often the pastor) looks over what's presented and offers suggestions to improve a particular worship plan. The planners then incorporate these suggestions and present the revised plan to the small group at their next meeting. Further revisions suggested by the small group are folded into the evolving plan and presented by the responsible pair to the centralized authority figure, and the revision cycle begins again. The more this cycle can be repeated, the better the final plan. Most congregations don't revise at all (except in the moment—"Oops! Guess we're skipping the Apostles' Creed this week!"); but in this model, revision is the key step where most of the plan improvement and most of the worship training takes place. Obviously, a few things are key to make this work. First, the key decision-maker in this process cannot be a power monger; he or she needs to be committed to and gifted at *empowering* ministry (Eph. 4:12). Second, most of the planning happens weeks and weeks ahead of time, not days.

An important point: when revising, be sure to employ a "don't take this personally" rule. It's altogether too easy for folks to misinterpret substantive critique as personal attack. You can help avoid this in two ways. First, be sure that evaluations are rooted in objective and agreed-upon criteria. (We use the seven adjectives described in a previously published *Reformed Worship* article: www.reformed worship.org/magazine/article.cfm?article_id=1119.) In other words, saying "I don't like that song" is *not* an acceptable comment in a revision meeting. However, "that song is too hard to sing" or "that skit seems irreverent and flippant" are acceptable appraisals. Second, I've found it helpful to suggest that a sincere compliment precede any critique. Even when the praise feels perfunctory, it softens the blow. So, for example, a suitable critique might be: "Erin, you have such a marvelous singing voice, that particular song isn't worthy of it."

## Realize

When a final worship plan is agreed upon (or when Sunday simply creeps up on you), the next stage is for the planners to clearly communicate the vision for the service to the worship leaders. It's fine if planners and leaders are two different groups—they're two different gift-clusters. But often the strategists have minimal contact with the folks who actually hoist the sails to catch the Spirit's wind (liturgists, musicians, technicians, etc.). No wonder, then, that some services feel stuck in the doldrums. It's important for those who will prompt the congregation to know the whys of the service plan. So tell them—there is no substitute for straightforward communication. It's a truncated and trivial preparation for worship when the band merely runs through the chord changes on a "set" of songs without a thought to the broader purposes of that particular service.

So, for example, at Calvin College's LOFT (Living Our Faith Together) services, student planners would create a service plan that made plain each song's liturgical function. This was then communicated to the musicians. Similarly, we'd often outline the point of particular prayers, but allow the individuals who were praying that week the freedom to express those thoughts in their own words. (For more examples of the sorts of service outlines we used at LOFT, see *Ten Service Plans for Contemporary Worship*.)

### Analyze

Finally, it's a good idea to periodically review previous services. Analyze less for technical miscues or taste preferences than for theological content. Again, using an agreed-upon measuring stick is a helpful strategy (like the seven adjectives mentioned on the preceding page). This keeps everyone focused on the main reasons God's people gather to worship. Surface-level snafus will still be noted ("we forgot to enter one of our songs into PowerPoint"), but they'll be properly contextualized ("it wasn't very hospitable to ask folks to sing without giving them any music or lyrics").

### Final Comments

All this is less daunting than it first appears. Keep in mind that the path through the diagram is for one service. But that doesn't mean your small group of experts meets three times each week (to Devise, Revise, and Analyze). Since the work is done far in advance, these three boxes represent the main agenda items for a once-weekly meeting with your team of experts. First, do any necessary winnowing and focusing work for new service plans. Then revise plans for the next, say, four weeks brought by individuals or pairs, then analyze last week's service.

This is not to minimize the time and personnel commitment necessary to be this intentional. There's no doubt—it's intense. But I'm not convinced this is a problem. My experience has been that people commit to worship planning more eagerly and enjoy it more when it demands a full measure of passion and creativity. And since worship here is preparation for our ultimate destiny with God, it's as worthwhile a task as there is.

# Assessing Songs for Congregational Use

Recent decades have seen an explosion in songwriting for worship unparalleled in church history. Given modern methods of distribution, these songs—in print and recorded versions—are available to the average worship leader by the tens of thousands. It's reasonable to assume that in all this ocean, a number of the fish are keepers, but many more are going to be bycatch. Add to this a little-known factoid: a congregation's stable repertoire of known songs hovers in the range of about two hundred.[1] The conclusion: there are *lots* of new songs your congregation doesn't need to sing *because there are so many better ones available*. So how does one choose the best ones?

In past centuries, it was the wisdom of the church's use over time that allowed certain songs to persist while the vast majority faded into obscurity. The same is true, even, of certain verses of songs. Did you know, for example, that Charles Wesley (who by some estimates wrote over six thousand hymns) wrote *twenty-seven* verses for "Oh, for a Thousand Tongues to Sing"? Most hymnals that include this song use between four and six—with good reason.

In the past, hymnal committees, made up of people with theological training and pastoral sensitivity, selected the songs that would be sung by their congregations. Even if not everyone appreciated all their choices, those in charge mostly chose with an eye toward providing a balanced diet of prayer—both praise and lament, confession and adoration, songs simple and complex, with comforting and challenging imagery, and so on. Nowadays, these concerns are either pushed to the side by market forces or submerged into more evident ways of slicing a congregation's repertoire—like fast songs and slow songs, or songs in the key of D and songs in the key of F.

All of this to say that the average pastor or minister of music in a church needs as much help as possible in identifying the better songs. There are many ways to make these sorts of assessments. One common way is to obtain repertoire from trusted sources where there is an adequate filtering system. But this limits one's choices unnecessarily. What happens when two young people in your congregation present to the minister of music a song they've written and wish to give as a gift to the congregation? What is the best way to assess its worth, given that its indigenous character already gives it a leg up on its consumer-driven competition?

The material provided below is only a suggested starting place, not a definitive checklist guaranteeing spiritual depth or musical excellence. It is also a better tool for assessing congregational song based in popular music forms than music based in classical musical forms. Even so, its limited helpfulness is a substantial improvement over selecting songs for congregational worship only based on a "what I happen to like this week" system.

### Aesthetic Assessment

A book on *words* for worship is treading on thin ice to offer guidelines for assessment of a song's *musical* qualities; even so, it seems important to say a bit about the sonic mechanism by which a congregation's sung engagement with God in worship is deepened or thwarted. Here are some basic principles to guide an overall assessment:

1. Congregational Participation. The primary assumption of assessment is that music in worship is intended to enable the congregation's full-throated, deep-hearted participation. Music that is rhythmically very complex, or melodically wide-ranging, or that has a harmonic surprise around every turn may be wonderful to listen to, but too difficult for a congregation to sing.

2. Congregational Fittingness. A corollary assumption is that wise music leaders select songs *for their particular people*. Your congregation may be able easily to sing that highly syncopated gospel number. Mine will need a little help to do so. Yours may thrill to the modal character of that choral anthem. Mine will find it weird. You are shepherds—know your sheep.

3. Liturgical Fittingness.[2] Every moment of worship is not the same as every other one. When the congregation raises its praise to God, music that is uplifting is just right. When it offers lament, "bounciness" is not the musical

quality the good pastor is looking for. Similarly, music that might be deemed too simple for a hymn of adoration may be just right for a sung response to a prayer of intercession. Likewise, a childish ditty may not be adequate to carry words with some theological freight.

4. Familiarity. Another corollary of congregational participation is that people respond well to familiarity—harmonic and rhythmic, melodic and formal. Many hymn tunes, for example, follow a familiar structure: A, A', B, A. This familiarity makes them easier for a congregation to sing. Of course, familiarity overdone can lead to boredom. The form A, A, A, A, B, B, B, A, A, A, A is not likely to engage a congregation for very long. But returning melodic and rhythmic motifs help to create a pleasing sense of musical resolution and singability.

With these broad assumptions in mind, here is a laundry list of the sort of things to look for when assessing a particular song's musical suitability for congregational worship:

*Form*—Is the form of the song identifiable? reliable? Do its parts cohere, or does the bridge lead nonsensically into a second verse form before returning to a chorus?

### Melody

- Does the song have a hook to draw you in and sufficient interest to sustain hearing it multiple times?
- Is the length of each phrase appropriate to sing in one breath (not too short, not too long)?
- Does the melody have an identifiable climax?
- Is the leading in the song either stepwise or arpeggiated according to the underlying harmony?
- Is the song in a reasonable (one octave) vocal range? Is that range neither too low nor too high?

### Accompaniment

- Does the song exhibit any harmonic sophistication?
- Does the song exhibit harmonic predictability?
- Does the song exhibit pleasing harmonic surprises?
- Is there fitting rhythmic interest in the song?

### Lyrics

- Is the language used in the song fitting for its purpose? Is it appropriately simple or elevated?
- Is the imagery innovative or surprising? Is it interesting and appropriate?
- Does the language exhibit pith? Or does it repeat excessively without offering another musical avenue for entering deeper into the song's message?
- Is the rhyme scheme interesting or simplistic?
- Do the accents of the words match the contours of the melody?
- Do the tone and content of the lyrics match the liturgical purpose (for instance, you wouldn't want a song quoting "be still" from the Psalms to call for loud, rhythmic intensity)?

### Theological Assessment

Because each congregation will have its own theological lights by which to assess a particular song's appropriateness, what we offer here are the sorts of questions one might ask of a song to discern whether it lines up theologically.

- What are the song's key words? What seems to carry the most freight?
- Is there an identifiable theological theme (such as providence or God's faithfulness)?
- Is there identifiable Christian content (remember the "Fred Test")?
- Voice—who is speaking to whom throughout the song?
- What is the song's liturgical function? That is to say, what does it *do* in worship (e.g., confession, adoration, dedication, proclamation)?
- What is the song's emotional function? That is to say, what does the song do *to us* in worship? Does it inspire joy or grief or longing or . . . ?
- Does the song agree with Scripture?
- If it is a paraphrase or interpretation of Scripture, is the paraphrase acceptable?
- Does the song agree with confessions or other denominational or congregational criteria? (For example, Calvinists would have difficulty singing the verse from Charles Wesley's "Love Divine, All Loves Excelling" that speaks of a "second rest.")
- How is God depicted in the song? Triune? Gendered? Monochromatic? Varied? Is God largely active (given good verbs) or passive, but with lots of adjectives?

- Is the song pastorally sensitive? Is it comforting or challenging? Which does your congregation need more of?
- Does the song articulate underexpressed theological themes, such as justice, diversity, concern for the environment, lament, and so on?

## Repertoire Assessment

A wise music minister not only assesses individual songs for inclusion in the congregational canon, but assesses the canon itself (or at least the working repertoire) with an eye toward the sort of theological and musical balance issues we've been discussing all along.

So, for example, think about the ratio of songs to the liturgical action they express. Are 80 percent of your congregation's best-known pieces songs of celebration? Are there songs of confession and dedication and intercession in your repertoire?

Here are a few similar questions you might pose to your one hundred most commonly used songs:

- Does your repertoire exhibit a wide range of theological themes (e.g., justification, revelation, ecclesiology, eschatology)?
- Does your repertoire depict a God who is both just and merciful, immanent and transcendent, a Christ both fully human and fully divine?
- Does your repertoire include a reasonable number of songs that tell the story of Jesus's life?
- Does your repertoire encourage certain fruits of the Spirit (love, joy, peace) and neglect others (self-control, faithfulness)?
- Does your repertoire contain songs that reflect the variety of biblical genres (e.g., are themes of prophetic literature expressed anywhere? themes of the Pauline epistles?)?

If these questions, and any like them that you devise, compel you to add songs to fill in some empty spots, one way to do so is to invite suggestions from your congregation. When you do so, you may get your congregation to think carefully about what they sing and why by asking that each suggestion be accompanied by a brief answer to questions like these:

- What significance does this song have for you as a worshiper?
- What biblically grounded worship theme does it express?

- What biblically precedented action does it enact (e.g., promise making, sacrifice offering, sin confessing)?
- What community characteristics does it help form? What Christian virtues does it promote?
- What is the story behind your love for this song?

I hope you will use your own creativity and wisdom to adapt these suggestions to your own situation. Perhaps the most important principles here are that (1) careful consideration is essential in choosing worship songs and (2) because of the ocean of songs available, you have the luxury of choosing only the best ones for your congregation.

Some materials in these assessments are adapted from Terri Bocklund McLean, *New Harmonies, Choosing Contemporary Music for Worship* (Bethesda, MD: Alban Institute, 1998), and from Greg Scheer's *The Art of Worship: A Musician's Guide to Leading Modern Worship* (Grand Rapids: Baker Books, 2007).

# Notes

## Introduction

1. Emily R. Brink and John D. Witvliet, eds., *The Worship Sourcebook* (Grand Rapids: Calvin Institute of Christian Worship/Faith Alive Christian Resources/Baker Books, 2004), 16.

2. For more on the fittingness of art for liturgical purposes, see Nicholas Wolterstorff, *Art in Action: Toward a Christian Aesthetic* (Grand Rapids: Eerdmans, 1980), 183–89.

3. Clayton J. Schmit's book, *Too Deep for Words: A Theology of Liturgical Expression* (Louisville: Westminster John Knox, 2002), has a helpful section on the importance and limitation of excellence.

4. James B. Torrance, *Worship, Community and the Triune God of Grace* (Downers Grove, IL: InterVarsity, 1997).

5. Schmit, *Too Deep for Words*, 117.

## Chapter 1 The Dimensions of Language in Worship

1. Alexander Gondo (Shona), tr. I-to Loh, alt., "Uyai mose/Come, All You People," text copyright © 1986 World Council of Churches and Asian Institute for Liturgy and Music. Used by permission. Please note that the WCC prefers the translation "Come and praise the Most High," although some congregations, including the one described here, sing "your Maker."

2. Don E. Saliers, *Worship & Spirituality*, 2nd ed. (Akron, OH: OSL Publications, 1996), 2.

3. Kendra G. Hotz and Matthew T. Mathews, *Shaping the Christian Life: Worship and the Religious Affections* (Louisville: Westminster John Knox, 2006), 70–71. For more on the relationship between worship and the generation of meaning, see Graham Hughes, *Worship as Meaning: A Liturgical Theology for Late Modernity* (Cambridge: Cambridge University Press, 2003).

4. From the Anglican Book of Common Worship, Authorized Forms of Confession and Absolution. Available online at http://www.cofe.anglican.org/worship/liturgy/commonworship/texts/word/confessions.html.

5. Greg Scheer, *The Art of Worship: A Musician's Guide to Leading Modern Worship* (Grand Rapids: Baker Books, 2007), 69.

6. Rich Mullins, "Awesome God," 1988 BMG Songs, Inc.

7. Kathleen Norris, "Incarnational Language," *Christian Century* 114.22 (1997): 699.

8. Text: original Portuguese: Silvio Meincke; Spanish: Pablo Sosa; English: Jaci Maraschin and Sonya Ingwersen (1989). See "Your Kingdom Come" on p. 228 for more on this song.

9. John D. Witvliet, *The Biblical Psalms in Christian Worship: A Brief Introduction & Guide to Resources* (Grand Rapids: Eerdmans, 2007), 20–23.

10. For an elegant treatment of the importance of new and old language in worship, see Gail Ramshaw's *Worship: Searching for Language* (Washington, DC: Pastoral Press, 1988), 87–90. Also, C. S. Lewis included extensive commentary on his favoring of standard Anglican liturgies over "innovation" in *Letters to Malcolm: Chiefly on Prayer* (San Diego: Harvest/HBJ, 1963), 4–8. His position is stated very strongly and works well to spark discussion. See "An Advocate for the Same Old Thing" on p. 84.

11. J.-J. von Allmen, *Worship: Its Theology and Practice* (London: Lutterworth, 1965), 34.

### Chapter 2  Worship as Dialogic Encounter

1. Walter Brueggemann, *The Psalms and the Life of Faith*, ed. Patrick D. Miller (Minneapolis: Augsburg Fortress, 1995), 68, italics in original.

2. For more on performative speech (words that *do*), see Nicholas Wolterstorff, *Divine Discourse: Philosophical Reflection on the Claim That God Speaks* (Cambridge: Cambridge University Press, 1995).

3. David Peterson, *Engaging with God: A Biblical Theology of Worship* (Downers Grove, IL: InterVarsity, 1992), 20, italics in original.

4. In fact, if we think of worshiping God in a fully trinitarian way, it is more than a conversation; it is a complex pattern of revelation and response: the Father is revealed to us in Jesus Christ by the inner workings of the Spirit; that same Spirit then prompts our response, which is mediated, perfected, and brought before the Creator by Jesus Christ. For more, see James B. Torrance, *Worship, Community and the Triune God of Grace* (Downers Grove, IL: InterVarsity, 1997).

5. Robert E. Webber, *The Divine Embrace: Recovering the Passionate Spiritual Life* (Grand Rapids: Baker Books, 2006), 232.

6. John D. Witvliet, "Words to Grow Into," *The Banner* 140, no. 10 (October 2005): 50; http://www .thebanner.org/magazine/article.cfm?article_id=175.

7. Witvliet, "Words to Grow Into," 50. See also John D. Witvliet, "Vertical Habits: Worship and Our Faith Vocabulary," Calvin Institute of Christian Worship, http://www.calvin.edu/worship/resources/ vocab.php.

8. Joyce Ann Zimmerman, CPPS, "Me to Thee to Me: Worship, Liturgy, & Devotion," handout for "The Last Thirty Years in Worship: What We've Learned along the Way," Calvin Symposium on Worship, January 2006. For a similar distinction between "Monastic" and "Cathedral" prayer, see Paul F. Bradshaw, *Two Ways of Praying* (Nashville: Abingdon, 1995).

9. Ruth C. Duck, *Finding Words for Worship: A Guide for Leaders* (Louisville: Westminster John Knox, 1995), 22.

10. Spanish traditional, "Santo, santo, santo, mi corazon/Holy, Holy, Holy, My Heart"; English trans. *Sing! A New Creation*. Trans. copyright © 2001 Faith Alive Christian Resources. Used by permission.

11. Cas Wepener, "Enriching Worship in Contexts of Poverty," unpublished paper, Stellenbosch University, 2007.

12. Chart reproduced from Emily R. Brink and John D. Witvliet, eds., *The Worship Sourcebook* (Grand Rapids: Calvin Institute of Christian Worship/Faith Alive Christian Resources/Baker Books, 2004), 25. Used by permission.

13. Chart reproduced from "Vertical Habits: Worship and Our Faith Vocabulary," Calvin Institute of Christian Worship, www.calvin.edu/worship/habits/index.php. Used by permission.

14. Ron Rienstra, *Ten Service Plans for Contemporary Worship* (Grand Rapids: Faith Alive Christian Resources and Calvin Institute of Christian Worship, 2002), 57–58.

### Chapter 3  On Chatter and Patter

1. Brian D. McLaren also discusses this sort of prayer in *A Generous Orthodoxy* (Grand Rapids: Zondervan, 2004), 226.

2. Gail Ramshaw, *Worship: Searching for Language* (Washington, DC: Pastoral Press, 1988), 159.

3. This phenomenon is called somatic memory. For more on ritual and worship, see the Nathan Mitchell–edited special issue of *Liturgy Digest* 1.1 (Spring 1993): 4–67.

4. *The Holy Observer*, March 15, 2004, http://www.holyobserver.com.

5. For more spoofing fun with language, see these Web sites: http://www.christilling.de/blog/2006/12/lords-per-minute-competition.html and http://www.larknews.com/august15_2003/secondary.php?page=5. Warning: these sites are not for the easily offended.

6. William C. Turner Jr., "The Musicality of Black Preaching: A Phenomenology," *Journal of Black Sacred Music* 2 (Spring 1988): 21–34.

7. Cleophus J. LaRue, *The Heart of Black Preaching* (Louisville: Westminster John Knox, 2000), 11. Alternatively: "Start low, go slow, rise higher, strike fire, retire."

8. Thomas G. Long, "Words, Words, Words," *Princeton Seminary Bulletin* 12.3 (1991): 314, 315.

## Chapter 4 On Repetition

1. Malcolm Gladwell, *The Tipping Point: How Little Things Can Make a Big Difference* (Boston: Back Bay Books, 2002), 126.

2. The "Cows in the Corn" joke is an Internet standard. Its provenance is unknown. Chances are you've only heard half of it.

3. For a more academic consideration of these varying musical structures, see C. Michael Hawn, *Gather into One: Praying and Singing Globally* (Grand Rapids: Eerdmans, 2003), esp. chap. 7.

4. John Bunyan, the free-church Baptist author of *Pilgrim's Progress*, makes precisely this argument in his "I Will Pray with the Spirit" (1663) in *The Doctrine of the Law and Grace Unfolded*, The Miscellaneous Works of John Bunyan Series, vol. 2, ed. Richard L. Greaves (Oxford: Oxford University Press, 1976). For a slightly broader view, see Christopher Ellis's "From the Heart: The Spirituality of Free Prayer" in *Gathering: A Theology and Spirituality of Worship in Free Church Tradition* (London: SCM Press, 2004), 103–24.

5. Preface to *The Book of Common Prayer 1559: The Elizabethan Prayer Book*, ed. John E. Booty (Charlottesville, VA: Folger Shakespeare Library, 1976), 14.

6. Annie Dillard, *Holy the Firm* (San Francisco: Harper Perennial, 1998), 59.

7. C. S. Lewis, *Letters to Malcolm: Chiefly on Prayer* (San Diego: Harvest/HBJ, 1963), 4–5. This excerpt is from a much longer passage on repetition and novelty in worship.

8. Lauren F. Winner, *Girl Meets God: On the Path to a Spiritual Life* (Chapel Hill, NC: Algonquin Books, 2002), 142–43, italics in original.

9. Jeremy S. Begbie, a theologian and a musician, writes eloquently about how repetition functions in music in a way that can teach us theological lessons. The same musical phrase, he says, repeated after an interlude of something else, provides satisfaction in the fundamental musical cycle of tension-resolution. But more than that, meaning clusters around the repeated phrase as it comes around again and again. Begbie speaks about how this might inform our understanding of repeated liturgical practices, such as celebration of the Lord's Supper. It might apply just as well to the notion of a refrain in a sermon as the thematic "tonic" or home chord. See Begbie's *Theology, Music and Time*, Cambridge Studies in Christian Doctrine (Cambridge: Cambridge University Press, 2000), 155–75.

10. For more on the use of responsorial psalmody and making good use of the prayer book of God's people, see John D. Witvliet, *The Biblical Psalms in Christian Worship: A Brief Introduction & Guide to Resources* (Grand Rapids: Eerdmans, 2007).

11. Robb Redman, *The Great Worship Awakening: Singing a New Song in the Postmodern Church* (San Francisco: Jossey-Bass, 2002), 69.

12. Sarah S. Miller, "Below the Frost Line: Hymns of the Faith," *The Christian Century*, December 12, 1990. Quoted in Brian A. Wren, *Praying Twice: The Music and Words of Congregational Song* (Louisville: Westminster John Knox, 2000), 92–93.

## Chapter 5 The Puzzle of Authenticity

1. Rob Bell, *Velvet Elvis: Repainting the Christian Faith* (Grand Rapids: Zondervan, 2005), 98–99, 101.

2. Andy Crouch, "Stonewashed Worship," *Christianity Today*, February 2005, 82.

3. Ruth C. Duck, *Finding Words for Worship: A Guide for Leaders* (Louisville: Westminster John Knox, 1995), 23.

4. Horatio G. Spafford, "It Is Well with My Soul," 1873.

5. For a more complicated example, as well as more detailed musical instruction, see Ron Rienstra, *Ten Service Plans for Contemporary Worship*, vol. 2 (Grand Rapids: Faith Alive Christian Resources, 2006), esp. 57–58.

6. "Ah, Holy Jesus," text by Johann Heermann, 1630; trans. Robert Bridges, 1899. The updated version of this hymn was taken from *The Psalter Hymnal* (Grand Rapids: CRC Publications, 1987) and reflects a revision from the 1980s.

7. "O Sacred Head," Latin Medieval; German trans. Paul Gerhardt, 1656; English trans. James Alexander, 1830. The updated version of this hymn was taken from *The Psalter Hymnal* (Grand Rapids: CRC Publications, 1987) and reflects a revision from the 1980s.

8. Robert Robinson, "Come, Thou Fount of Every Blessing," 1758.

9. For an example of another fan of this hymn, see Gary A. Parrett, "Raising Ebenezer: We Are Misguided When We Modernize Hymn Texts," *Christianity Today*, January 2006, 62.

10. For more about such choirs, see *Reformed Worship* 66 (December 2002): 45, http://reformed worship.org/magazine/article.cfm?article_id=1194.

11. Crouch, "Stonewashed Worship," 82.

12. James F. White, *Protestant Worship: Traditions in Transition* (Louisville: Westminster John Knox, 1989), 21.

### Chapter 6 Watch Your Figures

1. Sallie McFague, *Metaphorical Theology: Models of God in Religious Language* (Philadelphia: Fortress, 1982), 26. Quoted in Brian A. Wren, *What Language Shall I Borrow? God-Talk in Worship: A Male Response to Feminist Theology* (New York: Crossroad, 1989), 107.

2. G. B. Caird, *The Language and Imagery of the Bible* (London: Duckworth, 1980), 176. Quoted in Wren, *What Language*, 87.

3. Ulrich Zwingli, *An Account of the Faith of Huldereich Zwingli Submitted to the Roman Emperor Charles* (3 July 1530), trans. Samuel Macauley Jackson, *The Latin Works and the Correspondence of Huldreich Zwingli*, vol. 2 (Philadelphia: Heidelberg Press, 1922), 46.

4. Julia Kasdorf, "Same! Same! Pleasures and Purposes of Metaphor" (paper presented at Festival of Faith and Writing, Calvin College, Grand Rapids, Michigan, April 21, 2006).

5. This is a repeated theme in Ramshaw's writings. For an example, see *God beyond Gender: Feminist Christian God-Language* (Minneapolis: Augsburg Fortress, 1995), especially 93–99.

6. Robert Farrar Capon, *The Romance of the Word: One Man's Love Affair with Theology* (Grand Rapids: Eerdmans, 1995), 248. For those interested in a very rigorous treatment of the problem of theology (i.e., language about God) in a pluralistic culture, see David Tracy's *Analogical Imagination: Christian Theology and the Culture of Pluralism* (New York: Crossroad, 1982), especially the final chapter and epilogue. The benefits are worth the extra effort required to read and understand it.

7. For more on imaginative preaching, see Thomas H. Troeger's *Creating Fresh Images for Preaching: New Rungs for Jacob's Ladder*, More Effective Preaching Series (Valley Forge: Judson, 1982), and *Imagining a Sermon* (Nashville: Abingdon, 1990).

8. Gail Ramshaw, "Sin: One Image of Human Limitation," in *The Fate of Confession*, ed. Mary Collins and David Power (Edinburgh: T&T Clark, 1987). For full article, see *Concilium* 190.2 (1987): 3–10.

9. Thomas Lynch, *Bodies in Motion and at Rest: On Metaphor and Mortality* (New York: Norton, 2001), 271.

10. Adapted from articles by William T. Arnold and Daniel Doriani in *Evangelical Dictionary of Biblical Theology*, ed. Walter A. Elwell (Grand Rapids: Baker Academic, 1996).

11. Adapted from a blog post by Tom Trinidad on WorshipHelps.com (http://worshiphelps.blogs .com/worship_helps/2007/01/emerging_confes.html). Used by permission.

12. Brian McLaren, "The Last Thirty Years in Worship: What We've Learned along the Way" (lecture, Calvin Symposium on Worship, Grand Rapids, MI, January 26, 2006).

13. Brian McLaren, "Found in Translation," *Sojourners* (March 2006): 14–19.

14. For more on imagining the reign of God in our culture, there are at least three strands of thought to explore. One is the "missional church" strand that emphasizes the reign of God as relation, not location. A representative work is *Treasure in Clay Jars: Patterns in Missional Faithfulness,* The Gospel and Our Culture Series, ed. Lois Y. Barrett (Grand Rapids: Eerdmans, 2004). Another strand—perhaps understood as an alternative to the previous one—is well articulated in Bishop N. T. Wright's magisterial *Jesus and the Victory of God*, Christian Origins and the Question of God, vol. 2 (Minneapolis: Augsburg Fortress, 1997). This work has a fascinating appendix listing all early Christian references to the phrase in the Bible and other early sources. Finally, the "radical orthodoxy" strand includes authors like Stanley Hauerwas and John Milbank and is deeply concerned with the relationship between the kingdom of God and the church. Though fascinating to theologians in some quarters, the impact of this third strand on the church itself is still muted.

15. Text by David A. Robb and Amanda Husberg, "World without Walls," text copyright © 2005 Wayne Leupold Editions, Inc. Used by permission.

16. Lyrics for the song "Your Love Is Extravagant" are available widely on the Internet. For example, search for "extravagant" at www.integritymusic.com.

17. Lyrics for the song "Above All" are available by searching for "Above All" at www.integritymusic.com.

18. "Wal-Mart Rejects 'Racy' Worship CD," LarkNews.com, 1.4 (April 2003), http://www.larknews.com/april_2003/secondary_exclusive.php?header=header&page=walmart_cd. Copyright © 2003 Joel Kilpatrick. Used by permission.

19. Brian A. Wren, *Praying Twice: The Music and Words of Congregational Song* (Louisville: Westminster John Knox, 2000), 297–348.

20. An excellent book on the biblical translation debates is D. A. Carson, *The Inclusive Language Debate: A Plea for Realism* (Grand Rapids: Baker Academic, 1998). Carson is a conservative Bible scholar and a skilled linguist who fairly exposes the real issues, both political and linguistic, on all sides of the debate. For more resources on this question, see "Recommended Resources."

## Chapter 7 Naming God

1. Dr. Ruth's presentation was for a conference at the Yale Institute of Sacred Music (ISM). The conference was titled "The Place of Christ in Liturgical Prayer," and the proceedings of that conference are available from ISM. The full paper is included in *The Message in the Music: Studying Contemporary Praise and Worship,* ed. Robert Woods and Brian Walrath (Nashville: Abingdon, 2007). The Asbury Web site has a popularized version of this paper, available at www.asburyblog.net/articles/WarningToSong writers.pdf .

2. Despite our reluctance in this book to use the term *contemporary* as a descriptor of worship styles, throughout this chapter, in keeping with the nomenclature of Dr. Ruth's study, we will use the acronym CWM (Contemporary Worship Music) as shorthand for popular praise-and-worship-style music.

3. St. Augustine, *Confessions*, trans. Henry Chadwick (New York: Oxford, 1991), book 1, par. 4.

4. John D. Witvliet, *The Biblical Psalms in Christian Worship* (Grand Rapids: Eerdmans, 2007), 18–20.

5. Brian A. Wren, *What Language Shall I Borrow? God-Talk in Worship: A Male Response to Feminist Theology* (New York: Crossroad, 1989), 125.

6. Gail Ramshaw, *God beyond Gender: Feminist Christian God-Language* (Minneapolis: Augsburg Fortress, 1995), esp. 46. This is the first of many references to this idea.

7. Bill Lancaster, "Trinity Paper Approved with Amendments," 217th General Assembly News. Presbyterian Church (USA) homepage http://www.pcusa.org/ga217/newsandphotos/ga06044.htm.

8. "May God, Who Is Transcendent, Bless You," adapted from *The Book of Occasional Services 1994,* 171. Copyright © 1995, The Church Pension Fund. All rights reserved. Used by permission of Church Publishing, Inc., New York, New York.

9. Emily R. Brink and John D. Witvliet, eds., *The Worship Sourcebook* (Grand Rapids: Calvin Institute of Christian Worship/Faith Alive Christian Resources/Baker Books, 2004), 178.

10. Gail Ramshaw, *Treasures Old and New: Images in the Lectionary* (Minneapolis: Augsburg Fortress, 2002), 67.

11. "Tender and Compassionate God," in *Hymnal: A Worship Book*, ed. Rebecca Slough (Elgin, IL: Brethren Press, 1992), 746. Copyright © 1992, The Hymnal Project, Brethren Press. Used by permission.

12. Adapted from the Collect for the 5th Sunday in Lent, Contemporary. *The Book of Common Prayer of the Episcopal Church*, 1979. Available at http://justus.anglican.org/resources/bcp.

13. For an excellent but more technical discussion of metaphors for God, see Mary Therese DesCamp and Eve E. Sweetser, "Metaphors for God: Why and How Do Our Choices Matter for Humans? The Application of Contemporary Cognitive Linguistics Research to the Debate on God and Metaphor," *Pastoral Psychology* 53.5 (January 2005): 207–38. This article helpfully and fairly summarizes the debates over metaphors, names, and images for God, considering a range of prominent views. It applies philosophy, theology, and cognitive science to give a helpful account of how metaphor actually works. The conclusion of the article is similar to this chapter's approach: affirming the power and authority of the main biblical metaphors while also encouraging the intentional exploration of both the main metaphors as well as the full range of biblical depiction of God.

14. John Thornburg, "God the Sculptor of the Mountains," text copyright © 1993 John Thornburg. Used by permission.

15. The Reverend Judy Welles, parish minister, Unitarian Universalists of the Cumberland Valley, Boiling Springs, PA, "O Divine Source of Love," Prayers, Unitarian Universalist Association of Congregations Web site, http://www.uua.org/spirituallife/worshipweb/meditationsand/submissions/5603.shtml. Copyright © 1996–2008 Unitarian Universalist Association of Congregations. All rights reserved.

16. See D. A. Carson, *The Inclusive-Language Debate: A Plea for Realism* (Grand Rapids: Baker Academic, 1998), for an illuminating discussion of these challenges.

17. A careful and curious reader may note that in this book, in all of our own text, we have avoided the use of the masculine pronoun for God.

18. This entire discussion of the name *Lord* owes much to Ramshaw, *God beyond Gender*, esp. 54–56.

### Chapter 8  Something Old

1. G. K. Chesterton, *Orthodoxy*, chap. 4. See http://www.ccel.org/ccel/chesterton/orthodoxy.vii.html.

2. Robert E. Webber, *Ancient-Future Faith: Rethinking Evangelicalism for a Postmodern World* (Grand Rapids: Baker Academic, 1999).

3. This material was adapted from a previously published article: Ron Rienstra, "Roots and Wings: Musical Makeovers for Classic Hymns and Hymn Texts," *Reformed Worship* 66 (December 2002): 42–43. Also available online at http://www.reformedworship.org/magazine/article.cfm?article_id=1192. Copyright © 2002 Faith Alive Christian Resources. Used by permission.

4. This is Tom Long's phrase from *The Witness of Preaching* (Louisville: Westminster John Knox, 2005).

### Chapter 9  Something New

1. Tod Bolsinger, "It Takes a Church to Raise a Christian" (lecture, Calvin Symposium on Worship, Grand Rapids, MI, January 27, 2006).

2. Crossover Church's Web site: http://www.crossoverchurch.org.

3. Lutheran World Federation, "Nairobi Statement on Worship and Culture: Contemporary Challenges and Opportunities," published in *Ecumenical Review* 48.3 (July 1996): 415–17. For more on this statement, see chapter 10. For the full statement, see http://www.worship.ca/docs/lwf_ns.html.

4. From "Unashamed" by Crossover Church member Carlos "Los-1" Ramirez. http://www.cross overchurch.org/usatoday/usatoday.html. Used by permission.

5. "Hip Youth Pastor Now Completely Unintelligible," LarkNews.com, 3, no. 10 (October 2005), http://www.larknews.com/october_2005/secondary.php?page=3. Copyright © 2005 Joel Kilpatrick. Used by permission.

6. Lois Farley Shuford, "Ready My Heart," text and music copyright © 1995 Lois Farley Shuford. Used by permission.

7. Jonny Baker, Psalm 113 [urban remix '04], worship tricks [first series] no. 77: urban psalm. http:// jonnybaker.blogs.com/jonnybaker/worship_tricks/wt77.html. Used by permission.

## Chapter 10  Something Borrowed

1. Ronald P. Byars, "Creeds and Prayers—Ecclesiology," in *A More Profound Alleluia: Theology and Worship in Harmony,* ed. Leanne Van Dyk (Grand Rapids: Eerdmans, 2005), 102.

2. Based on Matthew 6:9–13 NRSV; from Emily R. Brink and John D. Witvliet, eds., *The Worship Sourcebook* (Grand Rapids: Calvin Institute of Christian Worship/Faith Alive Christian Resources/Baker Books, 2004), 4.4.10, p. 200. Copyright © 2004 Faith Alive Christian Resources. Used by permission.

3. See Brink and Witvliet, eds., *Worship Sourcebook,* 182–84.

4. C. Michael Hawn, *Gather into One: Praying and Singing Globally* (Grand Rapids: Eerdmans, 2003), 17.

5. Described in Hawn, *Gather into One,* 214.

6. C. Michael Hawn, *One Bread, One Body: Exploring Cultural Diversity in Worship* (Bethesda, MD: Alban Institute, 2003), 119–20.

7. This song, along with translations in English and Dutch, appeared in "I Am with You Always," the worship booklet for the Calvin Symposium on Worship, 2006.

8. Justo González, "Credo hispano," in *Mil voces para celebrar: Himnario Metodista* (Nashville: Abingdon Press, 1996), 69–70. Copyright © 1994 Abingdon Press. Used by permission.

9. Justo González, trans., "Hispanic Creed," in *Mil voces para celebrar: Himnario Metodista* (Nashville: Abingdon Press, 1996), 70. Copyright © 1996 Abingdon Press. Used by permission.

10. Augustus M. Toplady, "Rock of Ages, Cleft for Me," 1776.

11. "Kwake Yesu nasimama/Here on Jesus Christ I Will Stand," English paraphrase copyright © 2008 Greg Scheer, http://www.gregscheer.com. Used by permission.

## Chapter 11 Something Blue

1. John D. Witvliet, *Worship Seeking Understanding: Windows into Christian Practice* (Grand Rapids: Baker Academic, 2003), 43–44.

2. Witvliet, *Worship Seeking Understanding,* 40, with reference to Gordon Lathrop.

3. One useful resource for services of lament is J. Frank Henderson, *Liturgies of Lament* (Chicago: Liturgy Training Publications, 1994). See "Recommended Resources" for more information.

4. John D. Witvliet, "Prayers of Praise and Lament for Advent, Incorporating Psalm 80," *Reformed Worship* 45 (September 1997): 25, http://www.reformedworship.org/magazine/article.cfm?article_id=706. Copyright © 1997 Faith Alive Christian Resources. Used by permission.

5. "Um pouco além do presente/A Little beyond This Our Time." Text: original Portuguese: Silvio Meincke; Spanish: Pablo Sosa; English: Jaci Maraschin and Sonya Ingwersen. English translation copyright © 1992 Jaci Maraschin and Sonya Ingwersen. Used by permission.

## Chapter 12  The Embedded Word

1. We have discussed earlier how for Protestants this is part of our theological inheritance from Reformation theologian Ulrich Zwingli. For an excellent treatment of the relative "spirituality" of words and things, see especially the first five chapters of Leonard J. Vander Zee, *Christ, Baptism, and the Lord's Supper: Recovering the Sacraments for Evangelical Worship* (Downers Grove, IL: InterVarsity, 2004).

2. See Gregory Dix, *The Shape of the Liturgy* (London: Dacre Press, 1945). For a more contemporary articulation of this position, see Gordon W. Lathrop, *Holy Things: A Liturgical Theology* (Minneapolis: Fortress, 1993). Also see Paul F. Bradshaw, *The Search for the Origins of Christian Worship: Sources and Methods for the Study of Early Liturgy*, 2nd ed. (New York: Oxford University Press, 2002), for an articulation of some of the complexity.

3. Thomas G. Long, *Beyond the Worship Wars: Building Vital and Faithful Worship* (Bethesda, MD: Alban Institute, 2001), 47.

4. Long, *Beyond the Worship Wars*, 32.

5. Robert E. Webber, *Planning Blended Worship: The Creative Mixture of Old and New* (Nashville: Abingdon, 1998), 79.

6. Greg Scheer, *The Art of Worship: A Musician's Guide to Leading Modern Worship* (Grand Rapids: Baker Books, 2007), 88.

7. For more on the church year, see Robert E. Webber's *Ancient-Future Time: Forming Spirituality through the Christian Year* (Grand Rapids: Baker Books, 2004).

8. Ruth C. Duck, *Finding Words for Worship: A Guide for Leaders* (Louisville: Westminster John Knox, 1995), 122.

9. For more on "in between words," see Paul Ryan, "Consider Those 'In Between' Words: Spoken Transitions in Worship," *Reformed Worship* 79 (March 2006): 18–20, www.reformedworship.org/magazine/article.cfm?article_id=1665.

10. Scheer, *Art of Worship*, 108.

11. Walter Brueggemann, *The Psalms and the Life of Faith*, ed. Patrick D. Miller (Minneapolis: Augsburg Fortress, 1995), 50.

## Appendix 1  Practical Advice for All Occasions

1. Peter L. Haynes, "O God, You Refresh Us," Prayers for Special Occasions, copyright © 1991, Peter L. Haynes. Used by permission. http://rockhay.tripod.com/worship/prayers-etc/special.htm.

2. Laurence Hull Stookey, *Let the Whole Church Say Amen! A Guide for Those Who Pray in Public* (Nashville: Abingdon, 2001), 63.

3. Stookey, *Let the Whole Church Say Amen*, 27.

4. Some excellent resources with suggestions for organizing longer prayers are Emily R. Brink and John D. Witvliet, eds., *The Worship Sourcebook* (Grand Rapids: Calvin Institute of Christian Worship/Faith Alive Christian Resources/Baker Books, 2004), esp. 173–234; John Pritchard, *The Intercessions Handbook: Creative Ideas for Public and Private Prayer* (London: SPCK, 2003); Ruth C. Duck, *Finding Words for Worship: A Guide for Leaders* (Louisville: Westminster John Knox, 1995), 76–84; and Stookey, *Let the Whole Church Say Amen*, 99–104.

5. François de Salignac de la Mothe-Fenelon (1651–1715), in *The Worship Sourcebook*, 9.1.44, p. 359.

## Appendix 2  Worship Planning Process

1. This material was adapted from a previously published article: Ron Rienstra, "It Takes a Team: Examining the Worship Planning Process," *Reformed Worship* 74 (December 2004): 41–43. Also available online at http://www.reformedworship.org/magazine/article.cfm?article_id=1363. Copyright © 2004 Faith Alive Christian Resources. Used by permission.

## Appendix 3  Assessing Songs for Congregational Use

1. See John D. Witvliet, "We Are What We Sing," *Reformed Worship* 60 (June 2001): 4–9, http://www.reformedworship.org/magazine/article.cfm?article_id=1058.

2. For more on the notion of "fittingness," see Nicholas Wolterstorff, *Art in Action: Toward a Christian Aesthetic* (Grand Rapids: Eerdmans, 1980).

# Recommended Resources

While we have referred to many sources in the text of this book, we thought it might be helpful to list here a few works we have found most frequently and extensively helpful, both in understanding the issues raised by worship words and in day-to-day planning for worship.

## Studies of Worship

Hawn, C. Michael. *Gather into One: Praying and Singing Globally.* Grand Rapids: Eerdmans, 2003.

> A wonderful guide to help ministers and church musicians appreciate and use well the songs of the global church. Hawn does so through a sensitive examination of local cultures, significant composers, and salient examples throughout.

Long, Thomas G. *Beyond the Worship Wars: Building Vital and Faithful Worship.* Bethesda, MD: Alban Institute, 2001.

> Deservedly, this is one of the most popular books for guiding congregations and worship teams in thinking through worship renewal. Based on experience and field research as well as scholarship, Long identifies and explores nine characteristics of worship at faithful and vital congregations. At once accessible, educational, and even entertaining.

Lutheran World Federation. "Nairobi Statement on Worship & Culture: Contemporary Challenges and Opportunities." *Ecumenical Review* 48.3 ( July 1996). http://www .worship.ca/docs/lwf_ns.html.

> Written by an ecumenical team of pastors and scholars, this short work is an outstanding summary of key theological and practical issues concerning the relationship of worship and culture.

Plantinga, Cornelius, Jr., and Sue A. Rozeboom. *Discerning the Spirits. A Guide to Thinking about Christian Worship Today.* Grand Rapids: Eerdmans, 2003.

> This book is the product of a team effort to study the relationship between worship and culture in our rapidly changing world. The structure of the book reflects the four main divisions of the Nairobi Statement, and its style—filled with examples and sidebar commentary—reflects the lively personalities and insights of the study team.

Ruth, Lester. "The Trinity in Contemporary Christian Worship Music." In *The Message in the Music: Studying Contemporary Praise and Worship,* edited by Robert Woods and Brian Walrath, 29–42. Nashville: Abingdon, 2007.

> This is Ruth's summary of his research on trinitarian language in Christian contemporary worship music. The statistics are fascinating in themselves, but Ruth's analysis and commentary are equally illuminating.

Schmit, Clayton J. *Too Deep for Words: A Theology of Liturgical Expression.* Louisville: Westminster John Knox, 2002.

> Schmit uses aesthetic theory to explain why good words are important in worship. This is a friendly scholarly study with practical applications in the later chapters, including helpful exercises for preachers.

Van Dyk, Leanne, ed. *A More Profound Alleluia: Theology and Worship in Harmony.* Grand Rapids: Eerdmans, 2004.

> An interesting experiment in liturgical theology. Six theologians were given a particular liturgical moment (e.g., Confession and Assurance, Proclamation of the Word, Creeds and Prayers) and a theological head (Trinity, Soteriology, Ecclesiology) and were asked to write a chapter about the intersection of the two. The result is a surprisingly thorough exploration of what we mean and how we mean it when we worship well.

Witvliet, John D. *The Biblical Psalms in Christian Worship: A Brief Introduction & Guide to Resources.* Grand Rapids: Eerdmans, 2007.

> Everything you need to know about psalms in worship, concisely and engagingly explained. This book begins with a history of how the book of Psalms has been used in Christian worship, then, in the second half, gives a sweeping survey of contemporary uses. Practical and pastoral with scholarly underpinnings, the book includes many helpful references to other sources for psalm-use ideas.

## Prayers and Other General Worship Resources

Calvin Institute of Christian Worship Web site. http://www.calvin.edu/worship/.

> Thousands of pages of worship resources and diverse educational materials. A great first stop when trolling the Web.

Henderson, J. Frank. *Liturgies of Lament.* Chicago: Liturgy Training Publications, 1994.

> A Roman Catholic resource with an interfaith heart, this small book examines foundational principles for lament and then offers examples and points to additional resources. The main concern is for lament on crisis occasions.

The Hymnary Web site. http://www.hymnary.org/.

> This Web site is an online database of hymns and hymnals and is one of the
> most comprehensive hymn resources on the Web. Users can search the site by
> title, tune, hymnal, Scripture reference, subject, composer, and other categories.
> The site currently indexes over 16,000 texts and 12,000 tunes, with over 5,000
> full texts, full scores of many public domain hymns, and much more. With this
> site, worship musicians can save many hours and expand their congregations'
> knowledge and repertoire.

Pritchard, John. *The Intercessions Handbook: Creative Ideas for Public and Private Prayer.*
London: SPCK, 1997.

> From the Anglican tradition, this book is full of practical and creative ideas and
> models for intercessory prayer as well as private prayer.

Ramshaw, Gail. *Treasures Old and New: Images in the Lectionary.* Minneapolis: Augsburg
Fortress, 2002.

> This is an excellent resource for exploring biblical metaphors. The book is
> organized by major metaphors (fish, shepherd, tree, etc.), and examines the
> textual, cultural, and historical background of each.

Stookey, Laurence Hull. *Let the Whole Church Say Amen! A Guide for Those Who Pray in
Public.* Nashville: Abingdon, 2001.

> A practical, workshop-style guide. The examples are appropriate to a more high-
> church setting, though the general principles can apply anywhere.

Ward, Hannah, and Jennifer Wild, eds. *Resources for Preaching and Worship—Year A.* Louisville: Westminster John Knox, 2004 [also available for Years B and C].

> This lectionary-based book offers, for each lectionary text, a patchwork of relevant
> quotations, poems, and spiritual writings. Preachers can find fodder and ideas,
> although the book is not intended to address the quality of language the preacher
> finally delivers.

*A Wee Worship Book.* Chicago: GIA Publications, 1999.

> A wonderful book of litanies and service orders developed by the Iona
> Community. It models simple, contemporary language that is vivid and muscular
> rather than flimsy and flippant.

*The Worship Sourcebook.* Edited by Emily R. Brink and John D. Witvliet. Grand Rapids:
Calvin Institute of Christian Worship/Faith Alive Christian Resources/Baker Books,
2004.

> A resource created by the Calvin Institute of Christian Worship and intended as
> ecumenical. Stylistically much more diverse than other common worship-type
> volumes, it draws from an array of sources. The book features solid teaching
> sections on worship, but by necessity cannot go into great depth. Instead, it
> teaches by organization and example.

## Music

Scheer, Greg. *The Art of Worship: A Musician's Guide to Leading Modern Worship.* Grand Rapids: Baker Books, 2007.

> An engaging book combining solid theory with detailed instructions for practice. A great resource for musicians especially. Scheer gives worthy attention to words, although that is not his focus.

Wren, Brian. *Praying Twice: The Music and Words of Congregational Song.* Louisville: Westminster John Knox, 2000.

> Wren knows that singing is at the heart of the worship experience for many today, and in this book he explores a large sampling of issues raised when the people of God raise their voices. Rife with examples and pastoral wisdom, the book explores the poetic and theological character of worship songs, the purpose of singing and types of music used in worship, and more. Very helpful for church musicians especially.

## On Developing Worship Words

Duck, Ruth C. *Finding Words for Worship: A Guide for Worship Leaders.* Louisville: Westminster John Knox, 1995.

> Aimed at those who compose original words for worship.

## On Gender-Inclusive Language

Carson, D. A. *The Inclusive-Language Debate: A Plea for Realism.* Grand Rapids: Baker Academic, 1998.

> A level-headed and knowledgeable analysis of the debate over gender-inclusive Bible translations—perhaps the most important book to read on this subject. Carson, a language scholar, presents a fair and very illuminating study of the problems involved with translation. Although he is a conservative (complementarian) on gender roles, he exposes shortcomings of conservative positions on translation issues and critiques inclusive-language versions only in certain instances on linguistic grounds.

Cooper, John W. *Our Father in Heaven: Christian Faith and Inclusive Language for God.* Grand Rapids: Baker Academic, 1998.

> The book is a helpful summary of all points of view on the issue. Cooper, a conservative Reformed theologian, is quite fair to those who represent views with which he finally disagrees. We disagree with his final position theologically and find that it leaves key pastoral issues unexamined, but Cooper's argument is still instructive.

Ramshaw, Gail. *God beyond Gender: Feminist Christian God-Language.* Minneapolis: Augsburg Fortress, 1995.

> Concise, excellent summary of central issues. Ramshaw, a Lutheran liturgical theologian, is fully informed by feminist scholarship and theology while remaining dedicated to honoring tradition and to Christian orthodoxy.

Wren, Brian A. *What Language Shall I Borrow? God-Talk in Worship: A Male Response to Feminist Theology.* New York: Crossroad, 1989.

> A patient, thorough exploration of God-language, moving beyond the pronoun problem to views of masculinity and image systems for God. The book uses discursive argument, imaginative exercises, and examples to make its case. Wren's solutions are not feasible in every context but they are thought-provoking.

# Index